Running Up That Hill

Running Up That Hill

50 Visions of Kate Bush

Tom Doyle

ROWMAN & LITTLEFIELD

Lanham • Boulder • New York • London

Published by Rowman & Littlefield
An imprint of The Rowman & Littlefield Publishing Group, Inc.
4501 Forbes Boulevard, Suite 200, Lanham, Maryland 20706
www.rowman.com

Originally published in the English language in the UK by Nine Eight Books, an imprint of Bonnier Books UK.

Library of Congress Cataloging-in-Publication Data

Names: Doyle, Tom, author.
Title: Running up that hill : 50 visions of Kate Bush / Tom Doyle.
Description: Lanham : Rowman & Littlefield Publishers, 2023. | Includes
    bibliographical references.
Identifiers: LCCN 2023001457 (print) | LCCN 2023001458 (ebook) | ISBN
    9781538181164 (cloth) | ISBN 9781538181171 (epub)
Subjects: LCSH: Bush, Kate. | Singers--England--Biography.
Classification: LCC ML420.B897 D68 2023 (print) | LCC ML420.B897 (ebook) |
    DDC 782.42164092 [B]--dc23/eng/20230112
LC record available at https://lccn.loc.gov/2023001457
LC ebook record available at https://lccn.loc.gov/2023001458

For Karen and Eddy

CONTENTS

"I never wanted to be famous. My desire wasn't to be famous. It was to make a record. That's very different from wanting to be famous."

—Kate Bush

1

Moving Back into the Light

Facing fame, 2005

The car arrived just before 10.30 a.m. on a bright, early autumn morning to pick me up from my home in north London. It was September 22, 2005, a Thursday, and I was heading to an unknown destination. All I knew was that I was being driven to Kate Bush's house, somewhere in Berkshire.

Bush had been missing from public view, pretty much, for the past twelve years. But she'd finally agreed to break her silence with an extensive, exclusive cover story for *MOJO* magazine, and I'd been asked to do the interview. It was an equally exciting and unnerving proposition.

In the days and weeks leading up to this point, the anticipation had been ramping up. At the west London home-cum-office of Bush's then-manager Geoff Jukes, I'd heard her first album in a dozen years—the multi-layered and immediately brilliant twin disc *Aerial*—three times already. Listening intently as it blasted out from Jukes's posh audiophile hi-fi, I'd scrawled copious notes. After the relative disappointment of its patchy predecessor, 1993's *The Red Shoes*, it was clear that Bush's creativity was back in sharp focus.

Still, the people at EMI Records (her record label since 1976) were all a bit nervous, as I would soon discover they always were when tiptoeing around their most elusive artist. The increasing pressure of the pre-interview build-up had started to get to me. I tried to remind myself that it was, after all, just two people meeting up in a room to have a chat.

Bush's last encounter with the press, four years earlier in 2001, had been a polite, if evasive chat in a Harrods café with *Q* magazine, ahead of her attending the mag's annual awards ceremony in the Park Lane Hotel to pick up the Classic Songwriter trophy. Prior to that, eight years before, she'd put herself out there far more press-wise to promote *The Red Shoes*, appearing on various magazine covers. She had however suffered a particularly gnarly, borderline nasty encounter with the *Sunday Times* where the interviewer clearly hadn't liked her, and the singer had been forced to push back against uncomfortable prying into her personal life. It was said that she hated being interviewed.

As such, in recent years, she'd acquired the reputation of a media-shy, almost Greta Garbo-like figure who'd retreated from the real world, while at the same time attaining the reverential respect of a creatively controlling auteur in the mold of Stanley Kubrick. Out there in the world, her saintly patient fans gratefully absorbed every molecule of drip-fed information. Out there was a world of whispered rumors adding to an already towering myth.

The news that Kate Bush was due to return with a new album had prompted umpteen frothing headlines in the papers:

"Kate Bush Still Alive"
"She's Here Again!"
"Return of the Recluse"
"Dithering Heights"
"Wow! Bush Is Back!"

At a time when record industry profits were being hammered by free MP3 file-sharing services such as Napster and LimeWire, EMI were quite obviously getting worked up about the return of Kate Bush, and perhaps more importantly, the buying power of her devoted fanbase. "There is a lot of optimism in the business compared to previous years," a spokesman for the label commented. "We have our Kate Bush album, so it's shaping up to be a really strong quarter for us."

Ahead of the interview, a plan had been hatched for us to meet at Abbey Road Studios. The day before, Bush suddenly changed her mind and decided to move the location to her home. She wasn't about to give me the address, though, hence this air of mystery. As the car sped down the M4 in the direction of Reading, it became clear that the driver regularly ferried Bush around.

"Oh, it must have been *you* she was talking about the other day," he let slip to me. "She was in the back, on the phone, saying, 'Maybe we should just put a bag over his head.'"

It didn't feel like I'd been taken hostage, but it was, of course, brilliantly intriguing. An hour-and-a-half after we'd set off, the car pulled up outside a set of gates, and the driver reached out through his open window and pressed an intercom button.

~

This is how twelve years disappear if you're Kate Bush.

It is 1993, and she has just released *The Red Shoes*, her seventh album in a fifteen-year career characterized by increasingly ambitious records, ever-lengthening recording schedules, and compulsive attention to microscopic musical detail. Emotionally drained after the death of her mother Hannah the previous year, and against the advice of some of her friends, she then threw herself into writing and directing *The Line, the Cross and the Curve*, a film-cum-extended music video, which—despite its merits—Bush considered in retrospect to be "a load of old bollocks."

After taking two years off to recharge her batteries, in 1996, she completed a song in which she imagined Elvis Presley to still be alive somewhere, and named it "King of the Mountain." Another two years on, while pregnant, she teased out another song, about the unpredictable nature of artistic endeavor, called "An Architect's Dream." Following the birth of her son, Albert (or Bertie), in 1998, she and her guitarist partner Danny McIntosh found themselves "completely shattered for a couple of years." She moved house. She converted the garage into a studio. But, being a full-time mother who chose not to employ a nanny or housekeeper, it was hard to find time to actually work there.

Bit by bit, more ideas arrived, and a notion formed in her head to make a double album, although now as a mom, she had to adjust to a new modus operandi that involved stolen creative moments as opposed to her fourteen-hour days of old. Her son

4

began school, and suddenly time opened up. Two more years of concentrated effort later, the album was done. She looked up from the mixing desk and it was 2005.

Soon after, on a late September day, around noon, this writer turned up on her doorstep.

~

The affable Danny McIntosh welcomed me into the hall and through to the living room where, seconds later, Kate walked in, all wary smiles and nervous laughter. We shook hands, and my first impression was that she was surprisingly tiny (5 foot 3½). Dressed in brown shirt, jeans, and black-and-white trainers, hair clipped up in practical, busy-busy fashion, she was less the waif-like dancer of popular memory and instead exactly what she was: a forty-seven-year-old mother of one.

Kate's house turned out not to be the ivy-cloaked mansion of myth, where people believed she lived out some cloistered, possibly cobwebby, Miss Havisham-like existence. It was a large-ish Georgian mill house, filled with comfortable, airy, antiquey rooms, and a recording studio a short walk across the garden.

It was a disarmingly homely environment in which to meet such a vaunted figure. Surrounding her in the living room was all the evidence of a very regular, family-shaped existence—toys and kiddie books scattered everywhere, a DVD case for the Kenneth Branagh-starring 2002 film *Shackleton* lying under a Sony TV. The only clues to this room's dual purpose as the mix-appraising room for one of the most anticipated records of the decade were a pile of CDRs racked on a mantelpiece above black, floor-standing vintage speakers.

Atop the fireplace sat a painting, "Fishermen and Boat" by Joseph Southall, depicting weather-beaten seadogs wrestling with a rowboat, soon to be familiar to all as part of the inner artwork of *Aerial*. As she later showed me, balanced against a wall in the office next door was a replica of the Rosebud sledge burned at the dramatic conclusion of *Citizen Kane*, as commissioned for the video of Bush's return single, "King of the Mountain," and brought home as a gift for the seven-year-old Bertie.

Perching herself on the lip of her sandy-colored sofa in the living room, she sipped her tea, as I settled in an antique armchair to her left, and a palpable air of tension hung in the room. We were both a bit edgy. The prospect of the interview likely filled her with an acute dread. But over the course of four hours—"The longest interview I've ever done," she later pointed out—her initial fears melted away, and she proved to be excellent company: funny, insightful, and surprisingly sweary.

Rather than retreating from the normal world, it appeared that in fact Kate Bush had retreated *to* the normal world and far away from the unreal environments of music stardom. It's worth noting that possibly the happiest she'd ever looked in a promotional photograph had been as a grinning twenty-year-old in 1978 doing the dishes in the kitchen at her parents' home.

At the same time, Bush was, and remains, an utterly unique figure in modern music. Having gone from being a startlingly prolific schoolgirl poetess to overnight becoming the haunting, slightly unsettling pop star of "Wuthering Heights," she had since held many other, similarly individualistic positions, particularly for a female artist: intrepid aural explorer, fierce protector of her craft, publicity-avoiding megastar—and now, apparently—hermitic, glacially productive recording artist. By defiantly remaining true to her inner artistic voice, she had created some of the most original and surprising music of the past four decades and become the subject of murmured legend.

So could she understand why people built these myths up around her?

"No," she began, a touch apprehensively. "No, I can't. *Pffff.* I can't, really."

You once said, "There is a figure that is adored, but I'd question very strongly that it's me."

There was silence. A stare.

She did say it, I pointed out.

"Well, I supposedly said it. In what context did I say that, then?"

Just talking about fans building up this image of her as some kind of goddess.

"Yes, but I'm not, am I?" she responded, wide-eyed, incredulous. "I do really believe there's an element of people having a *feeling* of what I am. I think people, I *hope* people can feel that the intention in my work is to make something interesting creatively. It's not to do with making money. If I wanted to make money, I'd put a record out every year, whether it was shit or not. D'you know what I mean? And I'd do loads of TV to push it. That's not what interests me at all."

About half an hour in, likely happy enough with the direction the conversation was flowing in, she grinned and admitted, "I'm starting to relax now." At some points, she was almost breathless in her excitement to talk about her new record. She laughed enthusiastically and often, though there were moments where she grew distant, and you suspected she was thinking of three other things at once. Sometimes she sounded posh, sometimes almost like a wartime Cockney, while the slight woo to her r's was as strong in her speaking voice as in her singing voice. She didn't really do anecdotes, preferring instead to recollect past feelings (often self-deprecatingly) or theorize (in a more serious, considered tone; her most over-used phrase being "I think").

Occasionally, she was suddenly overcome with giggly, child-like wonder when explaining some of the concepts involved in *Aerial*, whether it be singing through the decimal places of a mathematical constant in "π," or vocally imitating birdsong in "Aerial Tal" and the album's closing title track. Then, the next minute, she'd adopt a faux plummy, luvvy, actorly tone whenever she felt she might be in danger of sounding pretentious.

Tellingly, at other points, she became semi-detached and almost regal, particularly if you complimented her on a song or album, and she'd say "Oh, thank you," in a manner well-practiced after years of accepting praise for her work. But she also admitted that she normally taped her interviews, too, to guard against being misquoted, as she believed she had been in the past. "But I didn't feel I needed to today," she enigmatically added.

Having in the weeks before read more than 100 of her past interviews, where she had so often seemed distant and unread-able, I was determined to try to meet the real Kate, the one who had spent years living in studios in the salty company of male musicians. It wasn't long before she revealed this side of her character, when she was addressing the rumors that she'd become some fragile being who'd chosen to hide herself away. She insisted the tittle-tattle didn't affect her.

"No," she said, before instantly becoming more animated. "A lot of the time it doesn't bother me, really. I suppose I do think I go out of my way to be a very normal person, and I just find it frustrating that people think I'm some kind of weirdo recluse that never comes out into the world."

Rising to the topic, her voice notched up in volume.

"Y'know, I'm a very strong person, and I think that's why actually I find it really *infuriating* when I read, 'She had a nervous breakdown' or 'She's not very mentally stable, just a weak, frail little creature.' It's like . . . Fuck off!"

At this precise point, the real Kate Bush may well just have entered the room.

~

If the outside world had been wondering whether Kate Bush would ever get around to finishing her long, long-awaited album, then it was a feeling shared by its creator.

"Oh, yeah," she sighed. "I mean, there were so many times I thought, 'I'll have the album finished this year, definitely. We'll get it out this year.' Then there were a couple of years where I really thought, 'I'm never gonna do this.' If I could make albums quicker, I'd be on a roll, wouldn't I? Everything just seems to take so much time. I don't know why it does take so long. Time . . . evaporates."

During the lengthy period when she was deep into recording *Aerial*, the people at EMI had been kept completely in the dark about Bush's creative activities. She pointed out that she wasn't on the hook to the label, financially either, which secured for her the creative freedom that had been hard-won down the years.

Only once a record was completed would she be paid a royalty advance by EMI.

"Well, I think a good way of playing it is try not to owe the record company money," she reasoned. "That's a good place to start from. And that way, you haven't taken any money for something you haven't delivered yet. With the first couple of records, obviously I made those quite fast. But gradually with each record, it's got longer and longer.

"I think quite early on, the company realized that they couldn't actually do anything to . . . y'know, what can they do? They can't say, 'Look, 'urry up!' cause it doesn't work that way. So . . . they just leave me alone to get on with it. I think sometimes it's frustrating [for them].

"Also, what I try not to do is say, 'Ooh, it's gonna be finished by such and such.' I try not to let them know it's going to be finished until it's finished. Because, y'know, it always takes me longer than I think.

"Even when I think I'm getting near the end," she laughed, "it still takes longer."

There had been a story floating around that some people from EMI had come down to visit her, and she'd apparently said, "Here's some stuff I've been working on," and produced some cakes out of the oven.

"No, I didn't!" she spluttered. "I thought that was quite funny actually. It presents me as this homely creature, which is alright, isn't it?"

She admitted, however, that it was getting harder to work with EMI, a company she felt was growing increasingly more faceless and corporate. "The whole world is gradually just becoming corporate, isn't it?" she stressed. "And I think a lot of people are really sad about that. It's the equivalent of the little corner shop turning into the supermarket, isn't it?"

Bush could, however, see eye-to-eye with the record label's then-CEO, Tony Wadsworth. "He's a really interesting combination of somebody who's very creative in a position of power at a record company. He used to come down, and we'd just chat and then he'd go away again."

But you wouldn't let him hear anything?

"(*Flatly*) No. But he's got a really good sense of humor. We ended up just laughing about it, really."

For his part, Wadsworth told me, "She's someone who's got a very clear creative vision, and the idea of conventional A&R is not applicable. I was very, very eager, like anybody else would be, to hear some new Kate Bush music.

"But," he added, with a knowing laugh, "you got a very clear sense when you weren't gonna hear anything. Though it didn't stop me from asking."

That's not to say, however, that Bush wasn't nervous when she first played *Aerial* to EMI's bigwigs.

"Um . . . yes, I was," she smiled.

Did she sit them in this room or take them to the studio?

"Well, the first time they listened in the studio. It's difficult because with the first listen, [for them] a lot of it's to do with sheer relief at the fact that it's something that hopefully isn't complete crap. So they're thinking, 'Phew, thank God for that.'

"I think, particularly with the record company, when they hear it the second time, they're in a much more relaxed state. The response the second time was really, really nice, and it felt genuine as well. I mean, you can never really tell with people, can you?"

"We were blown away," Wadsworth stated. "I never expected it to be anything but great. But there was relief that it was done."

~

Nonetheless, Bush admitted that the prospect of moving back into the bright light of fame was a daunting one. If there was a sigh of relief for her upon completion of *Aerial*, then its impending release brought with it a certain anxiety. One tabloid photographer had only weeks before being flown in a helicopter above her property, snapping her house from the air. Even the local drunks, wandering back home from the local pub, had started pushing the buzzer at the front gates late at night, before giggling or talking crap through the intercom.

Bush had even seriously considered whether it was worth actually releasing the album and inviting all that unwanted intrusion back into her life once again.

Did a part of her almost wish that she didn't have to put the record out?

"Well, this time I have actually said to Danny a couple of times—not that I can't put it out, because of course that's part of what I am—but I have said to him, 'God, y'know, *should* I put it out?'"

Just because you're letting all that outside noise in?

"Yeah, it's opening the door, isn't it? Because this [for me] is all about that creative focus, that quiet place. Being well-known is completely the enemy of this. Being well-known is all about this kind of [*imitating excitable crowd noise*] 'Waaaah.' Even more so now where you've got this truly silly preoccupation with celebrities.

People are sort of obsessed. Just because somebody's been in an ad on TV, so what? Who gives a toss? The people that really matter are surgeons, scientists, all these people who keep us alive."

She found it mind-boggling whenever she flicked through channels on TV and would see celebrities in a jungle being force-fed live bugs or dragging themselves through the dirt to keep themselves in the public eye.

"It's kind of Roman games stuff, isn't it?" she noted, visibly aghast.

In the end, of course, Bush knew that she had to face her own fame once again to release *Aerial* to the world.

"Well, I had this very interesting conversation with a friend years ago," she said. "They were suggesting that you didn't have to let other people hear it. But the way I see it is . . . look at a Shakespeare play. That wouldn't exist without the audience. And actually what I think is really important about art is not so much the art, it's the relationship between the observer and the art.

"Without wanting to sound *awfully pretentious*," she added, laughing and adopting her mock upper-class tone, "It's a lot to do with where the observer stands in relation to it all. To stand in a place of wonder at the planet is maybe exactly the most important thing that we can do being here.

"As the observer—receiving the Shakespeare play or seeing the beautiful painting . . . without your presence, it doesn't really exist in the same way.

"So, if you make music and you don't let people hear it, you could almost say it doesn't exist."

Still, it remained the biggest dilemma in Kate Bush's life: attempting to reconcile her intense need to create with her intense desire for privacy. A pretty tricky, or nigh on impossible thing for her to balance?

"Well, it hasn't been for the past twelve years," she pointed out, "because I've felt really privileged to be living such a normal life. It's so a part of who I am. It's so important to me to do the washing, do the hoovering. I don't ever want to lose contact with that. Friends of mine in the business don't know how dishwashers work. For me, that's frightening. I want to be in a position where I can function as a human being."

Did she ever feel she would've been happier if she hadn't become an instant pop star in her teens, and perhaps ended up more of a cult artist?

"I dunno. How can you ever say, 'If only?' You can't, can you? You can live all these scenarios in your head. But there's no point, it's of no purpose, because what happened is what happened, isn't it? And I was so driven to do what I did.

"I do think it's surprising in a lot of ways that I've been as popular. I mean, having such enormous great gaps . . . d'you know what I mean? I do find it fascinating. Because after such a long time, particularly this time, I thought, 'God, y'know, people are just gonna forget who I am.'

"But, y'know, it seems quite the opposite . . . that people are actually really excited about it. I have been genuinely touched by the sense of anticipation I've felt. I thought after five or six years, it was starting to get a bit dodgy. So, I feel really privileged that people have been waiting."

As to how some folk felt intimidated by her, particularly the staff at EMI, Bush was bewildered.

"I'm not sure if that's how I view it," she offered, carefully. "I don't think of myself as intimidating."

But she was to them, I pointed out. Everyone I'd met at the label seemed to get a bit jumpy when they were talking about "Kate Bush." Did she find that weird?

"I think it's totally ridiculous."

It could be useful though, couldn't it?

"It could be, couldn't it?" she smiled.

⌒

At the start of the interview, I'd done something I never did: I'd given Bush my mobile number. Just so that there wasn't a dramatic full-stop to the day and then I'd go away with my tapes, and she wouldn't have any further input. Just so that she wasn't always double-thinking herself during the conversation. I said I wouldn't instantly change anything she felt uncomfortable about, but at least we could have a dialogue about it.

She did call a few days later, wondering about a couple of tiny, trivial details that I was never going to bother with anyway.

"I mean, I'm not trying to *control* the interview, Tom," she joked.

"Perish the thought, Kate," I laughed.

In the end and through a few other conversations we had on the phone, I do feel I got to meet and talk to the "real" Kate Bush.

The hippie-dippy "Hello trees, hello sky" image is perhaps the typical caricature of her. But this cartoon rendering masks a far more complex personality: someone who is steely, gently controlling, painfully self-critical, and also the first person to happily puncture the reverential bubble that surrounds her.

In this way, *Running Up That Hill* is designed to be a multi-faceted portrait of Kate Bush: illuminating from fifty different angles the girl who lived in her imagination, reluctantly became famous because of it, then had to deal with unwanted outside forces, before battling on and emerging triumphant to become one of the most groundbreaking, idiosyncratic, and singular artists of our time.

2

Through the Back Door

East Wickham Farm, fourteenth century to today

Some 16 miles east of the one-time Hammersmith Odeon, 15 miles south-east of Abbey Road Studios, a dozen miles from where the Dance Studio in Covent Garden was once situated, and out beyond the great landmarks of Kate Bush's career, lies East Wickham Farm. A pastoral oasis amid the suburbs of Welling, Outer London (historically a part of Kent), it has maintained the air of a rural residence while being surrounded by the arteries of the city.

For more than two hundred years, the farm has remained largely unchanged, though its origins are far, far older, with its oak beams reclaimed from man-of-war ships that might have sailed as early as the sixteenth century.

"The house we lived in, the earliest part was fourteenth century," John Carder Bush, Kate's eldest brother, told me.

"When my father bought it in the early fifties, the whole thing was surrounded by thatched barns, which were really dangerous, so they had to be pulled down.

"But, as part of the original farm set-up, there were outhouses over the smithy's forge, a wheelwright shop where the carts were taken in and the wheels were sorted, and this wash house with stone-flagged floors and a central chimney surrounded by copper vats where all the linen of the household was washed. Leading up from that was a grain [barn and] loft where they used to haul bags of grain in from outside through a circular window."

It was to this rustic yet urban, former working farm setting that Catherine Bush was brought home in the days after being born on July 30, 1958, at Bexley Maternity Hospital: daughter to Robert, a GP; and Hannah, a nurse; sister to John (known as Jay) and Paddy, respectively fourteen and six years older than their new sibling.

The atmosphere of East Wickham Farm was to have a marked effect on Kate Bush's music and creativity down the years and was directly referenced twice in her lyrics—in 1980's "Warm and Soothing" and 2005's "A Coral Room." Both songs evoked images of stepping through its back door into a homely kitchen environment.

"That was the big thing about our home when we were all growing up," Kate recalled to me. "We'd come in the back door into the kitchen and that was the heart of our home. And we all did it every day."

Inside, as its visitors remember, East Wickham farmhouse was woody, welcoming and rambling. For a girl growing up, it was filled with opportunities to escape into different corners of different rooms. From the back of the house, the view was over the wildflowers of the eighty-four acre East Wickham Open Space, growing over earth covering the rubble of buildings bombed during the Second World War. At its furthest reach, across Upper Wickham Lane, there was Plumstead Cemetery, the perfect setting for Bush and her teenage friends to freak themselves out on Halloween.

As far as local myths and legends went, there was really only one: local publican Anne Muirhead, of mid-eighteenth-century hostelry the White Horse, was a co-conspirator of the fabled dandy highwayman Dick Turpin. At night, Anne—or "Fanny"— would light a lamp to let Turpin know that there were no rozzers lurking around. Muirhead was later to be remembered in the name of another pub, Fanny on the Hill, demolished in 1949. A second pub in the area bore the same name until it was, inevitably, turned into flats in 2014.

Down the years, modern housing crept up and closed in around East Wickham Farm, though it retained its bucolic spirit. Today, there is still a direct link to its farmstead and wheelwright past: Owen Bush, John Carder Bush's son and Kate's nephew, runs his bladesmith operation from there—the machine noise and metallic clanging emanating from the smithy now producing swords and knives for various TV shows, including *Game of Thrones*.

But, from the 1960s, through the 1980s and beyond, East Wickham Farm, on a normal street but somehow always half a world away from outside influences, was to utterly shape the artistic character of Kate Bush. Through those years, its grain barn and neighboring converted garages were to echo with the sounds of Bush's musical development, from her first wheezings on a pump organ to the recording of *Hounds of Love*.

3

The Sister in the Photographs

Cathy and Kate through the lens, 1966–2014

Home from school and time for dress-up. Whether, really, she was in the mood or not. Cathy Bush was always a willing participant in her brother John Carder Bush's photographic experiments, even if sometimes she looked tired or grumpy, or both, in the resulting images.

"She was always willing," he remembered. "I think part of the atmosphere of the photos, which was what I was really looking for, [is] there's this kind of almost sad look on her face. But that wasn't really consciously projected. I think that was cause she'd had a day at school and she's having to do these photographs for her brother, and she was just wanting to get on with something else. But she wasn't impatient. She was really cooperative, and it was good fun working with her.

"She was actually very quiet. Not withdrawn. Just wouldn't push herself forward. A really nice, sweet companion."

Inspired by the pre-Raphaelite children's book illustrators and the pen-and-ink Peter Pan fantasias of Arthur Rackham, the then-twenty-two-year-old hobbying photographer conjured up a world of furs and headbands and swords for his kid sister to inhabit.

"If you look at Rackham's illustrations for Peter Pan," Bush pointed out, "there's always something sinister lurking in the background. That's what I was consciously trying to get, the feel of those illustrators. So I wasn't really looking for anything cheerful. It was just trying to capture that atmosphere.

"[There's] one in the grain loft with the light coming through the circular window that could be a Rackham illustration. Then there's another one where she's sitting on steps and she's holding a goblet and there's a dagger [hanging by a chain] around her waist and some animal skins. That for me captures exactly what I was after. But looking at it again, it's an awful lot to do with the natural light. Summer afternoon light, soft."

These early photographs of Kate Bush as a sleepy-eyed child, which were later to become world-famous, were shot on a special 35mm camera that allowed two shots for every frame, meaning a thirty-six exposure roll would produce seventy-two pictures. "The main compulsion to use that camera was it was cheap," John admitted. "It diminishes your potential end quality, and the extent to which you can blow it up is very limited. [But] when I look at them, they're such amazing quality with such a primitive little tool."

Taken when their subject was between the ages of eight and twelve, many of the photographs captured the future Kate Bush's inherent otherness: whirling like a dervish on the family lawn or throwing a natural dancer's arch-backed pose in a poncho. Other images revealed the strong hippie influence of her older siblings (particularly one with her and brother Paddy in kaftans evoking the Incredible String Band), while a few which caught her grinning and looking scruffy revealed an impish, mischievous spirit. One later, faceless shot, taken from above, showed her trying out simple two-fingered chords on the family's time-weathered old pump organ with worn-out keys.

John Carder Bush said that it was at first "not that apparent" that his kid sister had an innate musical gift. "Certainly not at the age most of these photos were taken," he added. "The one of her sitting at the organ, [she is] maybe eleven-ish and, well, you can see the Kate person starting to emerge there. But you also can see with the overhead shot, of course, the two-finger technique that says what level of keyboard-playing she was at at that stage."

Nonetheless, no doubt aiding the concentration required for her to become a self-taught musician, there was always an air of stillness and apartness to young Cathy Bush.

"To say she was like a little mouse is an exaggeration," her brother stated. "But if she'd go off and do something with the school and she came back, she wouldn't spend hours talking about it. You had to really push hard to get the information out. She wasn't precocious in any sense, although you could say that it was a precocious talent when it did surface."

The photographs were first published as a book, *Cathy*, in 1986. It was limited to five hundred self-published, mail order-sold copies: "That was purely experimentation. I didn't at that time appreciate how interesting people would find it. So I published it myself, and myself and my partner posted them off to people."

The finished copies had however arrived back from the printer in what John Carder Bush remembered as an "awful yellow" slipcase that was impossibly tight. "A real mistake," he said. "When they turned up, we were on a very tight time schedule, and I think now if that had happened, I would have sent them all back. But we didn't have time, so we just went ahead with them. I knew some people received the book and actually couldn't pull it out of the slipcase."

Cathy was reprinted in 2014 following Kate's "Before the Dawn" shows, by which time the original copies were fetching anything up to £1,000: "It had become extremely rare, and people were paying a lot of money for it . . . which completely amazes me (*laughs*). Articles had been appearing in odd places. There was one in the *Wall Street Journal,* which seemed very obscure. I thought, 'Well, if that level of media interest is going on, then obviously that's sparked off by public or fan interest.'"

A trial by portraiture some of these sessions may have been for young Cathy, but they were to serve her well when creating her own imagery in the years to follow. As Cathy became Kate, John Carder Bush later photographed his sister for many of her album covers, most memorably in the iconic reclining pose on the front of *Hounds of Love* (and most recently for 2011's *Director's Cut*).

"I suppose a lot of people say to me, 'Ah look at that one, that's like the cover you did for *Hounds of Love*.' There were a few of the album covers I did that it really felt like I was doing the Cathy photos again. It was the same . . . not freedom . . . but relaxation because it's a brother photographing his sister. That certainly has a connection. You bring in a photographer who doesn't know the subject, it's gonna take a while for the photographer to build up anything with the subject, which for me and Kate was already there.

"Like the *Cathy* photographs, I suppose, all the stuff I did for her career was always done at home. We never hired a professional studio. It was always where either of us lived. For me, there was a big room, [where] I'd clear all my kids' toys out of the way, set up the backdrop and the lights and everything and turn what had been an ordinary household room into a studio. So we could do it for three days if we wanted to. There was no commercial pressure involved. And I think that has a lot to do with it as well, in terms of freedom to experiment. And also her knowing that any experiments would stay with me. They wouldn't go off out into the media and end up in places she wouldn't have liked to have seen them. I think that element of being able to trust the photographer is important."

As the decades passed, looking at Kate through the view-finder, it would often be Cathy that her brother saw.

"I can't see any difference, in the passing of time," he reflected. "The eyes are exactly the same. It's the same smile I see now. As soon as I look through the lens, she's back, through all the photos I've taken of her over the years."

4

The Artful Bushes

The family influence, 1960s onward

All the time she was growing up, Cathy Bush's home life was an ever-expanding universe of music and poetry. It was a place of wild imagination and esoteric interests, where each of the family members encouraged the others to explore their flights of fancy.

The air at East Wickham Farm was often filled with the sound of Robert Bush, a keen and dedicated piano player, practicing his Schubert, Beethoven, and Chopin pieces, sometimes for hours on end. The music magically produced by her father's fingertips (not to mention his discipline) were a formative inspiration for Cathy. When he pointed out to her the key of C Major on piano—easy, just all the white notes—she was off, soon inventing her own chords.

Her schooldays at St Joseph's Convent Grammar, two miles away in Abbey Wood, were, however, a drag. A posed photograph of Bush taken in her early years there captured her lack of enthusiasm: looking sullen, bashfully trying to hide her face behind her long curtains of dark hair.

"I found school wasn't helping me," she later reflected. "I became [an] introvert. I guess it was the teachers' system, the way they reacted to pupils, and I wasn't quite responsive to that."

A modern annexe aside, St Joseph's was a stiffly old-fashioned environment, filled with Victorian classroom desks and stern nuns. Together the students would be forced to sing the school song, "Potius Mori Quam Foedari"—which translates from Latin into English as "Death Before Dishonor." ("Not sure I understood what that meant," commented one former pupil on social media many years later. "Probably not eloping at 17!!?") In reality, it was a motto perhaps better suited to a meth-cooking biker gang than a bunch of teen and tweenie Catholic girls. Reinforcing the Hells Angels-like sense of toughness and bravado, the song's second verse included the line, "Girls of St Joseph's School will know no fears."

In this oddly confident but fusty world, Cathy proved herself to be bright. The subjects that she did well in are perhaps unsurprising in retrospect: English, music, Latin, biology. At school, she was taught violin, and apparently sailed through her grades. But, despite the fact she would later write a rocking, Roxy Music-ish ode to its famous players, from Paganini to the Devil himself ("Violin" on 1980's *Never for Ever*), she never seemed particularly enamoured with the instrument when it was in her own hands. At home, as soon as she'd practiced her scales or latest piece, she'd instantly get rid of it and move over to the piano.

Perhaps this was because it felt too intimidating to line up against the skills of her extended family. Summer holidays were often spent in or around Dungarvan, County Waterford, visiting assorted Irish relatives on her mother Hannah's side. The ferry from Fishguard to Rosslare was a well-traveled route for the Bushes, the family eventually arriving by car at Cathy's grandparents' cottage overlooking the crashing waves of the Celtic Sea. There, they'd soon find themselves amid a host of uncles all enthusiastically playing accordions and fiddles.

Back home at East Wickham Farm, traditional Irish and English folk records were a constant on the family stereo. Cathy's favorite was A. L. (or Bert) Lloyd, the London-born singer and folklorist with a penchant for drinking songs and sea shanties. Years later, for the B-side of the "Hounds of Love" single in 1986, Bush recorded "The Handsome Cabin Boy," a song she'd first heard via Lloyd's rendition with another British folk revivalist, Ewan MacColl. In its story, a pretty girl, Nell, disguises herself as a boy to gain employment on a ship, and is admired first by the captain's wife, before falling pregnant to the captain himself. As folk lyrics go, it was gender-blurring, risqué, funny, and clearly appealed to Bush. Bert Lloyd, she later said, was "*the* man as far as I'm concerned."

Other records on heavy rotation at the Bushes' home were the brothers' favorites: King Crimson, Pink Floyd, the Incredible String Band, Bob Dylan, the Beatles, the Stones. Cathy's own collection of 45-rpm singles included, by 1970, T. Rex and Dave Edmunds, while her favorite album, arriving the following year and leaving an indelible imprint on her fast-developing piano style from 1971 onward, was Elton John's *Madman Across the Water*.

In 2005, Bush told me she'd recently set up her turntable and given her original copy a spin for old times' sake: "I dug out some of my old vinyl and I put *Madman Across the Water* on, and I just thought it was absolutely fantastic. Obviously, it's a record that brought back a lot of associations for me, but it sounded so good . . . it was just great."

~

Music aside, there were always words floating around. John was a poet in addition to being a photographer. What's more, doubtless leaving a lasting impression on Cathy, he had the confidence to put his work out there.

In 1970, he published a poem, "The Creation Edda," in a four-page book issued by the Sceptre Press in a run of one hundred copies, which revisited the tale of Ask and Embla, the Norse myth of the first two humans. It was likely striking for its artistic bravery in other ways as far as his perma-receptive twelve-year-old sister was concerned: John Carder Bush's stanzas detailed the female Embla having sex with a volcano.

Before long, Cathy was inspired to write her own poems. One, "The Crucifixion," was published in the school mag at the end of her first year (1969–70) at St Joseph's and was a graphic depiction of the battered Jesus being hoisted onto the cross. Other poems that followed pre-echoed later Kate Bush song themes, such as invisibility ("I Have Seen Him"), ethereal romance ("Call Me") and the inner life of deceptively normal-looking humans ("You").

These poems, while clearly written by someone young, were far from juvenilia. John felt they were so accomplished that he sent them to a friend who edited a poetry magazine. The editor was willing to print them, if John's sister tweaked a few lines.

But, in the first display of the defiant and creatively autonomous character that she would become, Cathy refused, and let them go unpublished.

School friends of Cathy Bush would later recall that she often told them stories in the playground during breaks, spinning fantastical tales, such as the perhaps self-explanatory "The Haunted Mill," or riffing on Arthurian legends, or discussing in depth other typical early teenage preoccupations such as life after death or reincarnation.

Friends also remembered that when they were invited back to Cathy's house, her mother was a constant presence, but not one who restricted her. Hannah Bush had just turned forty in the weeks before giving birth to her and Robert's only daughter. Having already been through the process of parenting two older boys, the couple were likely more laidback and lenient when bringing up Cathy.

Middle child Paddy, meanwhile, was another strong influence: an energetic and contagiously enthusiastic individual, very much rooted in folk. Having in the 1960s played concertina for an outfit of Morris dancers, accompanying them in folk clubs during the decade that the genre was still powered by the British revival that had started in the 1950s, he subsequently involved himself with the English Folk Dance and Song Society, collecting records and further exploring the Irish tradition.

From here, he became fascinated by instrument making, and tried and failed to find an apprenticeship with a harp builder. It wasn't until 1973 that Paddy managed to enroll on a course in Musical Instrument Technology at the London College of Furniture in Shoreditch, where he specialized in instruments from the medieval era. There, as he later recalled, he threw himself into learning "piano tuning, violin making, harpsichord building, ethnic musicology." These interests soon veered into pure art.

"Toward the end," he remembered, "I started making instruments with arms and legs and out of very unorthodox materials. Instruments that didn't play and which demonstrated other sorts of principles. I had an exhibition at the Whitechapel Art Gallery and sold a couple of things. There was a great deal of interest, but not much success . . ."

Later, however, Paddy Bush was to play many unusual or bizarre instruments on his sister's records. Scan through the playing credits of her album catalog and his contributions include pan flute, musical saw, didgeridoo, koto, sitar, balalaika, mandolin, mandola, mandocello, valiha (a tube-shaped bamboo zither), singing bowls (mallet-struck metallic bells used in Buddhist practices), fujara (a Slovakian shepherd's flute), musical bow (a one-stringed zither), a bullroarer (an ancient device swung around the head to produce a loud, buzzing, motorbike-like tone) and, more prosaically, a fishing rod (impersonating a whip on the track "The Sensual World").

～

Meanwhile, back at East Wickham Farm in the early 1970s, John was introducing his sister not only to poetry, but to Shotokan karate, to Greek mythology, to Russian mystic and philosopher George Gurdjieff.

Often, when John and Paddy were practicing their kendo kata steps, Cathy would be upstairs in the grain loft, playing the pump organ, starting to set her poetry to her real and imagined chords, clearly pointing the way to her future.

Before all of that, though, there were more years at St Joseph's to endure. Given how much more she was learning at home, it's no surprise she couldn't wait to break free from the constraints of school.

5

The Girl at the Piano

The early songs, 1969–73

It was almost a race against time: could Cathy Bush learn to play the harmonium out in the barn before the mice managed to gnaw their way through its bellows?

The instrument that had been left to partial ruin at East Wickham Farm was actually a very rare and special one. Manufactured in the nineteenth century in Paris by Victor Mustel, it was one of only around five hundred highly prized "art harmoniums" that Mustel had made before his death in 1890. Similar models had once been treasured installations in churches, concert halls, and opera houses.

But it was on this old, neglected, and disintegrating Mustel pump organ that Cathy explored her fascination with chord structure. She would sit at it for hours, pedaling away until her ankles ached, usually working out the chords to hymns, attracted to their simple, but effective melodies. When she learned that if she moved one finger in a three-note cluster to another key, it opened up doors leading to other doors.

"This was the most exciting thing in my life: the chord," she remembered. "You could get completely different chords to work with the new note. That started my interest in the way things could sound and feel very different just by putting different chords to a tune."

Bush couldn't really read music and had no interest in learning. Equally, she wasn't much good at maths. But, still, she could see how chords were just mathematical patterns on the keyboard that seemed to easily appear to her.

Day by day, though, fewer of the organ's "stops"—the knobs that you pushed and pulled to control the flow of air to the pipes and change the sound from "flute" to "clarinette" to "hautbois" (oboe)—seemed to work. The mice were winning in their slow destruction of Victor Mustel's once-loved creation. It was time to move back inside the farmhouse and onto the piano.

~

Songs soon began to pour out of Cathy Bush. It was clear that even as a young girl, she had an intense desire to create.

"Uh . . . I don't know if I always had it," she stressed to me. "But I certainly got it really bad from, I suppose, about nine. By the time I was, I dunno, eleven or twelve, it was even worse."

Looking back, she realized that she'd been a pensive kid. She thought deeply, probably too deeply, about absolutely everything, and found it frustrating to be treated as a child when she didn't feel that she thought like one. As her pre-teen emotions began to become more difficult to process, she became more absorbed in the piano and her attempts to delve into songwriting. Writing, she realized, helped her to release the "excess of emotion I needed to get out of my system."

Paddy Bush recalled that his sister would "go and lock herself away and wind up spending five or six hours, seven days a week, just playing the piano."

Bush can't remember the very first song she ever wrote, except that it was at the age of eleven and it was "terrible . . . very overdone." By the age of thirteen and fourteen, she'd started taking songwriting very seriously, and approaching her lyrics as poetry. For her, the most amazing thing was the realization that she had the talent to create something out of entirely nothing.

Singing, however, was an agonising prospect at first. Her voice, she reckoned, was terrible: "I could sing in key but there was nothing there." The only solution, she realized, of course, was to keep on trying to sing, to keep on pushing forward.

Then, in January 1971, when Elton John arrived in the charts with "Your Song," it changed everything for her.

"My big hero was Elton John," she said. "I thought he was so brilliant because he played the piano. A lot of people were guitarists and writers and I just thought it was so fantastic that he wrote songs and played piano. And he's a brilliant pianist, kind of underrated really. So, he was a huge inspiration to me. I used to sit and listen to his stuff and think, 'Oh, it's so great,' and then I'd go off and (*making plonking and squealing noises*) 'Eee-ee-ee.'"

Looking back, Bush recognized that she'd obviously been intense as a young songwriter.

"Yeah, I think I was. Muted intensity. Cause that was kind of something that I did at home. I thought it was best not to mention it to . . . y'know, my best friends all knew, but I didn't make a thing of it at school. I didn't want to be hoisted up on the stage to do things at school. I suppose it was the equivalent to my hobby. Whereas some girls were off riding ponies, I was sitting, y'know, (*laughs*) writing my *rock opera*."

Ever encouraging, Robert Bush marveled at how easily his daughter seemed to be able to conjure compositions out of nowhere. "Her songs seemed to write themselves," he offered in a rare interview. "Whole stanzas at a time, in her head, while I'm struggling to put one word after the next." Realizing that it was perhaps best to capture Cathy's songs on tape, her dad invested in a pricey AKAI reel-to-reel machine. Soon, they even began to crudely copyright her songs by posting tapes back to themselves in sealed envelopes, stamped, and dated by the Royal Mail.

"I would put stuff onto tape, but I *was* the tape machine," she recalled. "I used to practice, practice, practice in order to remember the stuff. So it's what I did all the time.

"By the time I was about sixteen, I was on a mission from God, y'know (*laughs*). And I was the most positive person that I know. I must have been *completely* annoying. Cause I was just totally idealistic and really positive and so driven."

As she played through her songs, Paddy Bush would sometimes accompany Cathy on his mandolin, and before long he was encouraging his sister to start to play with other musicians, inviting a guitarist friend, Brian Bath, to East Wickham Farm.

Bath recorded in his diary on Friday, May 26, 1972: "I went to Paddy's, and he had his mandolin and my amp. His little sister sang through a mic and amp and sounded really incredible." Two weeks later, on Saturday, June 10, he returned, then afterward wrote: "Fit some guitar on Paddy's sister's song. Really feel honored to do it."

"She was really sweet and pleasant," Bath remembers. "She had this great voice and her songs, they were amazing. Really kind of interesting and beautiful, because they were just so different. They were going all over the place. The chord progressions were like nothing I'd ever come across before. She just seemed to go elsewhere."

Before long, the songs began to pile up. By 1972—when John Carder Bush first asked a friend with music industry contacts, Ricky Hopper, to listen to Cathy's tapes—she had over fifty original compositions.

"Oh, easily," Bush pointed out. "I was writing a song, maybe two songs every day. I must have had a couple of hundred."

~

The tapes that exist of Cathy Bush's earliest songs reveal a talent that, if not exactly full-formed, is like a rapidly developing Polaroid photograph. It's not always easy to date the recordings—some are from 1973; others, often re-recordings of the same song, are from 1976. More than two dozen of these since-digitized tracks are floating around online, in wildly varying degrees of audio quality. But here, in the author's estimation, are the top five:

1. "Something Like a Song"

Otherwise known to collectors as "In My Garden" or "Garden by the Willow," "Something Like a Song" is arguably the great lost track missing from the early Kate Bush albums. A visual and auditory hallucination of a song, it ties in with Bush's fledgling interest in Greek mythology, and appears to star Pan, the God of among other things, "rustic music." Another likely source is

"The Piper at the Gates of Dawn," the same chapter in Kenneth Grahame's *The Wind in the Willows* that so inspired Pink Floyd's Syd Barrett, and which features the appearance of Pan singing an entrancing song to Ratty and Mole, which they instantly forget.

In "Something Like a Song," the singer sees a spectral vision of a piper in her garden, whose playing she then starts to voice: gracefully vaulting up an octave into a bewitchingly hypnotic, wordless chorus of "ooo-ooo-ooo, aaa-aaa-ooo's," as pretty arpeggios of descending piano chords tumble below. Bush's voice here almost pre-echoes Elizabeth Fraser of Cocteau Twins, in the 1980s and beyond. Still, this being 1973, there are distinct traces of Joni Mitchell. More than anyone else, though, it sounds unmistakably like the Kate Bush we would come to know.

2. "You Were the Star"
Vamping piano chords, not a great distance from Carole King's *Tapestry*, drive along this narrative about the figurative "star": who might well be a famous but unnamed singer or artist, given their "genius," but clearly one who has fallen from the heavens. Bush addresses them to reassure them that even half of their star power will still shine brightly, as the chorus wends its way to a haunting melodic peak that recalls Joni Mitchell's "Woodstock."

3. "Sunsi"
A song whose roots can be traced back to Bush's lessons at Catholic school and those hours after school spent pumping out hymns on the harmonium. The general vibe is Elton John's take on the ecstatic stylings of Laura Nyro, while the title seems to obliquely refer to an archaic version of the Italian word "sumere": the act of a priest receiving communion. As ever,

young Cathy is seeking knowledge, this time some kind of key to spiritual enlightenment.

4. "Cussi Cussi"

Definitely a work-in-progress, but one that ambitiously flits between ornate arpeggios and a far more elaborate chord progression than many of her other early songs. "Cussi Cussi" is frenetic one minute, self-soothing the next. Lyrically, Bush seems to share some secret knowledge with the titular "Cussi": one that she warns them not to share with others. The stop-start, tempo-shifting arrangement would have been impossible for other musicians to follow and, as such, exists as a snapshot of Cathy Bush's creativity running free.

5. "Atlantis"

The idea of a drowned city would return much later in Bush's writing, in "A Coral Room" on *Aerial* in 2005. Lyric-wise, in some ways, this can be seen as a first draft of that landmark song, in which the metaphor was developed to signify the passing of time. Here the imagery is vivid but more on-the-nose: coral-covered buildings, herring swimming through the sails of sunken ships, while the narrator feels nothing but a sense of loneliness as she somehow inhabits the watery metropolis. Still, it's interesting to note that there is a direct line to be drawn between two songs written three decades apart, by a girl in her teens and a woman in her forties.

In a slightly mysterious footnote to all of this, in 1987, following the success of *Hounds of Love* in 1985—and likely attempting to cash in on both that and 1986's multi-platinum *The Whole Story* hits collection—a West German record company, Wild Wind, announced the imminent release of a compilation titled *The Early Years*, featuring ten of the Cathy Bush demos.

White label vinyl copies were pressed up, in a sleeve featuring a wonky cover image: a terrible yellow and brown daub of a lion's head in profile, framed in the black outline of a heart shape (which was in fact an even worse rendering of the already crudely drawn logo for Bush's 1979 Tour of Life). Wild Wind believed that they had somehow secured the rights to the tapes from a never-named source. When Bush and EMI learned of the scheme, a cease and desist legal warning quickly snuffed the project.

How the Cathy Bush tapes had arrived at this destination was via a circuitous route. In his zeal to bring Bush to the attention of record companies, her earliest champion Ricky Hopper had sent out a number of copies, which ultimately failed to stir much in the way of interest. One had fallen into the hands of a former EMI employee-turned-DJ, John Dixon, who in 1982 aired twenty-two of the unfinished songs on KSTM-FM in Phoenix, Arizona. Some fans were quick to record the broadcast, and the songs were then repeatedly bootlegged under various titles, including *The Phoenix Recordings*, *Alone at My Piano*, *Shrubberies* and *Cathy's Fantastic Works*.

No official release of these tracks was ever forthcoming, however. But if Bush was keen to keep her earliest, exploratory recordings under wraps, it proved to be a futile exercise in the end. In 1997, the songs leaked online and, as is the way of the digital age, the genie was out of the bottle.

6

A Songbird in the Garden of a Starman

Kate and David Bowie, 1972–2018

Fading in and fading out as its airwaves traveled over the North Sea or drifted up across the English Channel, Radio Luxembourg was always an exotic visitor to the homes of British pop fans.

Given its ropey reception, to its listeners it often felt like an echo of the 1960s ship-based pirate stations effectively killed off in 1967 by the launch of Radio 1 and held a certain faraway charm beyond the reach of the BBC's groovy, if a tad cheesy flagship chart station.

Fitting, then, that it was via the distant transmitter broadcasting from the Grand Duchy of Luxembourg that Cathy Bush first heard a strange new record coming in on a wave of phase. One evening in 1972, the thirteen-year-old was lying in the bath when the DJ played "Starman," the latest single from the at-the-time "Space Oddity" one-hit-wonder—and subsequent serial flopper—David Bowie.

To her teenage ears, everything about this alluring singer was instantly compelling: his weird name, his intimate and yearning voice, his trippy song about a benign alien waiting in the sky. When, along with an entire generation of future musicians, her young mind was subsequently blown by Bowie's appearance on *Top of the Pops* performing "Starman" on July 6, 1972, her intense curiosity turned to deep fascination.

"He was almost insect-like, his clothing was theatrical and bizarre," she remembered thirty years later in her foreword for a *MOJO* David Bowie special issue. "Was that a dress? No one was sure, but my conclusion was that he was quite beautiful. His picture found itself on my bedroom wall next to the sacred space reserved solely for my greatest love, Elton John."

Little was Cathy to know, and not that it meant anything at all to her in terms of having her two idols share her pin-up wall space, but David Bowie and Elton John were soon to become avowed frenemies. Bowie considered John's 1972 single "Rocket Man" to be a low-grade photocopy of the spaced-out astronaut blueprint of 1969's "Space Oddity." When the pair briefly met one another for the first time over tea in Los Angeles that year, passive-aggressive rivalry hung heavy in the air.

"We didn't exactly become pals, not really having much in common," Bowie sniffily recalled. "Especially musically." Bowie's wife Angie tried her best to puncture her husband's "Rocket Man"-shaped huff, reminding him, "Other people can sing about space, too."

"I know David has always wanted to be Judy Garland," Elton later carped, quite possibly having a dig at the octave-leaping "Over the Rainbow" steal in the chorus of "Starman."

Cathy remained unaffected by this pop star cold war, and three weeks ahead of her fifteenth birthday, traveled with the legion of Bowie's wide-eyed devotees to London's Hammersmith Odeon on the evening of July 3, 1973, for the final night of the Ziggy Stardust Tour.

As she excitedly waited only feet from the stage for the arrival of Bowie and the Spiders from Mars, she would have been entirely unaware that earlier that day, in the small hours sometime around 2 a.m. following the previous night's show, future Sex Pistol guitarist, the perma-thieving Steve Jones, had sneaked into the Odeon's auditorium past a security guard sleeping in the stalls and made off with a load of the band's equipment. Drummer Woody Woodmansey's cymbals, bassist Trevor Bolder's amp and Bowie's microphone (still bearing his lipstick traces) had all been silently carried off by Jones, stashed in his waiting minivan and driven away.

Neither would she have guessed that, close to the show's end, as Bowie stepped over to second guitarist John Hutchinson and whispered in his ear, telling him to hold off starting the final song, "Rock 'n' Roll Suicide," it was because he was set to make a jaw-dropping announcement. As if the gig hadn't been dramatic enough, Bush was about to witness a moment of rock history happening in real time.

"Ah, of all the shows on this tour, this particular show will remain with us the longest," Bowie declared into the microphone, to the accompaniment of clapping and squealing from the audience. "Because not only is it the last show of the tour, but it's the last show that we'll ever do. Thank you."

As the cheers quickly turned to sounds of shock and dismay, Cathy burst into tears. "I did, yeah," she recalled to me. "And it looked like he was crying too."

Bowie wasn't, of course, retiring, but rather killing the character of Ziggy Stardust stone dead (although he would keep his spikey red mullet for a bit longer). Bush's love for David Bowie was undimmed and continued to inspire her intense creativity. In 1973, she was moved to write a song that was to end up being named "Humming," but which can be traced back to its alternative title, "Maybe," and in its opening, sighing words—"Oh, Davy"—to its inspiration.

"Maybe" was one of the many songs taped in 1973 by Pink Floyd's David Gilmour on his reel-to-reel at East Wickham Farm, when he recorded Cathy Bush singing and playing piano after being tipped off to her talents by Ricky Hopper. It was subsequently recorded again in August 1973 at Gilmour's home studio with the Surrey country rock band Unicorn backing the young singer, and once more at AIR Studios in Oxford Street when the Floyd guitarist upped the ante by funding master recordings to further showcase Bush's prodigious skills.

In its earliest, home-recorded, piano-and-voice incarnation, the song bears the distinct imprint of the ornate, rhythmic playing style of Elton John as the singer ruminates on the star-like presence of "Davy," before declaring a fanciful wish to become one of the songbirds in his garden. The lyrical imagery having evolved by the time of the 1975 AIR recording, any reference to "Davy" is gone, though Bush makes the point explicit that the subject of the song is a rock singer. Stylistically daring to cross the David-and-Elton divide, with its mid-paced, rolling groove, piano arpeggios and weepy slide guitar, the overall effect is more "Tiny Dancer" than "Starman."

"Humming"/"Maybe" was ditched by Bush as one of the contenders for her debut album, *The Kick Inside* (even though the AIR sessions produced the master takes of "The Saxophone Song" and "The Man with the Child in His Eyes"). But she did allow the 1975-era full band version to be played once on Radio 1 in 1979 when being interviewed by DJ Ed "Stewpot" Stewart. It was a playful exchange revealing both Kate's quick humor and sometimes squirming assessment of her own music.

Ed Stewart: Well, actually, Kate has very kindly brought us in a tape of a piece of music you recorded . . . how old were you with this one, Kate?

Kate Bush: Oh, I was about fifteen [when it was written].

ES: D'you mind if we play it for everybody?

KB: (*Laughs*) I'll shut my ears, okay?

ES: Will you? Okay. Would you like to introduce it?

KB: Yeah. Here it is.

[*"Humming"/"Maybe" snatch plays for forty-eight seconds*]

ES: Kate had a very wistful look on her face then. Why was that?

KB: I was waiting for the flat note in the middle.

ES: Ah, you mean we saved it just in time?

KB: No, you caught it actually (*laughs*).

～

By this point, Kate was, of course, herself a star. One who often attracted comparisons—in terms of her creative bravery and shapeshifting characteristics—to David Bowie. Not that fangirl Cathy was ever far below the surface.

The precise date is lost, but somewhere in the early 1980s, Bush was recording in Abbey Road when she popped into another control room at the studio complex to visit an unnamed friend. There, sat behind the mixer, under a beam of light, coolly smoking a cigarette, was Bowie. She instantly froze.

"Hello, Kate," he said.

"Er, hello," she nervously responded, before immediately scarpering.

"I caught my breath outside the door and didn't dare go back in again," she later wrote. "We've met many times since then and I don't have to leave the room any more . . . or do I?"

History doesn't record whether or not Kate had to flee the room when she met Bowie, in 1994, at a private viewing at the Flowers East gallery in Hackney, east London, exhibiting bespoke artworks created by various musicians as a fundraiser for the War Child charity. A number of A-list names had made wildly diverse contributions to the collection, titled *Little Pieces from Big Stars*—Paul McCartney (a driftwood carving), Charlie Watts (a sketch of a hotel telephone), Bono (a music box), Pete Townshend (a model of a Rickenbacker guitar), Brian Eno (four plaster-and-nail sculptures and an ambient piece recorded in a Japanese forest, playing on a camouflaged cassette machine) and David Bowie (seventeen computer-generated prints).

Bush's contributions returned her to the adrift-in-the-ocean concept of "The Ninth Wave" from *Hounds of Love*, released nine years earlier. The small twin pieces, 7 x 6 inches apiece, were framed in black polished wood. Each featured a gold-colored plaque: one bore the words, "Someone Lost at Sea Hoping Someone in a Plane Will Find Them"; the other "Someone in a Plane Hoping to Find Someone Lost at Sea." In the center of each frame was a piece of black velvet, representing the night sky, with a single point of red light flashing from a battery-powered diode. Kate had signed both on the back using a gold pen.

Just after 8 a.m. the next morning, to promote the project, Eno and Bowie appeared together in a location segment broadcast live from the gallery on ITV's then-morning show *GMTV*. Interviewed by perky, if slightly confused presenter Anthea Turner, Bowie picked out Bush's artworks for special consideration. It proved to be a toe-curling encounter.

> David Bowie: These two pieces are quite lovely. Would you like to read the captions on the bottom?
> Anthea Turner: The captions say, "Someone in a Plane Hoping to Find Someone Lost at Sea."
> DB: And the other?
> AT: And the other one says, "Someone Lost At Sea Hoping to . . . um . . ." [*squints*] "Someone Lost at Sea . . ."
> [*Bowie raises his eyebrows, mock sighs and laughs in Eno's direction*]
> AT: . . . "Hoping Someone *in* a Plane Will Find Them."
> DB: I just wanted to check the reading ability (*grins*). That is Kate Bush. But these are quite delightful pieces and if they didn't have a name attached to them, I would have bid for these anyway. In fact I'm going for these . . . I think they're very romantic.
> AT: Well, I like those as well. It's just like the sort of . . . the white rabbit in the snowstorm, isn't it?

~

The previous evening, a Bush and Bowie fan named Neville Judd was waiting outside the Flowers East gallery and spoke to Kate as she went in, asking her for any information about the artwork she'd donated to the project. "It's about the sea," she told him, "and about me too, I guess."

After Bowie and Bush had left, Judd was allowed into the gallery and spotted film director Nicolas Roeg—who famously cast Bowie in his 1976 movie *The Man Who Fell to Earth*—eyeing up Bush's artworks. "One of us needs to buy them," Roeg told Judd, prompting the latter, two weeks later, to bid and buy the art pieces, for £1,150, at the auction held at the Royal College of Art.

Sometime later, Judd managed to ask Bowie why, in the end, he hadn't bid for Kate's works. "I thought they were the most fabulous things," Bowie told him, "and I intended to send in a bid, but something happened, and I never did."

～

For her part, Kate later revealed that in the various times she met David Bowie, and once she'd gotten over being utterly starstruck and prone to flight, she found him to be "really charming and playful." When Bowie died on January 10, 2016, Bush was one of the first to pay her respects, stating, "he created such staggeringly brilliant work . . . so much of it was *so* good. Whatever journey his beautiful soul is now on, I hope he can somehow feel how much we all miss him."

She added that she'd found Bowie's final album, *Blackstar*, which only revealed its hints, clues, and secrets after his death, "beautiful . . . very moving, of course, but one of the best things he's ever done."

Two years later, in 2018, Kate remastered and reissued her entire back catalog of albums. Along with them came the newly compiled rarities collection, *The Other Sides*, featuring—finally— her 1975 recording of "Humming." It slipped out without any hoo-ha, fuss, or fanfare, as a quiet tribute from an enthralled teenager called Cathy from Kent.

7

Guest Testimony

David Gilmour

"My friend, a guy called Rick Hopper, brought [Kate's] tape to me. I listened to it with him, and he said she was brilliant, and I said I agreed. I guess I thought that what was on it was not the sort of thing to take directly to a record company, to an A&R man. I thought a bit more was needed to be brought out of it. She was a girl plonking away on a piano with a rather squeaky voice and I didn't trust most of the A&R men that I'd come across to be able to spot what was in it.

"So I trundled off down to her house with a tape recorder one day and recorded a load more songs with her at the piano in her front room. Which was only to get more of it . . . not with the thought of taking that on to a record company. And then I sat and went through the whole amount of stuff that she had, which was a lot, at least fifty songs.

"I chose three songs out of her demos—'The Man with the Child in His Eyes' was one, 'The Saxophone Song' was another and I can't remember what the third one was ['Maybe']. There were no moments when we had any sort of arguments or discussions. She was just very happy. To be honest, when I chose the songs, I don't think she was even there. I just went through all these things on my own and said, 'That one will do, and this one'll do, and that one'll do.' I wasn't really trying to choose the absolute three best songs. I was trying to choose the best songs of a variety of styles, so that there would be a wider selection of her talent on view.

"I also then did one or two attempted demos on an eight-track in my home studio using the band Unicorn as backing musicians, but they didn't really achieve what was required. And then basically the decision was made that it needed to be done properly. I thought that we needed to actually record masters for an album and see where we got to.

"So I gave my friend Andrew Powell a ring—who was a producer and arranger—and we booked AIR Studios and Geoff Emerick the engineer. Andrew did some string arrangements and they cut those three songs as masters. I didn't even go in on the day of recording. Then some guys from EMI came to Abbey Road when [Pink Floyd] were making the *Wish You Were Here* album, and they were listening to some stuff with us. It was probably the final mixing for *Wish You Were Here* cause we usually wouldn't let 'em in until then.

"When that was finished, I took a couple of them off into another control room somewhere and said, 'Listen to this tape.' They listened to it, and they said, 'Oh well, we'll sign her.' So I put them onto Kate and all their subsequent dealings were directly with her and I just got repaid for the money I had put into it.

"Then it sort of sat for two or three years. This has generally come out as looking like they were nurturing her. There seems to be an element of revisionist thinking in the things I've read about it, because it seems to me that [EMI] then [considered] nearly every record producer who produced girls. There were all sorts of producers, from what seemed to me to be completely unsuitable other singers, that they tried out with Kate. Because for some reason they didn't want to use Andrew Powell.

"But anyway, the same guy [from EMI] I spoke to at some bash or other. He said to me, 'C'mon, this one just isn't working. You found the only good songs.' Or words to that effect. 'We've tried out all sorts of things and it just isn't working.' I said, 'Well, why don't you go back to Andrew Powell?' and he sort of ummed and ahhed and said, 'Okay, let's think about that.' Eventually, they did go back to Andrew Powell and that's when it all started rolling. Obviously, at least, for a while, [Bush and EMI] must have had some sort of reasonable affinity.

"I definitely thought she was a true original and a great talent. She was a deceptive little thing because she was just a very young girl who you wouldn't have thought would've been quite as definite about what she wanted, but she knew *exactly* what she wanted.

"I don't think she ever needed a guiding hand from me. I mean, I was very happy to do whatever I could do. But it was a very rare thing when she came asking for much in the way of advice. She'd be perfectly capable of dealing with everything. I think I gave her a little bit of advice on various aspects of the live thing when she was about to do her first tour . . . recommending people that she could work with. But other than that I have rarely given her any advice.

"I mean, people seem to have the impression that I've been a sort of consistent guiding hand all the way through. But it just isn't true (*laughs*). I wish I could take more credit for her success. But basically once I'd done my first initial little thing—which was not tiny, but it was very short-term—my involvement was pretty much over.

"She's a true artist. An auteur one would call her if she was in the cinema. She can see and hear exactly what she wants to get and then she has to struggle to try to achieve it, like anyone would. But she gets there in the end. I think she found that the Fairlight and the other computer systems gave her much more control and helped her to achieve her vision of what she was trying to do.

"I performed 'Running Up That Hill' and something else [the Beatles' 'Let It Be'] with her at the Secret Policeman's Ball [for Amnesty International, in 1987]. Then she got on stage with me and did 'Comfortably Numb' [at the Royal Festival Hall in 2002]. She was terribly nervous. I did have to push her rather. I think I probably caught her at a good moment, and she said yes and then she found it hard to pull out. I think she was tempted to pull out, but she stuck with it. She wasn't overjoyed with her performance on the night, and she said she'd rather I didn't include it in my [*David Gilmour in Concert*] DVD and that was fine. I would suspect that she likes to be in control and likes to know exactly what's going on.

"Does she ever remind me of Roger [Waters, in her creative determination]?"

"No. Much prettier, much nicer."

8

"The Man That Started It All"

Kate and Lindsay Kemp, 1975–78

It was the summer of 1975 when Cathy Bush turned seventeen. A friend had invited her along to the Collegiate Theatre in London's Bloomsbury to see a production titled Flowers, staged and starring Lindsay Kemp, the Birkenhead-born, South Shields-raised thespian and mime artist. Unbeknown to Bush at this point, Kemp was a former mentor and lover of David Bowie.

As the auditorium dimmed and the action began, revealing an opening scene depicting isolated prisoners mock-masturbating in cell-like circles of light, it was instantly clear to Cathy that the performance was not to be quite what she might have expected.

"It was called *Flowers* and I thought, 'Oh, that sounds nice,'" she recalled to me. "But, I mean, I couldn't believe what I was seeing. I'd never seen anything like it. It was so powerful. You couldn't call it dance and although strictly speaking you'd call it mime, it wasn't mime. It wasn't the sort of silly, y'know, 'Oh, where's the window?' kind of thing. It was, like, *theater*."

Based on French writer Jean Genet's largely autobiographical 1943 debut novel *Notre-Dame-des-Fleurs* (or Our Lady of the Flowers), depicting one man's journey through the Parisian demi-monde of outcasts and homosexuals, Kemp's *Flowers* was a fantasia with visual echoes of the Ziggy Stardust character he had helped to inspire. As the action progressed, Kemp's troupe, assuming the roles of priests, sailors, criminals, cross-dressers, angels and whores, enacted a dreamlike and not always easy to comprehend tale of a "journey to destruction," set to a soundtrack of Billie Holiday, Pink Floyd, Al Jolson and Mozart.

"It was the most wonderful combination of music and theater," Bush remembered. "Really kind of fun and really sexy. It just absolutely took my breath away. I thought, 'That's so powerful, visually, and using music with it is making it so much *more* powerful.' And it made me think that, 'Okay, so music is what I want to do.'"

John Carder Bush noticed an instant change in his sister after she returned from witnessing *Flowers*. "It seemed to me," he later noted, "that Cathy had come back as Kate."

~)

One poster for *Flowers* featured a banner quote from David Bowie, declaring of Kemp, "This is the man that started it all." It was an important, attention-grabbing endorsement of Bowie's former theatrical guiding light, and one quite possibly born partially out of guilt. In 1967, the twenty-year-old Bowie had first met Kemp after seeing the latter's one-man show at the Little Theatre in Covent Garden, and the two had become creatively and sexually entangled.

Soon after, the pair appeared together in a new presentation, *Pierrot in Turquoise*, which featured Bowie in clownish make-up and ruffle-necked polka dot blouse singing some of the songs featured on his recently released, self-titled debut album, including "When I Live My Dream" and "Sell Me a Coat." There was plenty of drama between the couple off stage, too. In the first days of 1968, the production moved to the Rosehill Theatre in the village of Moresby, near Whitehaven in Cumbria, where Kemp discovered that Bowie had also been conducting an affair with their mutual friend, costume designer Natasha Korniloff.

The revelation was to cause Kemp and Bowie to split, and the former to make a half-hearted attempt to end his life. "I foolishly and rather theatrically and not too seriously attempted to cut my wrists," Kemp related to the BBC's *Newsnight* in 2016. "I kind of scratched them and was taken to the hospital and the doctor looked at them and put a bit of sticking plaster [on them] and sent me back and said, 'Don't be so daft.'"

"Lindsay was a trip-and-a-half," Bowie commented in 1972, before adding queen bitchily, "I've never known anybody commit suicide so many times. He lived on his emotions."

Kemp and Bowie managed to continue their professional relationship in *Pierrot in Turquoise*, and Kemp was to act as the puppet master for many of Ziggy's choreographed moves, while also appearing as the Starman alongside the now far more famous singer at the Rainbow Theatre in December 1972. "He was a wonderful influence," Bowie averred. "His day-to-day life was the most theatrical thing I'd seen, ever."

Three years on, Kemp was to make an indelible mark on another future performer and recording artist. In the days after Kate had been wowed by *Flowers*, she was flicking through London's arts and listings magazine *Time Out* when she saw an advert for theatrical classes led by Kemp. These too were held at the Collegiate Theatre, often on the same days as afternoon or evening performances, and typically attended by members of Kemp's cast, excitingly allowing Bush to step into their world.

"All the people in his troupe used to walk around with bottles of Lucozade and St Moritz cigarettes," she colorfully remembered. "I'd do the classes and then sit in the front row and watch him do the show, so it was like living Lindsay. It was just a total inspiration. I still think that Lindsay is the most original artist I've ever met. Just extraordinary."

Kemp's rousing improvisational exercises, in particular, thrilled Kate. Suddenly, and without warning, he'd announce that everyone had to imagine themselves in a siege in a war, and wild scenes of raving and howling would break out. "People in the next room would say they just heard all these people screaming," Bush enthused. "It was really intense."

~

Kemp's classes then moved from the Collegiate to the Dance Centre in Covent Garden (50p entrance fee). In later years, he was to claim that he'd instantly spotted the fledgling Kate Bush in among the ranks of his students. She wasn't convinced.

"I'm sure he didn't even know I was there at all. I mean, I was just a little girl. I was just one of the girls in the class. There was nothing special."

"I remember very clearly the day that I first encountered Kate," Kemp recounted in his foreword to Italian photographer Guido Harari's book, *The Kate Inside*. "I encouraged her to show me her spirit dancing. She was transported. At times she looked like a swan gliding over water. As the music swelled, she let herself be swept away, twirling and leaping like a mad thing."

Further to that, in 2016, Kemp told *Newsnight*, "She was always at the back, and I was forever having to pull her forward. But once she'd started moving and improvising, she was dynamic."

Having no formal dance qualifications to her name, the open door policy at Kemp's classes was entirely freeing for Bush, both physically and—perhaps just as importantly—socially. It was the first time she belonged to a creative family outside of her own.

"Lindsay was lovely to everybody as well, really embracing," she said. "Then, after the classes, we'd all go to this little café across the street. It had this real feeling of being in a circus troupe."

When Kemp relocated shortly afterward to Australia for a planned six-week sojourn that turned into a year, Bush was keen to maintain momentum in her performance studies. In early 1976, she enrolled in classes held in an arts complex in Elephant and Castle, south London, taught by the Manhattan-born contemporary dance and modern ballet teacher Adam Darius.

"He wasn't the same kind of school of theater that Lindsay was," Kate pointed out. "I suppose you could call it more 'dance.' But he was also somebody who was very inspirational. He was really kind to me actually. In a way, he took me under his wing a little bit."

It would be another two years, though, before either Kemp or Darius witnessed the teenager's full transformation into a confident, fluid, and high-profile performer.

~

Of the two mentors, only Lindsay Kemp inspired Kate to write a song, however. "Them Heavy People" on *The Kick Inside* may have been addressed in her back-cover acknowledgments to "my teachers of music + movement," but the album's dreamy-headed opener, "Moving" solely focused on Kemp and the life-changing effect he'd had on Bush.

"He needed a song written for him," Kate told writer Phil Sutcliffe in *Sounds* in 1980. "He opened up my eyes to the meanings of movement. He makes you feel so good. If you've got two left feet it's still, 'You dance like an angel, darling.' He fills people up. You're an empty glass and glug, glug, glug, he's filled you up with Champagne."

One evening in early 1978, Kemp returned to his flat in Battersea, south London, to find a record had been carefully pushed under his front door. It was a copy of *The Kick Inside* upon which Kate had highlighted "Moving" and written the words, "This is dedicated to you."

He hadn't even known she was a singer.

9

Round the Pubs

The KT Bush Band, 1977–78

Amid a cloud of dry ice, wielding a fake rifle, the eighteen-year-old Kate Bush was for the first time performing for an audience her soon-to-be-famous mock-shooting routine as she reached the climax of the dynamic, shuffling rocker "James and the Cold Gun."

It was one of her three original songs, along with "Them Heavy People" and "The Saxophone Song," that she had worked into her set with the KT Bush Band, as part of their Tuesday night residency at the Rose of Lee pub in Lewisham, southeast London.

"That was our big number at the gigs," enthuses guitarist Brian Bath. "Especially at the Rose . . . it was just monumental."

The first week that the KT Bush Band had appeared at the Rose of Lee, in the spring of 1977, only around half a dozen people had turned up (three of them being Kate's father, Robert, and brothers, John and Paddy). By the second gig, there were still no more than twice that number.

"But then, in about three weeks, the word started getting around," Paddy Bush remembered, "and the club became more and more packed. I think maybe about the fifth or sixth week, you couldn't get in."

~

It hadn't been Kate's intention to join a band. But, in the months after she'd signed to EMI in July 1976, receiving an advance of £3,000 (around £20,000 today), it became clear that she would benefit from some stage experience. A career in music was entirely her chosen path now, and she knew she had to get serious about it. She had left school with an impressive ten O levels but walked out after sitting only her mock A levels, and there was no back-up plan. To start getting ready for whatever might come next, she needed to try singing in a live setting.

To this end, Paddy Bush got in touch with his friend Brian Bath (who had first witnessed Kate's vocal and songwriting talents when she was only thirteen). Bath in turn contacted his drummer friend Vic King and bassist, and soon-to-be Kate's long-term beau, Del Palmer. All were veterans of the south London pub rock scene, fronted by a novice who would nonetheless soon elevate their collective fortunes.

Over the winter of 1976 and into 1977, the quartet rehearsed in the one-time grain barn at East Wickham Farm, typically in freezing conditions. Initially, the repertoire of the KT Bush Band (a name Kate at first hated) comprised the standard covers band fare of the day: "Honky Tonk Women," "Come Together," "I Heard It Through the Grapevine," with diversions into more challenging material such as Hall & Oates's moody, slow-building soul track, "She's Gone," or Bob Marley and the Wailers' quietly rousing "No Woman, No Cry."

The first night that Kate set foot on the stage at the Rose of Lee, she was terrified. "I was so scared, I really was," she remembered. "But, once you're up there, it's different. Y'know, you just forget all about it because they're there to see you and you have to give it to them."

Appearing in a couple of regular outfits—long black sleeveless dress and flowers in her hair; white frock adorned with ribbons—Bush managed to adopt a stage persona and, as the weeks passed, increasingly lose herself in the moment. One evening, however, her performing bubble was instantly popped mid-set by a friend wandering over and saying, "Oh, hello, Kate," as if they'd bumped into one another in the street. The singer stepped off the stage for a chat.

"I was so ashamed of being such a poser," she later winced. "And I suddenly realized it was time for me to get back on stage, so I had to say to her, 'Oh, bye, then . . .'"

In those first months of the group's existence, there were faint rumblings that the KT Bush Band might be involved in the upcoming sessions for Kate's debut EMI album. On April 5, 1977, the quartet, with Paddy in tow, booked into De Lane Lea Studios in Soho to record demos of the three Bush originals they'd worked up together in rehearsals, along with a never-to-be-released song titled "Dear Dead Days."

"She just did her thing, really," says Bath. "She knew what she was looking for. It was just a great session."

Expanding outward from the Rose of Lee, the band ventured further afield into other pub venues on the gigging scene: the Black Cat in Catford, the Duke of Richmond in Earl's Court, the White Hart in Tottenham, the Target in Northolt, even traveling as far south as the Seven Stars in Brighton.

One memorable night, on June 3, at the Half Moon in Putney, the pub was invaded by an amiable, but utterly bladdered crowd of Scottish football supporters. Some of them indeed may have been among the horde who the next day—accompanied by Rod Stewart—invaded the pitch at Wembley Stadium and enthusiastically mangled the goal posts, following their national team's 2–1 victory over England.

"They were just mad," said Kate. "They had flags waving everywhere, and no one could see the stage because all the guys were getting up on the stage and putting their arms around you. It was a bit hard to keep singing."

For a time, the KT Bush Band appeared to be taking their career fairly seriously and upped their pub production values to include smoke effects and more elaborate lighting. Together, they also posed for a promotional picture in a field—Kate adopting a Patti Smith-ish stance with her fingers tucked into the pockets of her suit jacket, as the hirsute Palmer, Bath, and King lined up to throw jazz hands showmen poses in the background.

But, life on the working band pub and club circuit soon began to pall. The low point came one dreary Sunday afternoon with a slot at a cheesy disco in Harlow, in Essex, named Tiffany's. The booker seemed pleased enough and offered to put a return date in the diary, but the band politely rejected the offer.

The last club gig for the KT Bush Band was an EMI showcase for Kate at the altogether more swish White Elephant in Mayfair in June. Later in 1977, a brochure was produced by the record company to promote the upcoming artists on the label. In it, a shot of Kate in her white dress, in mid-flight on stage with the KT Bush Band, her face partly obscured by shadow, was accompanied by blurb featuring her name alone.

"Good things come in small packages and are worth waiting for," it clunkily began. "Whoever said that may have had Kate Bush in mind. Kate has been allowed to mature and develop her talents, and the results of this will be heard later this year when her first album is released. Kate Bush, definitely a name to be remembered."

A clichéd, showbizzy phrase it may have been, but it was to prove an accurate one.

~

The only existing footage of the KT Bush Band dates from the following year. In the February of 1978, the group traveled to Cologne to perform on *Bio's Bahnhof*, a music show (ranging from pop to classical) presented by Alfred Biolek and videotaped at the Depothalle, a former tram station. It was to be Kate's first ever appearance on TV.

The balding, bespectacled, brown-and-beige-wearing host was an avuncular presence, though in these post-punk times he appeared very much stuck in the early 1970s. After Biolek made a lengthy introduction to camera in German, Kate appeared in her red "Wuthering Heights" dress, shimmying with her back to the seated audience as jets of familiar dry ice shot into the air and the band launched into the reggae groove of "Kite." She cut an assured figure, those hours clocked up on the stages of smoky pubs having served her well. Behind her, the KT Bush Band did a decent job of getting their skank on.

A ripple of applause met the end of the song, before a backdrop unfurled from the rafters, cutting the musicians off from the singer, and featuring a godawful landscape painting depicting forks of lightning striking toward a fiery volcano. The backing track of the studio-recorded orchestral version of "Wuthering Heights" was ushered in, before Kate alone live-sang and elegantly moved through the steps of the unique and memorable routine that would soon become her visual signature. The band had literally disappeared.

10

Live in the Studio

The making of The Kick Inside, *1975–77*

Positioned four storeys above Oxford Circus in the heart of the West End of London, AIR Studios was one of the most state-of-the-art and in-demand recording facilities of the 1970s.

Opened in October 1970 by its co-founder George Martin, only six months after the announcement of the breakup of his most famous charges, The Beatles, it had in the years following been the scene of the creation of milestone records by Pink Floyd (*Meddle*), Roxy Music (*For Your Pleasure*), and Queen (*Sheer Heart Attack*).

It would have been an intimidating environment for any inexperienced recording artist, but perhaps especially for a sixteen-year-old schoolgirl committing her songs, entirely live to tape, for the first time in a professional setting.

Back in June 1975, in the test session funded by David Gilmour and overseen by producer Andrew Powell, Bush had begun making her debut album, *The Kick Inside*, before she was really aware of the fact. On that day, "Humming"/"Maybe" and "The Saxophone Song" (the latter making the final cut) were quickly recorded using a crack team of session musicians, including drummer Barry de Souza (David Essex), bassist Bruce Lynch (Cat Stevens) and guitarist Alan Parker (David Bowie).

If all of that wasn't quite thrilling enough, in the evening, an orchestra arrived to augment "The Man with the Child in His Eyes," Bush's most mysterious (and still-elusive) composition, involving nocturnal visitations from a guileless and empathic figure who, it seems, exists only in her imagination. "A very intimate song about a young girl . . . voicing her inner thoughts . . . to herself," was the closest she would ever get to really explaining it. That night, she captured what was to become the master recording of the song.

"When I look back at myself then," she reflected to me, "I think I was very brave. Because I was still at school, and there I was sitting in AIR Studios, singing and playing the piano live with, like, a thirty-piece orchestra. Then I'd go back to school the next day and, y'know, just try to get on with being a schoolgirl. I think it was very brave to do that and not just . . . run away from it.

"I think of myself in that room, and I think, 'Well done, that you actually had the guts to sit there and do that.' I wanted to leave school and my parents said, 'You've got to take your O levels. You can't leave school before.' There was an element of me wanting to show them that I really meant what I was saying . . . I wanted to make music. When I look back at it, they were really great about it. Because they probably saw I was so driven that it was what I was going to do anyway."

Cut to two summers later, and the making of *The Kick Inside* had begun in earnest.

In sessions beginning in July 1977—the month Kate turned nineteen—and spilling over into August, the remaining eleven songs that would feature on the record were confidently rendered in the studio. For these recordings, Andrew Powell had assembled a different band involving members of two pop/rock outfits he'd previously worked with as an orchestral arranger: drummer Stuart Elliott, keyboard-player Duncan MacKay (Steve Harley & Cockney Rebel), bassist David Paton, and guitarist Ian Bairnson (Pilot).

"She was nineteen, I was only twenty-four," Elliott remembers. "She was this little hippie chick. We thought nothing of it, y'know, just another session. Then, as soon as she sat at the piano and started playing songs like 'Wuthering Heights," oh my God, our jaws dropped. We thought, 'Flipping hell, this is just unbelievable.' The maturity in her composition. You can live a whole lifetime and never write a song half as good as Kate [can], no matter how musical you are."

A studio modus operandi quickly developed. The musicians would gather around Kate at the piano, and she would play through the next song to be recorded, before Powell handed out the chord charts.

Hour by hour, day by day, out from behind the grand piano flowed these astonishingly complex and captivating songs. Songs about the lunar effects on the menstrual cycle and the spook of weird coincidences ("Strange Phenomena"). Songs that brazenly addressed sex in a way that was uncommon for the era, especially for a young female artist ("Feel It," "L'Amour Looks Something Like You"), or that tackled taboos head-on, such as the rewriting of the eighteenth-century incest-and-murder ballad "Lizie Wan" to tell the tale of the suicide of a girl impregnated by her brother ("The Kick Inside").

For Stuart Elliott behind the drum kit, these vivid compositions were a pleasure to be required to rhythmically enhance. "It was an absolute joy," he remembered. "I just sat down at the drums, and I largely played to her vocal. Everything I did was in response to her top line and melody.

"It was really led by Kate because it was a complete picture. It's the greatest luxury to play with an artist like that. Cause quite often, [an artist will] write a great song, and then the producer will say, 'Right, let's do the backing track.' So there's no vocal. You've got to imagine what the top line is, and there's no vibe. But the vibe was there cause she was there on the sessions . . . sang it live, played it live.

"She didn't seem nervous at all. She was assured when she sat at the piano. There was a performance every time. She'd obviously played the songs over and over and over again. It was a very quick batch of sessions. We did all the backing tracks in four days. The chemistry of the whole thing was just incredible."

Songs such as "Kite" and "Them Heavy People" even suggested reggae grooves, before fun and games were had with the overdubs. On "Room for the Life," in first experimenting with the layers of strange sounds that would come to characterize Bush's music, along with the synths and clavinet and celeste parts, percussionist Morris Pert added boobams (small, stick-played, chromatically tuned bongos), while Andrew Powell was moved to blow "woo-woos" on the rims of beer bottles. Paddy Bush was brought in to play mandolin on "Oh to Be in Love" and add his distinctive basso profundo counterpoint vocals to "Them Heavy People."

Then, there was "Wuthering Heights," written on a night lit by a full moon, not long before work on the album was due to begin. Kate, who hadn't yet read Emily Brontë's 1847 novel of destructive love, was instead inspired when she caught the last ten minutes of the 1967 BBC series on TV. She later read the book "to get the research right," though in many ways made the story her own, not least through her strangely possessed-sounding delivery, nailed in just one take.

Kate had cast herself as a spectre and so appropriately sang the song in a ghostly, helium-high register, without any trace of self-consciousness or fear of ridicule. "Wuthering Heights" was an instantly entrancing creation: one that the singer knew could make her stand out from the typical pop crowd.

In the studio, as the track was played back in the control room, Kate danced along, already working out the choreography for her future performances of "Wuthering Heights." So enthralled were the singer and production team that they began mixing the song around midnight and stayed at AIR until dawn to make sure it was fully realized in every detail.

Upon release, "Wuthering Heights" was to fanfare the singer's arrival in an entirely attention-hijacking fashion. Some DJs would later think they were mistakenly playing the 45-rpm single at 78 rpm.

Years later, Bush talked to me about the single in a slightly weary, if still appreciative tone.

"They wrote all this shit about, 'She's obsessed with *Wuthering Heights*, and she's changed her name to Catherine,'" she mockingly stated. "For me, it's just a song I wrote a long time ago and I did think it was a wonderful story. It's so passionate, isn't it? It's the ultimate love story. Two people who are so . . . I don't know if you could really say they love each other, but it's all about passion between two human beings and that passion went beyond death. It's a fantastic story written by this very young girl. It's fascinating."

~

The bosses at EMI, however, were not keen on releasing "Wuthering Heights" as the first Kate Bush single, preferring the rockier and comparatively more straightforward "James and the Cold Gun." Bob Mercer, the record company's managing director, later claimed that the young singer had "burst into tears" of frustration in a meeting when she realized that she might not get her own way. In 2005, Bush insisted the story was utter rubbish.

"I find it *infuriating* actually," she quietly fumed. "Because it's portraying me as this kind of . . . I dunno. I've never burst into tears over anything. You've got to be really strong in this business, d'you know what I mean? And even though I was young at the time, I was probably just as headstrong and determined as I am now. Bob had hundreds of artists that he was doing deals with, but for me, that was my first record."

In fact, she could still visualize herself back in the meeting, and see all the faces around her.

"I remember that so clearly, like it was just a year or two ago. I can remember the people in that room and what the room looked like and everything, because it was such a big event for me.

"The great story with that, which I have seen misquoted, was we were all having this meeting and everybody else had ideas about other singles and I wanted it to be 'Wuthering Heights.' We were in the MD's office, and I'd said, 'I think it should be

"Wuthering Heights'" and a couple of people said, 'No no no no, we think it should be this and this.'"

Just at that moment, the door had opened and into the room stepped EMI's head of promotions, Terry Walker.

"He was known within the company as having quite a good instinct about stuff," Bush pointed out. "He walked in, put something on the desk and went, 'Oh, hi, Kate. 'Wuthering Heights' . . . great first single' and walked out. And everyone was like (*tuts*). The timing was just incredible."

11

"A Bag o' Cats!"

Reactions to "Wuthering Heights," 1978

"What is *that?*" —Unnamed EMI executive

"B-o-r-i-n-g. Rotten song." —*Record Mirror*

"Is she black?"; "No, I think she's from Devon." —Overheard conversation in staff canteen

"A weary rehash about 'cruel Heathcliff.'" —*Stereo Review*

"A munchkin falsetto." —*Crawdaddy*

"A squeaky, child-like intonation. And it's effective." —*Billboard*

"Bizarre. Kate is a complete newcomer, is nineteen, was first unearthed by David Gilmour, and has spent time with mime coach to the stars, Lindsay Kemp. The orchestration is ornate and densely packed, but never overflows its banks, Kate's extraordinary vocals skating in and out, over and above. Reference points are tricky, but possibly a cross between Linda Lewis and *Macbeth*'s three witches is closest. She turns the famous examination text by Emily Brontë into glorious soap opera trauma." —*Melody Maker*

"She sent me 'Wuthering Heights' and said, 'I'm thinking of releasing this as the first single.' I said, 'I wouldn't if I were you' (*laughs*). I was rather keen to release 'The Man with the Child in His Eyes' as the first single. But that was the second single and, even following 'Wuthering Heights,' it didn't do as well. So I was completely and utterly wrong and she was completely and utterly right, as she usually is." —David Gilmour

"'Wuthering Heights' is utterly mesmeric . . ." —*NME*

"Wuthering Wonderful!" —*Daily Express*

"Basil Bush's sister . . . responsible for 'Withering Tights.'" —Peter Cook

"I remember my mum, God rest her soul, when she first heard Kate Bush. I brought [the single] home. 'Oh Johnny, it sounds like a bag o' cats!' Those shrieks and warbles are beauty beyond belief to me." —John Lydon

12

Public Image Limited

Focusing the projector, 1978–80

It must be hard to become a pop star at the age of nineteen when, deep in your soul, you don't want to be one.

"The buzz for me wasn't being famous," Bush stressed to the author. "It was getting something interesting [done] creatively."

And so it must be hugely disorientating to find yourself suddenly yanked into a world of cosy mainstream TV programmes such as *Saturday Night at the Mill* (singing about a Russian mystic in "Them Heavy People") and *Ask Aspel* (singing about furtive homosexuality in "Kashka from Baghdad"). Or be especially dispiriting when one of the by-products of these promo appearances is having the piss taken out of you on BBC Two sketch show *Not the Nine O'Clock News*, as crimped-haired, leotard-wearing comedian Pamela Stephenson lampoons you by helium-shrieking, "People bought my latest hits, cause they liked my latex tits." Or to watch impressionist Faith Brown over on ITV in a bad black wig caricature you as a wide-eyed nutter squawking "Wow" while flailing through the air on fly wires.

Even if you laugh along—and send a long letter to Brown telling her you're happily in on the joke—it must be hard not to feel that it's all getting dangerously out of your control and that you're being reduced to a two-dimensional cartoon character.

Kate Bush's first UK TV appearance was also her worst. On February 16, 1978, in front of an estimated 15 million viewers, she squirmed under the lights at the *Top of the Pops* studio. Somewhere offscreen, the BBC orchestra, likely fresh from accompanying the latest singing turn on *The Two Ronnies*, were murdering "Wuthering Heights." Alone on the stage, the nineteen-year-old looked equal parts terrified and mortified, as she gamely attempted to sing over this lumpy, live rendering of her soon-to-be-number-one song. It was, as she would later assess with characteristic bluntness, "a bloody awful performance."

Luckily for Bush, the fast-developing medium of the pre-filmed promotional video would become a far more natural home for her: a place to visually magic up the characters in her lyrics. In fact, two clips were made for "Wuthering Heights." In the first (destined for the US market), wearing her red dress, she performed her carefully choreographed routine out on the Ministry of Defence's artillery range at Salisbury Plain. In the second, directed by former David Bowie/Black Sabbath sleeve designer Keith MacMillan and captured to video (rather than film) in a TV studio, the singer dressed in white and floated in front of a dark background over a floor of dry ice, her moves frequently dissolving into trippy trails through proto digital trickery.

"We set it up on a Monday morning," MacMillan remembered. "We shot it in the afternoon, we edited all night, and it was ready for *Top of the Pops* the next morning."

MacMillan's video was first screened on the BBC show on March 2, 1978, when "Wuthering Heights" was sitting at number five in the charts after having slowly moved up the rankings from numbers forty-two to twenty-seven to thirteen. The next week the single hit number one beginning a four-week stint, which involved being forced to return to the *Top of the Pops* studio for a run of performances that improved with each episode—Bush more confidently moving through her dance routine in a ghostly white frock or black dress (with rose in hair, à la the KT Bush Band look) and live-singing over the still-rotten BBC band, or performing behind a grand piano strewn with plastic orchids.

On March 16, Bush appeared on BBC One's current affairs programme *Tonight*, facing presenter Denis Tuohy, who proved to be a sympathetic and perceptive interviewer, asking if Bush's high singing register in "Wuthering Heights" was in fact her adopting the character of Catherine Earnshaw.

"Is the pitch of the voice there your natural, comfortable singing pitch?" Tuohy enquired. "Or do you deliberately heighten it to get . . . this ghost-like effect?"

"Yes, I do deliberately heighten it," Bush responded, "because that's what the song calls for."

Later in the interview, Tuohy wondered, "Were you surprised that a song as unusual as 'Wuthering Heights' made it in the way that it has . . . up to the top?"

"Yeah, I'm amazed," Kate grinned. "I mean, I always hoped that it would do something, and that people would like it. But the extent and the *speed* is just incredible. It really is awesome, and it makes me feel like that high (*indicating roughly an inch between thumb and forefinger*). Y'know, really, really small (*laughs*)."

It was a telling admission that Bush felt dwarfed by her overnight success. Equally revealing was her short onscreen chat with Irish TV host Gay Byrne on *The Late Late Show* at the RTÉ studio in Dublin.

"So absolutely you've decided that music and showbusiness is your career?" Byrne wondered.

"Music is, yes, for sure," Bush nodded, before pointedly adding, "the most important thing at the moment is that I get the time in order to write more and expand my, uh, inspiration and sources of stimulus."

And yet there were still a procession of showbiz hoops for her to jump through. Not least—and most bizarrely—when she traveled to Japan on a promotional trip in June 1978.

The singer had been invited to perform at the Seventh Tokyo Music Festival: essentially a song contest where she was to sing "Moving," the single that had been selected for the Japanese market. It was an enormous opportunity in terms of publicity. There were to be eleven thousand people—quite a leap from even the capacity crowds at the Rose of Lee only the year before—in the audience at the venue, the legendary Budokan. More terrifying still, an estimated 33 million viewers would be watching at home.

Existing footage of Kate's performance reveals her acute nervousness, as she sings live, her pitch wavering, on stage beside an orchestra, her eyes magnified by lilac eyeshadow to match her tights and lacy, puffy flower-adorned dress. In the final judgment, Bush tied in second place with US R&B group the Emotions, sharing the silver medal and 600,000¥ prize money (equivalent to a measly £5,600 today), while Al Green bagged the gold for his song, "Belle." More importantly, though, "Moving" was to reach number one in the national chart.

But there were even weirder scenes during the Japanese jaunt. The singer was encouraged to film two TV commercials for Seiko watches: miming to "Them Heavy People" while dancing in a silky dress, the colors of which bled from yellow to green to blue, as she self-consciously delivered in voiceover the slogan: "We have many varieties of mood within us. But it's up to you to choose."

More mind-bending still were Bush's guest contributions to pop variety show, *Sound in S.* Encouraged to solo perform a couple of The Beatles' cover versions—"The Long and Winding Road," "She's Leaving Home"—she then joined the show's one male and two female presenters for a cheesy ensemble rendering of "Let It Be." Elsewhere, in an utterly surreal moment, the two girl performers teamed up for a disco pop take on "Them Heavy People" before Bush burst onto the set with a troupe of male dancers to round the number off with a high-kicking, end-of-the-pier finale. She smiled her way through it all, but it was further proof that she was probably veering down the wrong route toward naff light entertainment.

Far classier was her December 1978 turn on comedy and music revue show *Saturday Night Live* in the US. During the rehearsals at the NBC studio in the 30 Rockefeller Plaza skyscraper, both Mick Jagger and Paul Simon turned up to visit and pay their respects to Britain's newest pop star. Invited onto the show by that week's host, Monty Python's Eric Idle—who introduced her to the programme's 22 million viewers as "very wonderful"—Bush performed the same quasi-yogic, gold-spangled leotard-wearing routine for "The Man with the Child in His Eyes" that had first appeared in the British-shot video for her follow-up single back in May. This time, however, she was atop a piano played by SNL's Paul Shaffer. Later, in a second number, she delivered her mac-and-fedora-sporting step sequence for "Them Heavy People."

Altogether, the highs and lows of these experiences offered proof that an artist could negotiate TV promotion entirely on their own terms. Nonetheless, for Bush, there lingered a nagging frustration that she now seemed to be spending all of her time promoting her records rather than making them.

"I felt it was all the wrong way round," she told me. "Because what I wanted to do was spend all the time and the focus on putting the record together and then do a bit of promotion to promote the record. Because, obviously, nobody would've been interested in me if it wasn't to do with the record. But the emphasis was all wrong. And so I wanted to just turn that around."

The first step was to stop wasting time shlepping around TV studios and to achieve some level of supervision over her videos, resulting, in 1980, in onscreen characterizations that reached beyond the precise choreography of her early promos: the plastic-bubbled foetus of "Breathing," the provocative swordmistress of "Babooshka," the wide-eyed soldier heading into battle in "Army Dreamers."

In Bush's mind, this clearly opened up a world of possibilities in which she would revel over four decades: "Telling a story, that's what's really a buzz for me. There's a huge amount of time and work goes into each video."

It was the untold battle of Kate Bush's career. With vision just as important to her as sound, her journey from performer to director involved a tussle for authority over her videography, which was to be as creatively defining as her battle for complete license over her music. From 1978 and on into the 1980s and beyond, Kate Bush slowly regained utter control of her career: inch by inch, record by record, video by video.

13

Lost in France

The making of Lionheart, *1978*

"I really didn't like my second record. It's just not what I wanted to say at all.

"It's not the way I would've done it . . . not having had the right amount of time to write the songs. Because with the first record, I'd had all the time from being twelve, thirteen, right up until when I made the record, to accumulate a big pool of songs that I then chose the best ones from. So, with the second record, it was made very quickly after the first, plus I was doing all this promotion, flying round the world promoting the first record, and it was all wrong.

"No offense to the musicians on the second record, but there was *conflict* between myself and Andrew Powell in the way that we saw it. And fair enough—Andrew was the producer, he wanted to do it his way, and I was the strong-headed artist who wanted to do it my way, so you're bound to get conflict. That was a really big turning point."

Only five months after the release of *The Kick Inside*, with Kate Bush's debut album already settling into what would become a seventy-one-week residency in the charts, EMI pushed her back into the studio to record its successor.

Kate had by this time left home, having moved out of East Wickham Farm at eighteen and into a Victorian house, owned by her dad and split into three flats, at the coincidentally named 44 Wickham Road in Brockley, London SE4, seven miles west across the city. Bush was now independent but still unobtrusively protected by her family: John Carder Bush lived in the ground-floor flat, with Paddy above him, and Kate at the top of the house.

Elsewhere, she was also keen to maintain another relationship: the one with the KT Bush Band that had apparently been severed with the making of *The Kick Inside*. And so, guitarist Brian Bath was invited to Bush's Brockley flat to work through the songs that were to feature on her second album, *Lionheart*.

"I'd sit with her at the piano," Bath remembers. "We'd go through songs, and I'd write up some rough kind of bar charts and we'd try to knock them into order. Like, 'Where's the intro, Kate? Are you really going to use that chord?' And we'd suss out what the chords were and just work out where we were with the guitar [parts]."

As successful as *The Kick Inside* was, both creatively and commercially, Bush was already trying to assert further control over her creative process as early as summer 1978. Back at East Wickham Farm, a demo studio was swiftly built in the barn.

"We converted it, with her dad," recalls Bath. "He showed us how to saw bits of wood up, and he did all the electrics and wiring. He was a clever man. We kind of soundproofed it and then we made a studio door."

The flagstone floor in the now ad-hoc live room was retained, while the grain loft, accessed via a set of steps, now served as the control room, where a small mixing desk and eight-track TASCAM tape machine were installed.

There, throughout June, at what was loosely named Summerhouse Studios, the test recordings for songs from *Lionheart* were committed to tape by the band, including early versions of "Wow"—a variously spacey and dynamic power ballad that explored the magic and artifice of showbusiness— and the jazzy, 1920s Berlin-evoking "Coffee Homeground," which originally featured heavy rock guitars eventually ditched from the final version.

For the vocal of the multi-movement "Hammer Horror," which shifted from muted verses through reggae bridges to rocking choruses, Paddy Bush encouraged his sister to immerse herself in the dread-filled subject matter by recording her vocal in total darkness in the barn.

"He had some boxes of matches," Brian Bath remembers, "and while she was singing it, he started throwing them through the air. We were upstairs listening to Kate doing her vocal. All of a sudden you just heard this 'Waaaaaaaaaaa!' She was apparently so scared. I thought she might've been putting it on, but she actually lost her voice. She couldn't sing for quite a few days after that."

∿

Scary fun and head games aside, *Lionheart* was to be recorded in a very different setting, 750 miles away, at Super Bear Studios in the village of Berre-les-Alpes, hidden away in the mountains northeast of Nice.

The vogue for location recording in France had continued in the years after the Rolling Stones had scandalized the inhabitants of the nearby Villefranche-sur-Mer during the drugged-out making of *Exile on Main Street* in 1971. Other premier league rock stars had sought creative—and often tax-related—refuge in rural France: notably Elton John and David Bowie at the Château d'Hérouville twenty-four miles northwest of Paris. Super Bear Studios, meanwhile, had been recommended to Bush by David Gilmour (continuing to be a gently guiding but unseen presence in her career) after he'd completed work on his first, self-titled solo album at the residential facility only four months previously. The singer, with the KT Bush Band in tow, arrived there in July 1978.

The building that housed Super Bear had previously been a high-end restaurant catering to the rich residents and holiday makers of Nice and Cannes. Now it was an idyllic getaway for musicians: its grounds planted with palm trees dotted around a long, narrow swimming pool, green-lit at night. Indoors, the wood-paneled studio boasted state-of-the-art equipment and a homely atmosphere. Down in the basement lay a recreation room equipped with Space Invaders and pinball machines. Brian Bath recalls the band in their downtime at Super Bear sitting around watching a low-grade video copy of *Star Wars*, at a time when VCR recorders were a rare and expensive luxury item.

An uneasy arrangement had been made with Bush and Andrew Powell to commence the *Lionheart* sessions with the KT Bush Band—Brian Bath on guitar, Paddy Bush playing his idiosyncratic array of stringed instruments and providing harmony vocals, Del Palmer on bass and Charlie Morgan on drums. At first, all seemed to be going well, especially when it came to the songs that the group had demoed at East Wickham Farm: particularly the explosively quiet/loud "Wow" and the dreamy "Kashka from Baghdad." But ultimately these two tracks were the only ones involving the band that ended up making the final cut for *Lionheart*.

It seemed as if this trip was a professional reward for the months that the KT Bush Band had spent developing their act around the pubs and clubs of southern England the previous year (not to mention rolling their sleeves up weeks earlier to build Summerhouse Studios). The only apparent disadvantage to the easy-going working arrangement at Super Bear, Bush later confessed, was that "you couldn't help but keep drifting off to the sun" outside the studio. In the sultry summer evenings, the group lounged around the pool.

"One night we were outside," Bath recalls, "and Kate was trying to break a wine glass, by singing the highest note possible. Trying to find where the glass vibrated. I said, 'Don't, Kate. If it explodes and goes in your face . . .' But we were only kids, really, weren't we?" As the days passed, however, work on the record soon became tougher and a lot less fun. Inside the studio, air conditioning maintained a cool temperature. But every time the door was opened, letting in a hot blast of the typically 28°C heat outside, the guitars instantly went out of tune. What's more, Powell was asking the musicians to do things they weren't used to: Paddy Bush struggled to double-track his hammered psaltery (or Greek zither) on "Kashka from Baghdad"; Brian Bath failed to nail a satisfactory swelling guitar part because he didn't have a foot pedal to control the sound.

"They gave us a good go for a couple of days," says the latter. "I mean, we were fairly experienced. But it just didn't seem to be working out right. Then there were a few meetings about what was going to happen, and what was not going to happen."

A representative from EMI flew out and a difficult compromise was reached: the core musicians who'd played on *The Kick Inside*—bassist David Paton, guitarist Ian Bairnson, keyboardist Duncan MacKay, and drummer Stuart Elliott—were to fly out to Nice to complete the album.

"We just had to swallow it and move away," Bath says. "The album had to be done, so they called the other guys in. We had the option of going home or staying there and I decided to stay there. Cause it was lovely up in the mountains."

"There was a crossover where we were all hanging out a bit together," remembers Elliott. "Andrew Powell kind of agreed to use Kate's musicians, but he also wanted to have a go with us as well. So I think they just sort of split the difference."

As the sessions progressed, it was clear that the relationship between Bush and Powell was changing. She was keen to get far more involved in the production. "I think that's a natural evolution for most artists," Elliott stresses. "Especially Kate, because she's very, very particular."

In fact, this was the point where Kate Bush's soon-to-be-fabled studio perfectionism began to make itself clearly and sometimes painfully evident. As a singer, and a self-critical one, Bush pushed herself hard. Powell felt that the guide vocal Kate had performed for "Wow" was "very musical." Nonetheless, she recorded it again and again, day after day, four or five times an hour, for anything up to ten hours at a time, seeking an emotional quality to the song that was elusive to the others.

Powell remembered it as being "physically very demanding and intensely frustrating for her."

The recording of *Lionheart* concluded at Super Bear in August (Queen entered the studio immediately after to continue work on their seventh album, *Jazz*) and the mixing commenced in September back at AIR in London. Here, in the same setting where *The Kick Inside* had been completed in the summer of 1977, it immediately became obvious what a difference a year had made. Kate was now famous and could no longer wander the streets of the West End without fear of being approached, or perhaps hassled, by fans and the general public. "She would still offer, if we were hungry, to go out and get the sandwiches," Powell remembered. "But we just couldn't let her. We'd have to send someone out with her."

When the album was released, on November 13, 1978, less than nine months after *The Kick Inside*, the credits on the label of the *Lionheart* vinyl told their own story: "Produced and arranged by Andrew Powell. Assisted by Kate Bush." But, while she'd successfully elbowed her way to a position beside Powell at the mixing desk, Bush was deflated by the end result. It was a textbook case, if ever there was one, of "difficult second album" syndrome.

~~~~

The problem wasn't, of course, that Kate Bush was short on songs, already having hundreds in her catalog. But she had for the most part decided to drive forward with new material for *Lionheart*. That, combined with the team change predicament with the musicians and her wrestle for power with Andrew Powell, resulted in an album that was rushed and underwhelming, particularly in the parts where she sounded like a fairly typical piano-based singer-songwriter.

Nevertheless, *Lionheart* is a vivid snapshot of this point in Bush's life and career. The lyrics often capture the now-twenty-year-old singer's ever-changing moods and conflicting attitudes toward the strange, suddenly spot-lit position in which she found herself. In "Full House," her head is filled with self-critical voices. But then, in opener "Symphony in Blue," she sings of how she was certain that she'd found her purpose in life.

"God, I don't even remember that song," she laughed decades later. "I mean, I do remember the title, but I can't remember what I was thinking about with that."

Similarly, Bush has perhaps unfairly distanced herself from one standout song on her second album, the quasi title track piano ballad, "Oh England My Lionheart." Within the space of three minutes and twelve seconds, she created a quietly powerful romantic ode for a part real, part imagined nation. Watercolor post-war images of orchards and apple blossoms sat alongside references to Shakespeare and Kensington Park, the ravens in the Tower of London and the meandering Thames, as its madrigal-like wistfulness was enhanced by harpsichord and recorder.

Still, and likely troubling EMI, it seemed as if Bush's commercial fortunes were already ailing: "Hammer Horror," her third single, released in October 1978, stalled at number forty-four—effectively flopping. Its follow-up, "Wow," fared better, climbing to number fourteen.

The *Lionheart* album itself—in the shops in time for Christmas—reached a very respectable number six but failed to match the success of *The Kick Inside*. It was time for a rethink, and she knew where to start.

"By the end of the second record," she reflected, "I was thinking, y'know, I don't want to be produced by somebody who sees it differently from me. Because obviously the production is such a big part of what the song is. It's every bit as much what the song is as the lyric and . . . I mean, it *is* the song.

"I didn't really know a lot about what you did in recording studios, but I'd made two albums and was getting the hang of it.

"So, I thought, if I could, I would try to take over."

14

"Your Hair Looks Really Nice"

Multi-Coloured Swap Shop, *1979*

Watched by millions of kids, parents, and hungover students, *Multi-Coloured Swap Shop* was a live, near-three-hour-long Saturday morning children's television programme that ran on BBC One between 1976 and 1982. Presented by bearded and blow-dried Radio 1 disc jockey Noel Edmonds, it featured cartoons, an outside broadcast hosted by the perma-chipper Keith Chegwin named the Swaporama (involving kids in towns and cities up and down the UK being invited to exchange their unwanted toys) and interviews with various celebrities, including the pop stars of the day.

On January 20, 1979, Kate Bush was one of the guests, cheerfully submitting herself to questioning by Edmonds and young fans phoning into the program via the famous (and famously always engaged) number 01 811 8055.

Most tapes of the show were erased down the years by the BBC. Now, the only existing, typically wobbly recordings are ones that

89

were made by viewers with access to a VCR. Luckily, the footage of Kate on *Swap Shop* has survived, since it was up until this point her most happy and relaxed appearance on TV. As such, the interview is worth offering in its barely edited entirety:

[*Noel Edmonds holds up some fan art to the camera, featuring an array of melted-looking Kates*]

Noel Edmonds: Lovely. I hope you can see that in full color. Marvellous. It's been sent into me by Laurie Pearce. Laurie, congratulations. I shall give that to Kate in just a moment. Because the wish of Victoria Peters has come true. She's in Wirral, Merseyside. Victoria says, "Please, could you have Kate Bush on *Swap Shop* in real life?" She is here in real life. (*Kate giggles offscreen*) And I can see from here she's breathing. What's more, Victoria, [I'm] chatting to her in a moment. But let's have some "Wuthering Heights."

[*A video plays of Bush performing "Wuthering Heights," shot the previous May 1978 in the mock graveyard-like setting of "The Haunted Castle" at the Dutch amusement park Efteling*]

NE: "Wuthering Heights," of course, the number that brought my next guest to prominence last year. Kate, welcome. That must mean an awful lot to you that song actually, mustn't it?

KB: Yes, it does. It means an awful lot. I mean, that's really why my name is known, because of that song and because of the book.

NE: Yes. How did the interest in the Brontë subject come up?

KB: Well, it was originally from a TV series years ago, and I just caught the very end of it. And it was really freaky cause there's this hand coming through the window and whispering voices. And I've always been into that sort of thing. And it just hung around in my head. And the year before last I read the book. And that was it. I had to write a song about it.

NE: When did you write the song? Because the record came out at the beginning of the year, was it January or February?

KB: That's right. And I'd written the song in the summer before. Really just before we recorded the album. It was my latest song.

NE: So, what, six months before that first single came out, you were planning to start a strong record career?

KB: Oh, yeah. I mean, I think I've always wanted to record since I was a kid. That's what I wanted to do. I wanted to be, if not a singer, a songwriter. I never thought I'd be a singer. And I still in a way really don't consider myself a singer. It's just fantastic for me that other people do.

NE: Yeah. Well, from an observer's point of view, an amazing year last year. But you were dubbed by lots of journalists as the voice of '78, the singer of '78. Is that a problem, do you think? That you made such an impact? Do you feel that could become a little bit of a burden?

KB: I've no idea. I think possibly I could get a problem with the fact that most people associate me with just one song. But then again, I'm so lucky that people even remembered me for anything. Y'know, I mean, I've been so lucky in this last year. And really all I'm concerned about is just carrying on doing what I can and hoping that people will still like it. That's all you can do, and I just take it as it comes.

NE: True. I was lucky enough to be on your first *Top of the Pops*.

KB: It was my second one, actually.

NE: Was it the second one?

KB: Yeah.

NE: That was with that song. I remember you being incredibly cool when things were getting a little bit heavy because you couldn't get the timing right with Johnny Pearson's orchestra. [*This was, of course, also the second time Bush had been exposed to the musical crimes of the BBC ensemble.*] And Johnny was trying to be sympathetic and sort it out. And the terrible time problems with recording *Top of the Pops*, you really kept calm about the whole thing. I thought that was quite amazing. Have you found it difficult to adapt at all to some of the pressures of television or live appearances?

KB: Well, it's such a strange process, the whole thing. Like, you get very nervous before you come on. And then when you're actually doing it, you're so concerned about giving your best that I was quite happy to say, "Um, excuse me, can we just stop and do it again?"

NE: Yeah. There was a problem with orchids or something all over the piano, as well, wasn't there?

KB: Oh yeah, plastic orchids. They were worried that they were gonna [catch on fire under the lights], y'see, and the whole place would go up in flames.

NE: Well, you carried it off absolutely brilliantly. What about live appearances? Are you doing very much at the moment? Are you going out?

KB: No, not really. It's something that I've done very little of, live work. Really, the main place I did it was in pubs a couple of years ago and, I mean, that was great. But it was on a very different level.

NE: What were you doing then?

KB: Uh, standards. "Honky Tonk Women," all that sort of thing.

NE: Just standing up in a pub and letting rip?

KB: Oh yeah. I had a little band. It was great.

NE: Marvellous. Ooh, I didn't know about that. That sounds really interesting. If you'd like to pick up the phone there, we might be able to dig up some nasty questions about your past for you. And on line five. Hello?

Caller: Hello, Noel.

NE: Hello, who are you?

Caller: Elaine Drury.

NE: Hello, Elaine. You're the first one through to Kate Bush.

ED: Hi, Kate.

KB: Hello, Elaine.

ED: Oh, I'd like to ask you, do you know your highest note that you can sing?

KB: (*laughs*) Uh, I've no idea. I'd have thought I can sing higher notes in the bath than anywhere else.

NE: You do have an amazing range, don't you? Has it ever been sort of written down, how far you can go?

KB: Oh, no, that's the last thing I'd do. Because if you set yourself a limit, then you're probably never gonna get over it.

NE: Give us a high note.

KB: What now?

NE: Yeah, break the phone.

KB: (*laughs*) *Eeeeeee*. It's very early in the morning.

NE: Alright. Thank you. Do you find your voice alters during the day?

KB: Oh yeah, incredibly. It's very interesting.

NE: Do you wake up as a tenor, do you? Line six. Hello. Who are you?

Caller: David Lang.

NE: Hello, David, what's your question?

DL: You know one of your songs, "The Man with the Child in His Eyes?" I want to know what the meaning of the song's about.

KB: Oh, well, it's something that I feel about men generally. [*To unseen crew*] Sorry about this, folks (*laughs*). A lot of men have got a child inside them. They're more or less just grown-up kids. [*Laughter from crew*] No, no. It's a very good quality. It's really good because a lot of women go out and get far too responsible. And it's really nice to keep that delight in wonderful things that children have. And that's what I was trying to say, that this man can communicate with a younger girl, because he's on the same level.

NE: (*Adopts childlike squeak*) Thank you very much, David. [*Crew laugh heartily*] Line two. Hello, who are you?

Caller: Martin Smith.

NE: Hello, Martin. A question for Kate, please.

MS: Um, hello, Kate. What would you be if you weren't a singer?

KB: Ooh, dear, probably working in Woolworths. Something like that. I dunno.

NE: That's very good. You've just floored her. I bet Woolies are pleased, but uh, but when you were at school, were you aiming at a career of any sort?

KB: Well, yes, I was really into being a psychiatrist.

NE: Well, that's a bit of an amazing answer, really. "Well, I was gonna be a psychiatrist. When the brain surgery fell through." Thank you very much for the question. Line three. Hello, who are you?

Caller: Kim Susan Neville.

[Name flashes onscreen as Kim Susan Revell]

KSN: Um, I'd like to ask Kate, um, how long have you had your hair like that?

KB: *(laughs)* How do you mean? Do you mean the color?

KSN: No, I mean, the style.

KB: Ooh, long time. I mean, it's just how it is, y'know. It does what it wants. [Sometimes] I put it in plaits.

KSN: Oh, cause I've tried to do that. And it's always come out well.

KB: Oh, good.

KSN: I think your hair looks really nice.

KB: Oh, thank you. I'm sure yours does.

NE: Okay, thank you very much. Bye bye. Line four. Hello, who are you?

Caller: Monique Vinson. Hello, Kate. Where do you get all those clothes when you sing?

KB: I go and get them from shops. Normally antique shops because older clothes are just generally more interesting, y'know? I get them specially for the things I sing.

MV: Oh. I like your hair, like the other girl said.

KB: Oh, thank you.

NE: Compliments flowing. Thank you very much for the call, Monique. Line one. Hello, who are you?

Caller: Sarah. Sarah Tooley.

NE: Hello, a very good morning to you. And what's your question?

ST: Hello, Kate. How young did you discover your musical ability?

KB: Cor. I'm not sure if that's something that you discover yourself, really. Since I was a kid, I've always been singing and playing the piano. And it was really only through the things that have been happening to me recently that I realized that I could actually do it as a living.

ST: Oh, I see. And also, what's your favorite of your records?

KB: What's the favorite? What, you mean out of all my songs? Ooh, that's quite a hard question. I guess I'm pretty fond of "Oh England My Lionheart."

ST: (*Sounding a tad confused*) Oh, yeah.

KB: Yeah.

NE: Right, thank you. You can put the phone down for a minute because I want to ask you a question. The dancing is a very important part of your work. Are you going to incorporate that skill at all in any concerts?

KB: Um, that's something I've yet to find out for myself. Like, I can say, "Oh, yeah, I want to do this and this." But when you actually start working out, you find you have very obvious limitations. Like, you can't leap up in the air twenty times and keep singing a high A, y'know. You'll just sort of explode into little pieces. But I'm going to try to do something like that (*i.e., singing while dancing, as opposed to exploding*). I think theater is a very important part of concerts.

NE: Great. (*Gestures toward circular coffee table where a variety of prizes Bush has brought in*) Well, you've got loads of *things* here.

KB: (*Picks up a pair of none-more-1970s gold satin shorts*) Well, we've got some shorts here from Italy. (*Picks up grey satin bomber jacket*) This is from New Zealand. That's a jacket that they gave me. In fact, it's too small for me. And I thought someone might like that. This is a box from Japan. They've got a very traditional drink out there called sake, which is a rice wine. And you drink it from here and you put some salt on the corner, and you drink it through the salt.

NE: Okay. What about a question, please, Kate?

KB: Well, the question is, on the end of my album, *Lionheart*, there's a message been scratched for everyone. And what is the message?

NE: Actually on the disc?

KB: Actually on the disc at the end.

NE: Lovely, superb. Well, we had Eric Simms, a naturalist, on the program last week. (*To unseen props man*) Could you drop in Eric Simms's correct answers, please?

[*Wire-held stuffed seagull drops into view, perched on edge of fake nest containing postcard entries*]

NE: Thank goodness it's housetrained. Would you like to pull one out very quickly? We wanted to know which was the heaviest bird in Britain. The heaviest flying British bird.

KB: It says that the heaviest British bird is the mute swan. What's a mute swan?

NE: I haven't the foggiest idea. It's a swan anyway. Certainly it's a swan.

KB: And the lady that's won it is Jane Gray from (*reads out full address, including house number*). So, well done, Jane.

NE: Thank you very much for that. Thanks for coming on. And we were talking about "The Man with the Child in His Eyes." We get a chance to hear it now. Kate, thank you very much.

KB: Thank you, my pleasure.

[NB: the winning answer—the inscription on the runout groove of *Lionheart*—was "Hope you like it!" The name of the viewer who won the satin jacket and shorts and masu sake cup the following week is, sadly, lost in the mists of time.]

15

"The Fear and Sparkle"

Tour of Life, 1979

It started with a horrible, freak accident. In the hours immediately after the preview show of Kate Bush's first—and, as it would transpire, only—tour, as the crew were finishing packing up, lighting technician Bill Duffield was carrying out what they called the last-minute "idiot check," making sure no items of equipment had been left behind.

It was April 2, 1979, at Poole Arts Centre, a facility that had opened only the year before. Its 1,500-capacity Wessex Hall, where Bush had performed earlier that evening, boasted a state-of-the-art design enabling the tiered seating to be pulled back under the stage and the entire space flattened for banquets or dances.

In the semi-darkness, Duffield rushed up the steps of an aisle back toward where the lighting desk had been positioned, not realizing that someone at the venue had already removed a floor panel in preparation for the rows of chairs being stored away. He fell more than 5 meters down through the gap, onto concrete. After being rushed to the nearest hospital, and placed on life support, he died a week later.

Bush and the others were back at a nearby hotel when the terrible news of Duffield's accident came through to tour manager Richard Ames. The official opening night at Liverpool Empire was less than twenty-four hours away. Along with the immediate shock, there was an agonising decision to be made: go ahead, or cancel?

"Bill was a professional like the rest of us," Ames stated in the aftermath. "I think any professional would have wanted the thing to carry on and be a success, and we rallied together."

"It was such a tragedy," Bush reflected, more than two-and-a-half decades later. "We'd just started getting this circus troop off and running and he was one of the team. It wasn't even our first proper night, it was our warm-up night, the very first night. So, it saddened us all. It was an awful thing to happen."

Five weeks after Poole, on May 12, 1979, at Hammersmith Odeon in London, the singer performed a benefit show for the lightning tech's family, modifying her show to incorporate guest appearances by two other artists who had previously employed Duffield's skills, Steve Harley and Peter Gabriel.

Furthermore, Duffield was memorialized on her next album, 1980's *Never for Ever*, in the title of "Blow Away (For Bill)." Years later, in "Moments of Pleasure" from *The Red Shoes* in 1993, his name appeared in the song at the end of her roll call of departed friends.

～

Aside from the pubs and club gigs in 1977 where she'd fronted the KT Bush Band, and the various live-sung TV appearances she'd made—or suffered through—since, Kate Bush had very little experience of performing live. With her instant success, however, she had inevitably been faced with the prospect of leaving the recording and TV studios and going out on tour to promote her two albums.

In 1978, Bush received an offer to open for Fleetwood Mac on the final leg of their high-profile US tour in support of their mega-selling *Rumours* album. Frustrating the people at EMI, she turned it down. In retrospect, it was probably a smart move: The arena and stadium crowds at the Cotton Bowl in Dallas or the Omni Coliseum in Atlanta were likely to have been far more interested in loading up on beers and hot dogs ahead of the headlining act than paying much attention to a strange young singer from England with her songs about period pains and strange phenomena. What's more, it would have by necessity been a straight band-based affair, and probably one involving a struggle with the limiting conditions that support acts were forced to endure.

If Bush was going to commit to touring, she had something far more theatrical in mind. And so, six months of planning went into what was at first named either the Kate Bush Tour or the Lionheart Tour, but which would become in later years known as the Tour of Life. It was to be a production in three acts, involving dramatic staging, dancers, poetry, magic and video effects, and seventeen costume changes.

Characteristically, the singer oversaw every tiny detail of the staging, at the center of which sat a huge, heavy ramp, which could be raised or lowered, depending on the number. A magician, Simon Drake, was brought in to provide illusions. He later remembered that there had been a couple of ambitious schemes that failed to make it to the final show, and that he'd taken Bush to meet "some strange chap doing video synthesis in west London and a robot builder in north London."

A nine-piece band was put together involving Brian Bath and Del Palmer, alongside new faces including drummer Preston Heyman, guitarist Alan Murphy, keyboardist Kevin McAlea and synth/acoustic guitar player Ben Barson. Together they began rehearsing at Wood Wharf Studios in Greenwich, with Kate arriving after she'd put in an arduous three-hour morning shift at the Place dance studio near Euston with choreographer Anthony Van Laast. Whether or not she could perform these involved routines while singing was the big question. To free her up, she asked tour sound engineer Gordon "Gungi" Paterson if there was any way he could fashion a cordless, hands-free radio microphone set-up. In the end, it was to prove to be a revolutionary device.

"I said, 'I want to be able to dance and sing, so it's theater, and not be wandering around all the time with a hand-held mic,'" Bush explained to me. "'You've got to come up with something that I don't have to hold.' So Gungi came up with this sort of headset that was basically a coat hanger that you could put into shape, with a mic in the end.

"I remember the first time I tried it, it was this feeling of being amplified without holding anything, and it was really weird. You sort of wanted to get away from it so you could cough, but it was just there all the time. We used to pick up cabs quite regularly on it cause it was such a prototype version.

"Basically, we invented that," she added. "I said to him, 'We should patent this' and he said, 'How can we patent it? It's a wire coat hanger with a mic on the end.'"

As ever, the tour involved Bush's family, with Paddy performing mandolin and singing backing vocals in the band, and John marking the intervals in the show with poetry readings. In addition, the latter, along with his wife, even provided the vegetarian tour catering. Interviewed on camera for a half-hour TV special on the tour, screened by BBC One's *Nationwide* current affairs program, John appeared behind a tableful of typically 1970s veggie fare (nut bakes, salads) and responded to the presenter enquiring, "It's almost a vegetarian tour, isn't it?" by smiling and stating, "Yeah, you could say that. Well, it's good food. Because it lets people carry on working afterward. They're not walking around really laid out with an enormous great meat meal."

Lunch and dinner aside, other details of the work-in-progress production—as it moved from Wood Wharf in Greenwich to a soundstage at Shepperton Studios in Surrey, to the Rainbow Theatre in Finsbury Park, north London—were kept secret. At the Rainbow, however, a freelance photographer managed to sneak in and furtively shoot a few rolls of film before being caught, reportedly told off by Kate, and then thrown out by security.

Bush's handwritten letter to her fans that appeared at the beginning of the official program spoke of her excitement and apprehension ahead of the tour. In it, she recalled her days of training at the Dance Centre with Lindsay Kemp, of performing with the KT Bush Band, of the exhausting intensity of her recent record-promoting schedule—all leading up to this point where she (a touch clunkily, if still evocatively) described feeling "the fear and sparkle in my stomach."

$\sim$

Anticipation was high in the audience on the night of Tuesday, April 3 at the Liverpool Empire. For such a grandly designed stage show, Kate Bush had to make a suitably dramatic entrance. As the house lights fell, blue and green waves were projected onto a front-of-stage gauze, accompanied by the whale song that opened "Moving." The singer's amplified silhouette then appeared on the screen, before it was pulled aside to reveal her in a blue leotard, wearing her hands-free microphone, and she began to sing. For her fans, hearing Bush's voice live was a first-time experience, and they erupted in cheers and applause.

During much of the first act, the band remained in shadow, letting the spotlight focus upon and trail the singer and her two dancers, Stewart Avon Arnold and Gary "Bubba" Hurst, as they rocked her back and forth in a huge, red-lined shell for "Room for the Life" or donned the now-familiar macs and fedoras for "Them Heavy People." The stage was further lit up through new songs "Egypt" and "Violin," with Bush wearing a glittering gold belly dancer belt and red skirt and, in the latter, the dancers hiding inside enormous, Muppet-like foam fiddle costumes.

Theatrics aside, as the show unfolded, it was clear that Bush in fact needed no props or gimmicks. Equally, if not more powerful, were the songs she performed alone at the piano— "The Man with the Child in His Eyes," "The Kick Inside," "Feel It"—which fully showcased her fluid voice and arpeggios.

At the other end of the spectrum, the promo video routine for "Hammer Horror," in which Bush was tossed around by a black-hooded figure, was re-enacted on stage as purely a dance number, and performed to a version of the song that had been re-recorded by the band so as not to fall foul of Musicians' Union rules. There were plenty other highlights—the wire fences and leather biker jacket shenanigans of "Don't Push Your Foot on the Heartbrake," the whirling dervish moves of

"Wow," the mock-shooting routine at the climax of "James and the Cold Gun"—but it was the two encores that sealed the deal.

In the first, for "Oh England My Lionheart," Bush sat on the stage, in a flying jacket, with goggles affixed to her khaki cap, and a tangled parachute behind her, as if she was a Second World War pilot who'd somehow crashed through the roof of the venue. Then, she returned, amid dry ice, for a showstopping "Wuthering Heights," at the end of which she reverse-walked back up the ramp, waving goodbye.

The next day, the reviews were glowing, and sometimes filled with flowery prose. "Kate Bush is a love affair," declared the *Liverpool Post*. "A poignant exposition of the bridges of dreams that link the adulated and the adoring." The writer from *Record Mirror*, meanwhile, worked himself up into a froth in a way that would have seen him instantly cancelled today: "Throughout, she remained full of poise and in complete control of her vocal dexterity which reached a peak on the more sensual songs. Her unabashed obsession with sex manifested itself on 'Feel It,' 'In the Warm Room' and 'The Kick Inside' where she revealed a soft spot for incest. The soft focus porn continued with 'Full House' where the salivating audience was treated to a face full of thigh tied in black nylon."

This was sadly the sort of thing a twenty-year-old female singer had to put up with at the fag end of the 1970s. Ten years later, when talking to Adam Sweeting in *The Guardian*, Bush remembered how she'd felt at the time about being sexually objectified.

"I felt that my sexuality, which in a way I hadn't really had a chance to explore myself, was being given to the world in a way which I found impersonal. When I started in this business, I felt very at home in my body. I was a dancer, that was the area

I explored. And it was very scary for me those next few years, because whatever I wore, whatever I did, people were putting this incredible emphasis of sexuality on me, which I didn't feel."

~

As the tour progressed, Bush played to sold-out theater houses everywhere and she began to grow ever more confident on stage.

"The first couple of nights I was really frightened," she remembered. "But then, once I realized I could do it and I had the confidence to *know* that I had the ability to do it, it was fantastic."

Date after date, the reviews maintained their effusive tone . . .

"Kate Bush's eerie dance and mime works twice as well on stage as on *Top of the Pops.*" —*Birmingham Evening Mail*

"There is no doubt that such a performance merited nothing less than the five-minute standing ovation it received." —*Southern Daily Echo*

"Each aspect was perfect in itself. Spectacular entertainment." —*Bristol Evening Post*

"Oh yes, Kate Bush is amazing. Her stage performance evaporates all doubts and adds a totally new theatrical dimension to the rock medium." —*Manchester Evening News*

"What an ambitious adventure it is for a singer on her first concert tour—and how mediocre does she make most of her pop contemporaries seem." —*Daily Mail*

In Manchester, Labour Prime Minister James Callaghan, on the springtime election trail in his determined (but ultimately failed) effort to ward off Margaret Thatcher, was pictured alongside Bush, hoping that some of her potential youth vote-winning star power would help illuminate him. In Sunderland, fans were photographed queuing overnight for tickets, some of them tucked up in sleeping bags on the pavement.

In Edinburgh, an after-show party at the Caledonian Hotel provided the only rock-'n'-roll moment of the tour—a messy pillow and water fight that caused £1,000 worth of damage (the bill footed by EMI). In London, ahead of the first of five shows at the Palladium, the singer revealed in a press conference that she'd already turned down offers to appear in musicals and even a couple of horror films.

"I was given a choice of two roles opposite Dracula-type characters," she said, "and I don't see myself in that sort of role. And I don't consider myself an actress, anyway. There is still so much I want to do musically."

Further underlining the fact that she felt she was an artist rather than a "star," Bush also declined a request to sing the theme for the latest James Bond film, *Moonraker*. (In the end, it was handed over to the stalwart Shirley Bassey.)

Following the final Palladium date, a party was held at the Dial 9 Club in London, where a *Record Mirror* reporter snippily noted that "Kate and her entire family smiled happily in the bordello-like gloom. 'I was feeling just a little tired tonight,' confessed an ever-radiant Ms Bush, although no signs of such a condition were visible."

Still, Kate was clearly exhausted by the tour, and when it moved on to Europe, shows in Copenhagen, Hamburg, and

Amsterdam had to be cut down in length, owing to her having developed problems with her throat. Back in London, there were three Hammersmith Odeon shows—including the Bill Duffield benefit—to complete.

By the final gig, on May 14, 1979, an air of closing night giddiness infected the performers. Two of the road crew secretly hired a pantomime camel costume and wandered on stage inside it during "Egypt" (Bush, already the trooper, hugged it around the neck as she sang). In "Wow," meanwhile, performed by the singer at the end of the ramp which had been made to resemble a seaweedy pier, a frogman appeared.

"On the last night, I looked down and one of the crew came out in scuba-diving gear and a snorkel and kind of swam around the stage," she recalled. "Then, at the end of 'James and the Cold Gun' where I used to shoot a couple of people with my gun . . . that night, every time I turned round there were, like, ten more of them. The stage was littered with bodies."

Incredibly, it had only been six years since the fourteen-year-old Cathy Bush had cried when she'd witnessed David Bowie killing Ziggy Stardust on the same stage at Hammersmith Odeon. The final night of Tour of Life was to be freighted with the same kind of drama, even if it was only recognized in retro-spect. When she waved her goodbyes at the end of "Wuthering Heights," no one was to know that it was to be Kate Bush's last full concert for thirty-five years.

~

Post-tour, in August 1979, the BBC's *Nationwide* crew, looking for an update, followed Bush to Studio 3 at AIR on Oxford

Circus, where she'd begun recording her third album, *Never for Ever*. It was a filmed encounter that revealed something of the outside pressures on her, only weeks after she'd turned twenty-one.

"Don't you have a problem now?" probed the offscreen interviewer. "What next? How [are you] going to follow the success?"

"Well, you see, people say this to me, and I don't really look at it that way, because it's not a matter of following success," she countered. "It's things [that] have happened, you've done them in the past, and you see things wrong in them. And you want to go on and you want to do them right. And I think that's all it is, y'know. It's just the desire to want to keep doing things better. And I don't really see it as following a great success. Because if I did, I'd get *really* paranoid. And I probably wouldn't be able to do a thing."

"Do you ever worry that your confidence might go?" pushed the reporter.

"It goes," Bush confessed. "Yes, it goes a lot."

~

Twenty-six years later, Kate Bush sat in her front room in Berkshire and insisted to me that the reason she'd never toured again hadn't been due to a crisis of confidence.

"It's not really that I stopped touring, cause I only did the one," she pointed out. "Loads of people think I didn't like it, but I loved it. It was exciting, but it was exhausting. I mean, it nearly killed me, really. And I was very young and very fit. I mean, I was kind of athletic fit, y'know. It was two-and-a-half hours on stage dancing and singing and it was really hard work."

She'd said afterward, though, that the tour had left her feeling "exposed?"

"I don't know what I meant about being exposed other than that transition coming out of touring into a much more self-sufficient world.

"It's very strange when you do a tour—I mean, it's only that one I've done and it's a long time ago now—but it's almost like you live in this little microcosm. It's not like living in the real world. And I think sometimes that's why bands tour for years and years . . . they're afraid to come out of that microcosm. Cause you have everything done for you. It's like, 'Tea, please!' Then suddenly you go home, and you've got to make your own tea. It's very different and I think sometimes it's quite a shocking transition."

Bush claimed that her original plan following Tour of Life had been to make another two albums and then return to live work.

"I thought, 'Right, if I do another two records, then we'll tour that.' So it would be like every two records we'll have a show that goes with it. But, of course, by the time I'd got to the end of that second record [*The Dreaming* in 1982], it was another world. Because I'd got so involved in all the production and everything. And the time was passing, and I hadn't performed for a long time. [Making albums] somehow felt more important . . . to stick with the whole thing of learning how to put a record together. If you want to try to keep the focus, it's quite difficult.

"And also, the thing about shows, I think, is that although they're creative, because you're slightly reinventing things every night, it's not the same as actually writing a piece of music from scratch. It's not making something totally new."

So you're just repeating yourself?

RUNNING UP THAT HILL

"You are, really. And that in itself is an art form and it's very interesting. But it's not the same as making something out of nothing."

Through the years, Bush had limited her live appearances to the rare one or two songs performed at charity events or as guest spots with other artists. At this point, her last on-stage appearance had been with David Gilmour at London's Royal Festival Hall in 2002, for her audibly nervous rendition of Pink Floyd's "Comfortably Numb" that she'd requested to be snipped from Gilmour's subsequent live DVD.

"I was completely terrified," she laughed. "I've done this a couple of times for friends, and I'm so terrified because it's such a long time since I've been on stage. There was another time I did it, [with Peter Gabriel at Earl's Court in 1987, for "Don't Give Up'] and the same thing happened. Fantastic reaction from the audience and you're thinking, 'That's so great. People are really sort of warm and receptive to me being here.' But I'm so terrified, y'know, that I'm just making a complete arsehole of (*affecting mock shaky voice*) my-ss-eeaa-ll-fff. They kind of wheel you off and you don't have time to *not* be nervous. I mean, maybe if I was up there for half an hour, I might start being less nervous.

"But also, I suppose there's an element of, y'know, coming out from (*laughs*) my Hoover and the school run to being on-stage in front of all these people. It's something that if I could do more, then I would have this confidence in my ability to be able to do it and then I probably wouldn't feel nervous any more. It's something that if you do a lot . . . it's like being an actor, isn't it? You learn how to do it. So, yeah, it's totally terrifying."

Looking back, she said that she had no regrets whatsoever in terms of having effectively disappeared from the stage.

"I don't regret not having done more shows, because the one [tour] I did was very interesting creatively. And I suppose the further I got away from having done that tour, the more I felt nervous about getting on stage. But, y'know, I've toyed with the idea, several times. I really would like to do some shows. But I dunno, I'm in a different space now. There's no way I'd tour again. But I would like to do some shows."

Was she never tempted to do a one-off night at the Royal Opera House, maybe? Or to just play with a piano and a band at Shepherd's Bush Empire, or somewhere? People weren't necessarily expecting her to perform elaborate dance routines . . .

"No, I know, I know. Yeah, I mean, I do toy with the idea. I would really love to do some live stuff. But I suppose in a way, it's the creative challenge that I find so interesting. I mean, who knows, maybe I will? Grab me Zimmer frame and waft out there."

People really still did want to hear her sing live . . .

"(*Long pause*) Well, maybe I will one day."

~

As a footnote, Bush said that she sometimes caught current pop stars on TV, using far more professional, updated versions of the hands-free headset microphone she'd helped develop for Tour of Life.

"I see odd clips of people doing stuff now," she smiled. "I see them wearing my little mic and dancing and singing, which is what people didn't do when I did that show. And actually, I think, (*tuts*) 'Oh, I was doing that years ago.'"

16

Smash!

A journey into sound, 1979–80

The first glass hit the famous tea-colored parquet floor of Abbey Road's Studio Two. Another quickly followed it. Then another, and another. Before long, the place was a mess: jagged shards strewn everywhere. Later, the canteen staff at the world's best-known recording facility would be none too chuffed to learn of the reckless destruction of their glassware.

In the spring of 1980, as she was nearing the completion of her third album, *Never for Ever,* Kate Bush had fallen in love with the sound of breaking glass. Miked, recorded, and stored on the high-end and costly sampler, the still-new-fangled Fairlight CMI (or Computer Music Instrument), the smashing sounds were looped and played amid the balalaika crescendo of "Babooshka," destined to be a top-five single.

Then it was onto the rifles, the percussive cocking of their hammers sampled to enhance the bodhran beats of another future hit, "Army Dreamers." For Bush, it was a revelatory experience: the moment she could begin to paint with colors of sound that, until now, she'd only heard in her head.

It was at this point that the recording studio became a playground for her wildest imaginings. But while as an artist the Fairlight gave her an enormous array of samples to manipulate within her songs, it was also an important tool in her striving for creative control. Now, she could write a part using the sound of an instrument that she couldn't actually play, such as an acoustic guitar or cello, and then bring in a session musician to perfect it.

Bush had been introduced to the Fairlight by Peter Gabriel the previous autumn, around the time she'd added her distinctively haunting backing vocals to two tracks from his third self-titled solo album—"No Self Control" and "Games Without Frontiers" (singing in the latter the breathy "Jeux sans frontières" hookline that helped give Gabriel his biggest UK hit up to that point, reaching number four). Gabriel subsequently lent one of the bulky and expensive new instruments to Richard James Burgess and John L. Walters of the electronic band Landscape and asked the two to cart it over to Abbey Road to give Bush a demonstration. She didn't need its potential spelling out.

On *Never for Ever*, as opener "Babooshka" slipped into the tangential track two shapes of "Delius (Song of Summer)," Kate Bush the artist we know today was born. There was a good reason for this—three albums in, she was now in command of her production, albeit for now working in cahoots with Jon Kelly, the engineer of *The Kick Inside* and, for her, its too-hasty *Lionheart* follow-up. The two had begun to explore a working relationship when together they mixed the tapes for the four-track live EP,

On Stage, recorded at the second Tour of Life Hammersmith Odeon show in May and released in August 1979.

"So, with the third album, I said [to Kelly], 'Shall we produce it together?'" she recalled to me. "That was the first big step.

"I think music is very visual," she added. "On *Never for Ever*, there was quite a bit of that . . . trying to imagine being there. It's that thing of being in this place, isn't it? That you're talking about or singing about. So then you're trying to create what it looks like and who's there."

Looking back down through her catalog, Bush agreed that *Never for Ever* was the first of her albums to sound entirely like "her" . . .

"Yeah, I think so," she nodded. "I could do some of the experimentation which for me is such a part of the process. I discovered the Fairlight, and I was using the musicians that *I* wanted to use."

So futuristic was the Fairlight that, in 1980, it earned itself an item on BBC One's science and technology show, *Tomorrow's World*. Presenter Kieran Prendiville indulged in some daft tomfoolery with the device, playing tramping feet and woofing dog noises up and down the keyboard, but then perceptively pointed out, "The scope it offers musicians in being able to create any sound you care to name is nearly limitless."

The Fairlight CMI had been developed the previous year by two Australians, Kim Ryrie and Peter Vogel. The latter flew to England in late 1979 and demonstrated it for Peter Gabriel, sensing that the former Genesis singer and now art-rock-minded solo artist might be impressed by the device. Gabriel was blown away and subsequently formed a company, Syco Systems, to sell the Fairlight in the UK with an eye-watering £12,000 price tag (the equivalent of £64,000 today).

Gabriel would be filmed in 1982 by the makers of ITV's arts programme *The South Bank Show* in scenes that depicted him as a modern-day Stig of the Dump, clambering over mounds of metal in a scrapyard, trailed by an engineer with a tape recorder, as the singer smashed a car windscreen and blew through a metal pipe to create sounds to feed the Fairlight. These were to feature on his fourth eponymous album, released that year.

But, by then, Bush had beaten him to using the Fairlight on *Never for Ever*, its first appearance on a commercial release. Nonetheless, she thanked Gabriel on the record's sleeve for "opening the windows" in terms of her creativity.

"It was suddenly being let loose in a situation where I could actually get my hands on things and play around," she recalled of the making of her crucial third album. "It was fantastic. There was this lovely feeling of creativity and freedom and fun."

~

Still, at first Bush had to get her head around the reality of actually producing her own album. One trick she'd learned from *The Kick Inside* and *Lionheart* producer Andrew Powell was to keep a notepad close to hand and devote a page to each song so that she could scribble down ideas for instrumental parts or audio effects or vocal harmonies. Tougher to acclimatize to was the fact that she was now the one who had to marshal the all-male musicians, who were often her friends.

"After all, I am only little, a female and an unlikely producer!" she stressed at the time in a newsletter to her fan club, which revealed much about the prevailing attitudes of the day. "But as I squirmed and contorted my way through explanations of visuals and audials," she went on, "they stood patient, calm and open, and not one uttered 'You weirdo!' unless in jest."

The initial sessions in the latter half of 1979 at AIR were straight-forward enough, employing much of her Tour of Life band to cut four tracks: "Violin," "Egypt" (slowed from the funkier stage version into a more atmospheric piece), "Blow Away (For Bill)" and the murderous tale of "The Wedding List," wherein she cast herself as a woman widowed on her big day when the groom was shot dead, driving her to gun-toting revenge (a plot line inspired by François Truffaut's 1968 film *The Bride Wore Black*).

"Our first 'productions,' with the help of ideal musicians, were a success," she recorded in her newsletter.

"The band had just come off the tour, virtually," Brian Bath points out. "There was a real good working unit, and a couple of the songs we'd actually performed live already, although the arrangements were changed for the album. But you could see it was taking a new direction. There were influences from Steely Dan. It had a different kind of spark to it."

Working hours were long, and the days at Abbey Road would spill over into the evenings and leak through to the early hours ("A very creative time," Bush stated). All the while, she was learning her production craft, even though, as she pointed out in her newsletter missive, she was still at this point struggling with inarticulacy when it came to the gnarly task of explaining in words precisely what she wanted to hear coming out of the speakers.

"Each song has a very different personality," she reasoned, "and so much of the production was allowing the songs to speak with their own voices—not for them to be used purely as objects to decorate with 'buttons and bows.'

"Choosing sounds is so like trying to be psychic," she further offered. "Seeing into the future, looking in the 'crystal ball of arrangements.' 'Scattering a little bit of stardust,' to quote the immortal words of the Troggs."

(Bush was here referring to the notorious Troggs Tapes, the widely bootlegged 1970 recording of the on-the-slide Hampshire band having a hilariously sweary, cartoony argument while attempting to record a song named—brilliantly—"Tranquillity."

The actual quote was one from drummer Ronnie Bond: "You gotta put a little bit of fucking fairy dust over the bastard."

"Oh, we'll put some fairy dust over it," responded producer Dennis Berger. "I'll piss over the tape.")

~

Through the doors of Abbey Road Studio Two in the first five months of 1980, the latter stages of the recording of *Never for Ever*, passed a procession of musicians—their parts sometimes kept, but often erased from the tapes and replaced by others. After the smooth start to the album's recording, progress had slowed, as Kate Bush searched on and on for intangible qualities to the performances. Many of the players felt lost or frustrated and simply didn't really understand what the singer-turned-producer was looking for. Drummer Stuart Elliott did, however.

"It's something that resonates with her emotionally," he says. "I mean, I've been replaced a couple of times, and I've replaced other musicians . . . some very famous ones who'll remain nameless. She knows what she wants, and she goes for it and gets it, and it doesn't matter how long it takes . . . The lovely thing about Kate is that she's relaxed, patient. It was a process of layering music really, which was the big change in Kate's approach."

"We had so many musicians, cause it never seemed to work," says Brian Bath. "It was always a problem with the bass or the drums. We had like, I dunno, about twelve different bass players for 'Breathing' or 'Babooshka.' We'd all be sitting around waiting for the next bass player to turn up. There'd be logs of names of people turning up at the studio and we'd run the song and if it didn't work, they'd sit out."

For both "Babooshka" and "Breathing," Bush decisively benched Tour of Life drummer Preston Heyman and brought in Elliott to play.

"Stuart Elliott came in, and he's very orchestrated," Bath says. "Fabulous drummer. He's so inventive."

"Music is . . . you have to break your back before you even start to speak the emotion," Bush ventured, in explaining her methods.

"I hate the term 'thinking out of the box,' but I can't think of another one," Elliott laughs. "That sort of sums Kate up really. I used to make suggestions: 'Why don't we try this? Why don't we try that?' And she'd very gently sort of smile, but then get on with it. Which I totally respect.

"It's not a case of being blinkered," he continues. "[It's whatever] it takes to get what her vision is, and if it doesn't work with one musician or one bunch of musicians, she'll just get some other guys in. She often does. It's just part of the process of Kate getting what she envisions, really."

Brian Bath remembers that while there had been various bassists brought in to play on the Pink Floyd-like, post-apocalyptic ballad "Breathing," the breakthrough moment came when John Giblin contributed his slinky, simpatico fretless part. "All of a sudden the song just took off," he says. "He was just weaving, like he was a plant growing on the song. What he did to that song was incredible."

This layered approach of painstakingly etching individual performances onto tape was slowly producing the results that Kate was continually striving for. Nonetheless, she admitted at the time that hearing Pink Floyd's 1979 double LP opus *The Wall*—particularly Side Three, running from "Hey You" through to "Comfortably Numb"—had initially frozen her creatively and almost made her want to give up since, in her opinion, "they'd said it all."

Her vividly realized response was the crackling, atomic "Breathing," written from the perspective of an unborn fetus (or, in her words, "future spirit" who had lived previous reincarnated lives), addressing the listener from amid an atmosphere of poisonous nuclear fallout. "Before I put the lead vocal on," she recalled, "the backing track alone made me want to cry, it was so perfect."

"Breathing" was to prove mildly controversial when it was released as a single in April 1980 and made number sixteen—*Top of the Pops* cutting its video before Bush's band were depicted being hit by a blinding white, bomb blast flare. An EMI employee visiting the session at Abbey Road had predicted the single could get Bush into trouble, but for a different reason entirely. "[They] caught the 'in-out, in-out' bit," she remembered, "and said, 'You're not seriously thinking of releasing this, are you?' He really thought it was pornographic . . ."

Ultimately *Never for Ever* was the first album where Kate Bush successfully rendered in audio the "visual connection" that she felt her music needed to convey. It's there in the buzzing bee that flits from speaker to speaker at the close of "Delius (Song of Summer)" and with the appearance in the chorus of "Army Dreamers" of a drill sergeant issuing shouted commands repurposed as counter-rhythm. In "All We Ever Look For," noisy footsteps move from the left to right speakers or earphones, the clomping pedestrian opening doors and discovering behind them chanting Hare Krishna devotees and tweeting songbirds and cheering crowds. In "Breathing," three minutes in, a distant faux radio report can be heard, the broadcaster chillingly attempting to measure the power of a nuclear explosion by the duration of its flash and extent of its mushroom cloud.

Meanwhile, the tales in the songs themselves were even more imaginative, subtle, and affecting. The grieving mother in "Army Dreamers" isn't merely blaming a military system that chews up naïve recruits for the death of her son but wondering if she could have done more parentally to guide him. The wife in "Babooshka" who attempts to stress test her marriage and honey trap her husband isn't the innocent victim she initially appears, since she herself has become emotionally remote and part of the problem. (Bush explained the narrative as being about "the way in which we often ruin things for ourselves.")

Having explored incest in the title track of *The Kick Inside*, "The Infant Kiss" appeared equally provocative. The source of inspiration was 1961 movie *The Innocents*, based on Henry James's Victorian horror novella *The Turn of the Screw*, in which a governess fears that the children in her charge may be pos-sessed. Although the lyric of "The Infant Kiss" was left wide open to interpretation—the narrator seems aroused but deeply disturbed by the mature goodnight kiss of the child with the man in his eyes—Bush fretted that it would be misconstrued and sensationalized.

"Well, it's not actually that [i.e., about paedophilia]," she argued to *Melody Maker* writer Colin Irwin, "and it would worry me if people mixed it up with that because that's exactly what worries *her* so much. I find that distortion very fascinating and quite sad. And frightening. The thought of someone old and evil being inside a young and pure shell, it's freaky."

Her point, in other words, was that the central character of "The Infant Kiss" was terrified by her confused sexual feelings—and what others might think if they knew about them—and absolutely not reveling in them. It was further proof that often Bush's lyrics were oblique, finely nuanced, and easily misunderstood.

Elsewhere, the title of *Never for Ever* (also the name of a song that was recorded for *Lionheart* but never released or even bootlegged) was almost Zen-like in its message: feelings and situations, whether good or bad, are impermanent. In other words, all things must pass.

~

Although startling, strange, and original, *Never for Ever* did nothing to diminish Kate Bush's stardom. In the wake of its release on September 7, 1980, she made record signing appearances in Edinburgh, Glasgow, Newcastle, Liverpool, Manchester, and at the Virgin Megastore in London, the latter drawing a lengthy queue down Oxford Street.

This dedicated promotional graft paid off when the album went straight in at UK number one the following week. Even more incredibly, it became the first-ever chart-topper by any female solo artist. The fact that it only stayed there for a week didn't dent that accomplishment, especially since it was knocked into second place by her teenage idol David Bowie's equally excellent *Scary Monsters (and Super Creeps)*.

Never for Ever also reached number one in France and made the top five in Australia, Israel, Norway, West Germany, and the Netherlands. The commercial success of her uncompromising and decidedly idiosyncratic third album encouraged Bush to go further in her sonic adventuring. Much, much further.

17

A Right Royal Mishap and Blunder

Embarrassing encounters with the monarchy, 1982/2005

It was with the vocal exertions of the second chorus that Kate suffered what would later be termed as a "wardrobe malfunction." As she fiercely emoted her way toward the climax of "The Wedding List," the straps of the singer's halterneck top pinged loose.

It was July 21, 1982, the Prince's Trust Rock Gala at the Dominion Theatre, London. On stage with a starry band of her contemporaries, including Genesis' Phil Collins, the Who's Pete Townshend, Ultravox's Midge Ure, and Japan's Mick Karn, Bush was for the first (and last) time performing live the dramatic, dynamic cut from her *Never for Ever* album. As Prince Charles watched on from the audience, the singer unleashed a series of what can only be described as orgasmic shrieks. Just over three minutes in, the moment captured in close-up by a film crew, the straps of the top, tied behind her neck, unknotted and slipped free. Ever the professional, Bush quickly covered her bosom and gripped onto the plunging garment with her left hand, trying to suppress an embarrassed smile, though still bold enough to thrust her microphone-wielding right arm aloft in triumph as the song drew to a close.

"Whoops," exclaimed Townshend, after the band had arrived at a precise dead stop, and as Kate tiptoed off into the wings following the hasty recovery of her dignity.

"My dress fell off in front of Prince Charles at the Prince's Trust," she later recalled to me, wide-eyed. "I don't have a very good track record with royalty."

Twenty-three years later, on March 1, 2005, Bush was invited to Buckingham Palace to attend, as the official statement described it, "an Evening Reception to recognize the excellence of British Music and the contribution it makes to the culture and economy of the UK."

Under the chandeliers, in a room filled with such diverse characters as Dame Vera Lynn, Queen guitarist Brian May, the omnipresent Phil Collins, rave DJ Pete Tong and non-rave DJ Terry Wogan, Kate was presented to the Queen. Standing beside her was 1960s pop star Sandie Shaw, who later let slip to a reporter that Bush had guilelessly asked Her Majesty for her autograph—an absolute protocol no-no.

"I made a complete arsehole of myself in front of the Queen," she admitted to me. "I think the Queen's absolutely wonderful, and I have met her before, and she does *glow*. She's gorgeous. I'm ashamed to say that when I told Bertie that I was going to meet the Queen, he said, 'Mummy, no, you're not, you've got it wrong,' and I said, 'But I am!'

"So, rather stupidly, I thought I'd get her to sign my program. (*Adopting "Cockney sparrow" accent*) 'Oh, s'cuse me, Ma'am, would you sign me program for my little boy? He's your biggest fan,' sort of thing. She was very sweet. Cause it was a stupid thing for me to do, really. The thing is, I would do anything for Bertie and making an arsehole of myself in front of a whole roomful of people and the Queen, I mean . . . I'm just sort of living up to my reputation."

18

Echoes in the Walls

Kate and Abbey Road Studios, 1980–2011

When a sound hits a wall, part of its energy is reflected and part—sometimes only a tiny fraction—is absorbed. So it's easy to believe that the building at 3 Abbey Road, St John's Wood, London NW8, is a studio complex that has stored up the echoes of all the greats who've performed there in the past near-century.

Paul Robeson's bass-baritone voice delivering Hoagy Carmichael's "Rockin' Chair" over a haunting orchestration back in 1931. Beniamino Gigli's resonant vibrato in "Song of Songs" in 1946. The Beatles' "yeah, yeah, yeah's" in "She Loves You" in 1963. Shirley Bassey's long, high, blasting note (that almost made her pass out) at the end of "Goldfinger" in 1964. Syd Barrett offering you a ride on his "Bike" in 1967.

No surprise, then, that when Kate Bush first entered Abbey Road Studios to record in 1980, she sensed that she was somehow not entirely alone.

"I felt there were at least ten other people with me," she told author Brian Southall for his 1982 book, *Abbey Road.* "The place had tremendous presence. I don't think it's just the fact that The Beatles recorded there, but a combination of all the people who have been there over the years and all their combined creativity."

In his preface for the same book, George Martin expressed similar sentiments, stating his belief that a building is "capable of absorbing the personalities and emotions of its inhabitants." In the case of Abbey Road, it meant for him that because "countless performances of masterpieces by the greatest musicians and artistes in the world have been captured by her mikes . . . there is no need for the photographs on the walls to remind me of their presence."

"Being on your own in Studio Two is a fascinating experience," Bush further elucidated. "I felt tremendous vibes in there, both positive and negative. It's built on ley lines which means there are very powerful forces at work."

~

Bush didn't express to me her feelings about Abbey Road—which had become her spiritual home from home—in quite such esoteric terms. But it was clear nonetheless how much the legendary recording facility still meant to her, decades after she was initially given access to its hallowed spaces.

"Being at Abbey Road, I was so excited," she enthused. "Y'know, it was *the* studio. Elgar had worked there, and The Beatles."

Her choice of words was telling—Elgar first, Beatles second. She obviously looked back down through the entire lineage of giant figures who had made classic recordings there, beyond rock and pop.

Sir Edward Elgar had officially opened what was at the time known as EMI Studios, on November 12, 1931. On that date, he conducted the London Symphony Orchestra in Studio One for a recording of "Pomp and Circumstance March No. 1"—best known for yielding deathless British patriot anthem "Land of Hope and Glory"—before an audience of grandees including George Bernard Shaw.

Little wonder, perhaps, that on their first visit to the studios on June 6, 1962, for their EMI audition, longhaired Scouse nobodies The Beatles were made to use the tradesman's entrance. Post-success, however, they were to turn the studios into their own fiefdom: often scrubbing other artists' bookings from the diary in order to fulfill the intensive record-making demands made of them by Parlophone. For the world-famous Fabs, 3 Abbey Road became an oasis of calm and concentration away from the screaming white noise of Beatlemania.

The exception being the day they discovered fans hiding up in the roof of Studio Two. "We were recording," Paul McCartney told me in one interview, "and we heard some sort of noise, and somebody said, 'What is that? Quiet, please.' And they eventually found out that high up in the ceiling there's maintenance ducts and there were a few fans who'd managed to get in there who were getting a bird's eye view of the session. So that was like, 'Oh, boy.'"

Weird distractions aside, The Beatles, with George Martin's guidance and expertise, famously expanded the envelope of recorded sound in their eight years between 1962 and 1970 at Abbey Road, setting the experimental tone for many others to come. One significant moment was when a psychedelic spark passed from the Beatles to Pink Floyd in March 1967. The four members of the Floyd were invited to sit in and watch the Beatles ("God-like figures to us," said drummer Nick Mason) putting the finishing touches to "Lovely Rita," with its comb-and-paper-parped overdubs and Lennon's "chk-ah-chk-ah" vocal percussion. The following day, next door in Studio Three, the Floyd recorded in one take their strange and gently wistful ballad "The Scarecrow" to a beat made from the clip-clop of horses' hooves lifted from the same BBC sound effects records used by the Beatles on *Sgt Pepper.*

Kate Bush was clearly part of the brilliant parade of audio innovators who through the decades walked through the doors of the former Georgian mansion, which in 1970, following the release the previous September of The Beatles album that immortalized it, was officially renamed Abbey Road Studios.

A decade on, Bush was photographed in the Studio Two control room, posed in front of one of the old-fashioned "lever fader" EMI TG mixing desks. Reminiscent of the workings of a steam train cab, it was the same piece of equipment that The Beatles had famously been pictured with, underlining the sense of continuity.

"They had a lot of the old equipment still, the valve desks and valve microphones," she recalled. "It had a fantastic feeling, it was a bit like a school. There was this feeling of all these school children working there."

The first time Bush had herself ever gone to Abbey Road was in 1975 during Pink Floyd's sessions for *Wish You Were Here,* by which time they'd become a very different and vastly more successful band, eight years after the acid-lost Syd Barrett had been replaced by Bush's now-mentor David Gilmour. It was a head-spinning experience for a sixteen-year-old.

"I was absolutely staggered," she told Brian Southall, "and I really thought I would never be able to record in a place like Abbey Road. But when I started recording, I wanted to go back there . . . it's always been a special place for me."

~

Still, Bush wasn't at first sure if Abbey Road would be the right fit for her, sonically, and in early 1980, she booked Studio Two to do a test recording. Alone at the piano, she committed to tape her quiet song of family reminiscence, "Warm and Soothing," with its delicate arpeggios and soft falsetto vocal notes. "Really, the only way we could tell if it was going to sound good was if I went and did a piano/vocal," she said. "So I did and it sounded great."

In the inner sanctum of Studio Two, with its echoes in the walls, Bush felt truly inspired, and even thought about using it as purely a songwriting room. "But," she acknowledged, "it would have been an enormously expensive way of writing."

During the months there completing *Never for Ever*, Bush didn't treat Abbey Road with utter reverence, as highlighted by the glass-smashing shenanigans involved in "Babooksha." She, co-producer Jon Kelly, and engineer John Barratt also played a daft game, daring one another to see who could be quickly spun around and around in a revolving control room chair the most amount of times without keeling over or being sick. Bush, used to gyrating as a dancer, secretly employed the "spotting" technique—focusing your vision on one spot to avoid dizziness—and won every time.

Bush became such a regular user of Abbey Road that she was quickly seen as a big part of the studios' story. By 1981, there was an enormous black-and-white shot of her positioned on the wall at the foot of the stairs leading to Studio Two. When, on November 12, 1981, a huge party was held to mark the studios' fiftieth year, she was asked to symbolically cut the cake—a ludicrous 5 foot by 4 foot cream sponge monstrosity topped with kiwi fruit—alongside 1960s pop star Helen Shapiro, in the middle of a throng including George Martin and Yehudi Menuhin.

As she later revealed in her newsletter, Bush didn't exactly feel comfortable being in the center of such a starry music biz bash. "Having cut a huge slice of cake," she wrote, "I started to cross the room that was very hard to move in because of the swirling crowds. But, with a cream cake aimed at their party clothes, the room practically cleared like the parting of the waters."

During the epic, troubled making of her fourth album *The Dreaming*, Abbey Road was to be one of the studio facilities that Bush pushed to the limit. But, even as she subsequently retreated, from *Hounds of Love* onward, into her private studio set-ups, she always returned to St John's Wood to record strings: a routine she continued up to 2011's *50 Words for Snow*.

From 1989's *The Sensual World* through to 2005's *Aerial*, the various ensembles were arranged and conducted by her regular scorer, Michael Kamen, a kindred spirit in terms of pushing and experimenting with the typically buttoned-up, rigid, and reading-from-the-page orchestral players. Bush and Kamen's final session together at Abbey Road for *Aerial*, in the weeks before Kamen suffered a fatal heart attack aged fifty-five in November 2003, was characterized by playfulness.

"It was the most fun," she told me. "When you work with orchestras, you have to work very fast and very efficiently. Obviously, it's very brave to try changing [the arrangement] when you've got thirty or forty people sitting, thinking, 'Oh, what're they doing?'

"We got to one bit, and I said, 'Hey Michael, d'you remember those seagulls we did years ago?'—this effect you get from strings where they go up and down and they sound like seagulls—and he went, 'Oh yeah, oh yeah . . . seagulls, everybody!'"

Back in June 1981, in footage that was set to become iconic and long-remembered in her career, Kate Bush made her own filmic mark on Studio One. In the same room where Elgar was captured in scratchy black and white footage conducting "Pomp and Circumstance . . ." in 1931, and where the Beatles had live-broadcast "All You Need Is Love" to an audience of over 400 million in twenty-five countries in 1967, she and her two dancers roller-skated across the parquet floor in the video for "Sat in Your Lap."

Written at home the day after Bush had seen Stevie Wonder perform at Wembley Arena in September 1980, and left impressed by the show's rhythmic power, "Sat in Your Lap" was the key that was to unlock the door into the next phase of her career. The angular beats and cut-up elements of its studio version were less Emily Brontë, more David Byrne (the Talking Heads' frontman's pioneering 1981 collaboration with Brian Eno, *My Life in the Bush of Ghosts* was also to be a key influence). As the singer introduced a cast of voices—faux naïve, growling, shrieking, operatic—she sang about the human hunger for knowledge conflicting with the lethargy or impatience that stops people from actually gaining it.

It was a brilliant, truly original, if challenging new direction that could potentially test her wider audience. Released as a single on June 21, 1981, the avant-garde pop of "Sat in Your Lap" was certainly weird, but still catchy enough to reach number eleven in the UK chart. In the scenes shot on the Abbey Road studio floor, Bush—in a halter top and tutu—threw flamenco shapes, her dancers variously wearing bull horns and court jester get-ups. In other scenes, the singer was hoisted aloft by them, wearing a white cloak and pointy cap displaying a "D" for dunce, as they rolled toward the camera.

On the surface, it was entertaining pop oddness, but there was also something ritualistic afoot. "Abbey Road's past," she told the keen readers of her newsletter, "full of dancing and singing spirits, was to be conjured up in the present day."

Kate Bush was now in an artistic class of her own, and yet still so young. The next month, July 1981, she would turn twenty-three. She may have been wearing a dunce cap in the video for "Sat in Your Lap," but clearly, she was no fool, and learning more and more all the time.

19

Guest Testimony

Ian Rankin

"I discovered her with 'Wuthering Heights.' That was a very early, exciting statement. It was not only based on a novel, but she used the same title for the song, so she got a lot of people interested in the story of *Wuthering Heights*. I mean, she's probably responsible for more folks picking up that book than any English teacher at high school.

"She hadn't read the book? (*Laughs*) She knew the *story*. It's a classic trope of doomed romance, isn't it? And it's got a spooky, supernatural element to it. So, it really appealed. And such an unusual song to get to number one. They always stay with you. I was in my early teens, and I was interested in books, and I was interested in becoming a writer. Here was somebody from the world of pop scoring a big number-one hit single with an incredibly literate song based on a novel.

"If you were a teenager and you were a wee bit arty, you were discovering all these things [such as the reference to Russian mystic and spiritual teacher Gurdjieff in 'Them Heavy People'] as well. You were dabbling in bits and pieces of philosophy and romantic poetry. You were looking for your road in life. You were looking for answers to big questions and there she was dealing with some of it in her lyrics.

"And she continues to. But, at the same time, she's also capable of writing about very mundane matters. I mean, how many folk have written songs about washing machines or songs where they recite the number pi? So one of the exciting things is that, as her career continued, you never quite knew what you were going to get. And, of course, a lot of the songs are open to the wildest interpretation you want to give to them.

"She compels as a lyricist because it's great use of words. There's great imagery, great poetry, there's a bit of mystery. I don't know how many times I've read the lyrics of Side Two of *Hounds of Love* ['The Ninth Wave'], looking for what it's actually all about. You can read her the way you would read a poet or a novelist. You keep going back. As I get older, I keep digging out new things that I hadn't noticed before. Or things that I think might be relevant, or things that might make sense to me. The Peter Pan references [on *Lionheart*]. In some ways, she makes me want to go back and read the books or see the play again, and I love that.

"She's painting pictures, isn't she? She's an extraordinarily kind of visual lyricist. These images just flash up in front of you as you listen to the record, or you read the lyrics. When she's singing 'The Big Sky' and you've got that kind of thumping beat behind her, you're looking at a big sky, because it's such an expansive song.

"I've just got an incredible amount of respect for her because she doesn't always make it easy. There're these three-minute pop songs, but they're incredibly difficult lyrically, and she's obviously worked really hard at doing them as well.

"Collecting lyrics together in a poetry book worked really well for Van Morrison [as Kate Bush did in 2018 with her volume of lyrics, *How to Be Invisible*]. There are certain musicians, like Van Morrison or Leonard Cohen, where you can read their words without actually having the music there in front of you. Now why it works, I don't know. But it does. I think if you're that kind of lyricist, if you're someone who has put a lot of work into your lyrics, to your fans you feel like a poet. She's definitely a poet when she writes, and her words can be read without the music behind them. But that takes a very special lyricist."

20

Let the Weirdness In

The making of The Dreaming, *1980–82*

The cannons were firing at them from across the valley. Or at least that's what Kate Bush wanted the beat to sound like. For the booming ending of the dark and unsettling "Leave It Open," the song had to feel as if it was under attack. It was down to engineer Nick Launay to help make that happen.

"We got corrugated iron from a building site and put it around the kit," Launay remembers. "We were making loops and just experimenting madly. I think the word 'wow' was used a lot. It was like being in a toy shop."

The location was Town House Studios in Shepherd's Bush, a state-of-the-art recording studio located on the grimy Goldhawk Road, a very different setting from leafy St John's Wood and Abbey Road, or the buzzy West End and AIR. Really, though, apart from trips to the nearby shops for supplies, Bush and Launay could have been anywhere. Bunkered in the studio for weeks on end, they were indulging themselves in flights of imagination.

Mainly, it was all about drums, drums, drums. Chinese drums, military drums, African drums. Nick Launay, at the time a punk rocker in his early twenties, had just come off the back of recording the beats-heavy *The Flowers of Romance*, the third post-Sex Pistols album by John Lydon and his amorphous band Public Image Ltd (or PiL). The young engineer had been given the job of co-producing the record after the artist formerly known as Johnny Rotten, fired up on Red Stripe lager, had locked the studio door on the original, clueless engineer and, as Launay vividly recalls, "told him to fuck off."

The sense of attitude, madness and freedom on *The Flowers of Romance* left a distinct imprint on the sessions for *The Dreaming*.

"We actually used some of the same instruments as the Public Image record," Launay says. "Kate was absolutely incredible. It was this almost child-like enthusiasm that both of us were driven by. It was just like, 'Let's try this, let's try that.'"

"Leave It Open" was one of the twin peaks of strangeness—along with *The Shining*-inspired horror story malevolence of "Get Out of My House"—on *The Dreaming*, with Bush's vocal dramatically cutting between demonic male spirit and cartoon banshee. At the end, as the drums turned to warfare, she repeated a deliberately obscure phrase that sounded as if it was wafting in through the ether.

When the album was finally released in September 1982, Bush set a challenge for her fans to guess exactly what she was singing at the end of "Leave It Open." For a while, she went with the theory that it was "we paint the penguins pink." Then she tipped them off, signing one of her increasingly irregular fan club letters with a reminder to "let the weirdness in."

It could have been the mission statement for the making of *The Dreaming*.

∽

Outside, as recording began in earnest the year before in the overcast and suffocatingly close British non-summer of 1981, riots were breaking out up and down the country. Unrest, fueled by the provocative stop-and-search Metropolitan Police strategy (mainly targeting black youth), spread from Brixton in London to Toxteth in Liverpool, to Chapeltown in Leeds, to Moss Side in Manchester.

"I've been lucky enough to be tucked away in the studio through all the riots, and only catching the muggy weather in-between sounds," Bush noted in her summer 1981 newsletter. "I hope everything has been good for you during this summerless time. We all know that 'things they are a-changing.'"

Inside the various London studios that the singer moved around as she sought to create her fourth album, other battles were being fought. After sharing the credit with Jon Kelly on *Never for Ever*, Kate Bush was determined to go it alone in producing its successor.

"I was off into this world of fighting to be a producer," she told me. "To take creative control of my music."

But even some of those close to Bush had their doubts about the wisdom of her overseeing the making of her next record entirely alone. "The usual one was, 'Are you sure you should be producing this, Kate?'" she remembered. "And this was from people that I was working with, not even record company people. I had to really batten down the hatches, [but then started to] really feel, 'God, maybe I shouldn't be producing it.'"

Yet she had a very clear vision for *The Dreaming*: a combination of the influences she'd recently absorbed and the techniques she'd accrued.

First of all, she splashed out thousands of pounds on her own Fairlight, having increasingly found the top-flight sampler "invaluable for my music."

Secondly, she'd fallen under the spell of Brian Eno and David Byrne's kaleidoscopic 1981 album *My Life in the Bush of Ghosts*, with its hypnotic looped polyrhythms over which the pair had ingenuously placed "found sound" vocals, including those of a radio talk show host, a preacher, an exorcist, and the soulful wailing of a Lebanese mountain singer named Dunya Younes. To Bush, the album was "really revolutionary and I think it was very underrated as well. Such a successful combination of ideas."

Thirdly, she'd learned a lot from Peter Gabriel in terms of his oblique approaches when making his third solo album, on which she'd appeared. To clean up the top end of his productions, Gabriel had banned his drummers, Phil Collins and Jerry Marotta, from playing cymbals. Bush followed suit on *The Dreaming*.

The sessions began with Hugh Padgham, who at the time had co-created Gabriel's "gated" drum sound—the beats enlarged by natural reverb but unnaturally clipped at the end—which his assistant Nick Launay had recreated on *The Flowers of Romance*. Phil Collins had then made the drum sound famous when Padgham and Launay reproduced it for him on the eruptive tom-tom roll on his 1981 single, "In the Air Tonight."

Hugh Padgham had racked up recent hit-making credits with Collins, Gabriel and XTC and, as Bush pointed out, was "at the time the kind of star engineer. He'd worked with Peter, but his big claim to fame was he'd done the drums on the Phil Collins track, so I was really knocked out that I'd managed to get him because everyone wanted to work with Hugh. So, that was interesting. [The Town House] was a total departure from Abbey Road as well. I mean, I loved working at Abbey Road, but it was like trying to step into a new era, I suppose."

When Padgham quit early on in the sessions for *The Dreaming* to fly to Montserrat in the Caribbean to work with the Police on their fourth album, *Ghost in the Machine,* Bush carried on regardless with Launay. And the drum adventures (and challenges) began.

"At the time I had this thing about no hi-hats, no cymbals!" she laughed. "On *Never for Ever,* I was really pleased about the experimental stuff we did. But I always felt there was this slightly sort of MOR quality to hi-hats. It just sounded a bit passé. So that was one of the key things, make sure there's no hi-hats . . ."

"That was a challenge," notes drummer Stuart Elliott. "We had to rack our brains to find things that were not traditional. So we just looked for tiny little hand drums and bits of metal and just bashed the hell out of those. Del Palmer, who was the engineer/bass player [and Bush's then-boyfriend] did a lot of sampling with the Fairlight. Y'know, aerosols, *pss pss,* and they'd use those as hi-hats. It was a very creative period."

The backing tracks that Bush created in her three months working with Launay at the Town House were ambitious and wide-ranging. "Houdini," via chamber orchestral passages crashing into PiL drum hammering, revisited the story of the escapologist's dangerous stunts and his promise that after his death he would prove the existence of the afterlife by contacting his wife Bess through a medium.

Title track "The Dreaming" evoked the dusty atmosphere of Australia, for a tale of Aboriginals cleared from their sacred grounds or being hit by vans and left lying on roads and in ditches. Spotlighting the anything goes approach, seemingly unthreatening visual artist/entertainer Rolf Harris, a regular on British TV, was brought in to play bass-like digeridoo (although his name was quietly expunged from the credits on the 2018 reissue of *The Dreaming*, following his jailing in 2014 for multiple historic counts of indecent assault). On the same song, unlikely television and radio star Percy Edwards, famous for his uncanny vocal impersonations of animals, was employed to provide the sounds of Australian magpies, dingoes, and sheep.

One of the most affecting passages of audio on *The Dreaming* meanwhile was the result of an accident. Bush had arrived home and pressed "play" on her answering machine, which malfunctioned and let her hear only the ends of the messages where callers were saying goodbye. Inspired, she dug out other old answering machine cassettes and edited these onto the end of "All the Love," a song filled with the last-days regret of someone who had kept themselves remote from their family and friends. The fact that the messages at the close of the track were genuine, as they said to her "bye" and "cheerio" and "I'll see ya, love," were all the more haunting.

Meanwhile, at Abbey Road, with engineer Haydn Bendall, Bush worked on "Night of the Swallow"—an emotional dialogue between a pilot and his partner; the latter warning him not to fly an illicit, dangerous mission (and the former trying to reassure her). It was a high-concept production involving the fiddles and pipes of Irish traditional group Planxty recorded during a flying visit to Dublin. At one point, back in London, Bush ended up using all three of Abbey Road's studios at once, including feeding the drums into the cavernous Studio One to capture some of Elgar's reverb.

All in all, it was progressive stuff. But Bush soon became mired in the recording of *The Dreaming*. "We actually ended up dragging round loads of different studios," she said. "[I used] loads of different engineers and actually I ended up back at Abbey Road at several points."

As Launay notes, "She's obviously got this incredible talent and her mind is very complex. The time I spent with her was great fun and all very creative and we got a lot done in the three months.

"When I listen to that record now," he adds, "two-thirds of what I hear is what we did at the Town House. That's not to take away any massive effort that was made afterward with the vocals and top line overdubs. But with the mind she had, she probably got very detailed and procrastinated over things.

"Anyone will tell you, the early stages of making a record are the fun times because you're being more loose with things. It's very easy to overthink the fine-tuning and get worried that it's not right. I wouldn't suggest to any artist that they produce their own record. You need someone to bounce ideas off and, between the two of you, you form a conclusion. That's what producers are there for."

~

As the months passed, and 1981 turned to 1982, things had grown more complicated. "By the time we were going through so many different studios," said Bush, "I was starting to get worn down by it all. Cause, of course, you're full of self-doubt."

It was an emotion tangentially expressed amid the angular beats of "Suspended in Gaffa." Bush's explanation of this most cryptic of songs—which referred to the strong, sticky gaffer tape much used by roadies and studio techs—was that it involved the frustrating effort some people put into gaining a "glimpse of 'God.'" If it actually sounded altogether more personal, then she later admitted that the lyric was "reasonably autographical" and "about seeing something that you want—on any level—and not being able to get that thing unless you work hard."

In the chorus of "Suspended in Gaffa," the singer's feet are stuck in the mud. Moving forward is hard, and emotions are difficult to process. It was easy to read it as a metaphor for the creative quagmire she was forcing herself to wade through. But still, Bush *knew* inside that she was right to forge on toward her vision, shimmering tantalisingly on the horizon.

"If you believe that it's worth it, you've just got to not listen to what other people say," she stressed. "It used to be almost like the acid test. If somebody sort of went [*sharp intake of breath*], 'Not sure about that,' I'd think, 'Yes! Great. I'm onto something here.' This resistance became the sign that I was onto something (*laughs*). If you've got people around you all the time, going, 'You can't do that,' it's a really good test.

"I think that's very much the sort of English thing," she added. "Cause in the States, y'know, even if you come up with a really crap idea, everybody'd be going, 'Oh Gawd, that's so fantastic.' And actually in some ways, that's also what Americans are really good about—they're so positive and enterprising. That's why they get things done that we don't.

"But you can still have some idea flailing around in this country. Nobody will back it . . . they're all too busy slagging it off. But it's also an incredible test of intention, because if you really mean something and you fight it through, then you *really* mean it."

As the months rolled on, executives at EMI Records were increasingly beginning to wonder if Bush should be producing herself at all, or even if the record would ever be finished. The pressure from the label began to weigh her down. She credited engineer Paul Hardiman, who came onboard in the latter stages—as the project moved to Odyssey Studios near Marble Arch and onto Advision Studios in Fitzrovia—with giving her the confidence to push on.

"He really treated me as a producer. He made me feel like he trusted me. Really, from that point onward, I felt like I had somebody who was there for me, and it meant so much. It was like a breath of fresh air suddenly coming in after all this flailing and fighting and thinking, 'I'm not going to do this, they're going to get me.' I don't mean in a paranoid way. But they were going to beat me down and I wasn't going to have the strength to see it through. I mean, it's only an album for Christ's sake, d'you know what I mean? But when you're in it, you're in it."

Bush's vocals for the album, perhaps unsurprisingly by now, "took weeks." Experimenting further, she effected her singing with flangers and harmonizers and echoes and squashed her voice using studio compression until you could hear every breath, lending it added intimacy. "The breath . . . for me, that's as important as the words," she explained at the time. "It's the space in-between." She also said that another big desire for her was to "put some balls into my voice for the first time."

The Fairlight, which was usually added late in the recording of any track, was pushed into action to add the sounds of car crashes and fluttering birds and snatches of strings. By the end, the music, as its creator colorfully described it, was a "sea of overdubs."

At the very heart of *The Dreaming*, though, there seemed to be a lot of anger.

"Yes, that was my 'I'm very angry' album," Bush admitted to me.

Was she personally angry at that time?

"Yeah, I think I was. I think I was angry, and I think that's there in the music. There was just this real creative need to say what I wanted to say, I suppose. Because in a lot of ways I'd been very lucky to have the creative control I had up to that point. But it was still that one step away from really being able to get my hands on it.

"Always, somehow, I'd been having to work around other things and suddenly here I was being able to actually try to do it. But I met a huge amount of resistance, and maybe that was what I was kind of angry about. I felt I was having to fight continually."

But was there a point after she'd finished *The Dreaming* when she raised her head and thought to herself, "Maybe I'm a bit out of tune with what's going on?"

"In what way?"

Well, commercially. "Sat in Your Lap" was a mental single, obviously.

"Yeah, I think it was all mental. But that's what I really liked about it, was that it was 'Fuck you, you record companies! Trying to pin me down!'"

The highpoint of this frustration appeared on record at the very end of the album, on "Get Out of My House," where in the terrifying lyric the singer is faced by an evil, shape-shifting spirit and turns into a demented, braying mule to scare it away.

"I played that to a couple of friends and when it got to the bit where it was going, 'Hee-haw,' they just absolutely broke up and pissed themselves laughing and said, 'God, you've totally lost it, girl.' I was thinking, 'No, but that's *great*. That's one of my favorite bits!'"

Time has proven *The Dreaming* to be a classic. For many—the author included—it's their favorite Kate Bush album.

"Do you know, so many people say that to me," Bush smiled when I offered that opinion. "It's really nice for me because I had such a hard time making that."

In the end, the struggles were worth it. As she reached another milestone in her career, *The Dreaming* was the point at which Kate Bush became a truly unique artist. Nonetheless, selling it to EMI and the wider public, beyond her most devoted fans, was to involve other clashes entirely.

21

"Pull Out the Pin"

From The Dreaming, *1982*

**"Pull Out the Pin" airlifts the listener directly into the
southeast Asian jungle.**

The first full realization of the cinematically minded music
that Kate Bush began striving to make on *Never for Ever*, this
five-and-a-half-minute-long track was the centerpiece of—in
the old money—Side One of its wildly ambitious successor, *The
Dreaming*. The scene was set by Preston Heyman's echoing, stick-
played bongo pattern, Danny Thompson's snaking double bass
and Brian Bath's choppy guitar shrunk to a fizzy noise emanating
from a transistor radio amid the bamboo.

Dropping herself into the middle of the action, Kate casts herself as a dirt-bellied, patiently stalking Viet Cong soldier.

While recorded in the sizeable cultural wake created by the
release of *Apocalypse Now* in 1979, the track was in fact inspired
by a TV documentary viewing the war from the Viet Cong perspective. In the studio, this stimulated an act of sonic visualization.
"We sat in front of the speakers trying to focus on the picture,"

Bush remembered. "A green forest, humid and pulsating with life."

Bush was captivated by the idea that a Viet Cong soldier would sometimes trail one of his American counterparts for days, using olfactory sense to follow the stink of his city-raised enemy—perspiration, aftershave, dope—before delivering the decisive act of violence. Track him until he buckles under the weight of exhaustion. Then cap him before he knows anything about it.

Vocally, "Pull Out the Pin" is deftly complex—Bush's electronically double-tracked delivery at first calm and composed before turning sinister, then desperate, in her repeated cries declaring her will to survive. By inhabiting the thoughts of this tenacious soldier, she performs an impressive act of lyrical ventriloquism.

At its heart, more than even "Breathing," "Pull Out the Pin" is Bush's first truly Pink Floyd-like track, with its rotoring helicopter sound effects and brooding-turned-explosive qualities reminiscent of the moody-to-manic energy of *The Wall* that had awed and inspired her upon its release in 1979, the year before the difficult and protracted sessions for *The Dreaming* began.

The Floyd connection is made explicit by the appearance of David Gilmour on the chorus vocal counterpoint of "Pull Out the Pin." Never before (or since) has Gilmour as a singer sounded so cooly menacing, and never up until this point had Bush sounded so deeply immersed in such an unlikely role.

"I'm able to oversee the whole thing in a way that I can treat myself almost like an actor on a stage," she said of her almost method-like approach. "It's not just being a singer. The voice is just part of trying to create an atmosphere or a little story or a picture and it's very much about the emotional content . . ."

22

Back in the Lens

"The Dreaming" and "There Goes a Tenner" videos, 1982

The roller-skating, dunce-cap-wearing moves in the video for "Sat in Your Lap" may have been captured to video in a spare afternoon on the parquet live room floor at Abbey Road's Studio One, but for the oddly shaped, Australian-accented follow-up single, "The Dreaming," Kate Bush began to flex her creative muscles. Ambitious on record and increasingly ambitious on screen, she became deeply involved in the realization of the promo films for the singles from her fourth album.

Paul Henry was brought in to direct both "The Dreaming" and "There Goes a Tenner." A former art director at the Arista and United Artists record labels, he'd designed record sleeves for the Stranglers and Buzzcocks and in 1979 made the striking part-live action, part-animated TV promo clip for Simple Minds' second single, "Chelsea Girl." Having recently been sacked from his position as marketing and art director at Island Records, by 1982 he'd decided to pursue his career behind the camera.

"Somewhere along the line, Kate came into the frame," he says. "But I didn't come the formal route and I think that was a disadvantage. Because obviously she was a big artist." From the off, it was clear that Bush wanted to have a large input: "She was very thoughtful, very creative, very open about what she wanted to get from the films. She had very specific ideas."

One aspect for "The Dreaming" video being to break directorial norms, which forced Henry to creatively push back straight away. "She wanted the whole thing shot as a wide shot. Which obviously you don't do, because you need other shots in order to make a film move along. But she was very keen on showing off the dance routine."

Henry's task was to create a dusty antipodean environment within the walls of Ewart Television in Wandsworth—a feat accomplished by shooting through a pane of glass upon which a landscape had been painted. "It wasn't an easy track to visualize," he stresses. "So that sort of slightly grungy look that it ended up having, with lots of dust and smoke and so on, was a departure, really, for her. I thought it was brave to go that route."

For a video high in ideas but not the budget to match, Bush and her troupe of dancers performed on a floor covered over with builders' sand, amid polystyrene rocks and spindly trees, and in front of a sun and moon made of cardboard. Bush, wearing a distressed, silver-white, space age jumpsuit, also took some giant, walking-on-the-moon steps, hoisted aloft on hidden flying wire.

"It was just a day's shooting," Henry points out. "And a lot of it was put together on the day. Which meant that obviously at times we had to accept sort of second best. So there were some shots that I look at now and cringe. But we were up against it [because of time constraints]."

One memorable scene involved Bush and the dancers pulling on a "rope" that was in fact a green laser. In 1982, this still looked futuristic. Later in the video, the singer seemed to command live birds to fly into the air by waving her hands.

"The animal handler said to us, 'All you have to do is just turn the lights out in the studio, open the doors and the birds will fly out,'" Henry remembers. "It was obviously not shot in sequence, so at a point in the day it was felt that this would be the right [moment] to shoot that particular shot with the birds. Then, we spent an hour trying to shoo the birds out of the studio. They all sat in the gantry. The occasional feather would drift down into the shot."

The director remembers the filming being relatively pain-free. The editing process, less so. "We had an ongoing discussion about wide shots and close ups," he says. "We sort of had to dance around each other to get what we needed. And, actually, because Kate was paying for it, she felt that she had complete control, and quite rightly, y'know.

"In the end, she just didn't want the closer shots. So the edit was a compromise and caused a lot of problems with EMI. They were unhappy with the cut. There was no support forthcoming from EMI. Plenty of criticism, of course, but no support."

The people at Bush's label then instructed Paul Henry to take a firmer stance when it came to the video for her next single,

"There Goes a Tenner." "I'd been told, 'Don't be bamboo-zled,'" he recalls. "So I had to be a lot tougher, if you like, on the second one."

The storyboard for "There Goes a Tenner" mirrored the bungled heist, Ealing comedy caper narrative of the song. Del Palmer played a getaway driver. Bush, breaking into a building with her two dancer accomplices, was keen to look like a mucky robber.

"We talked about the fact that she'd ended up looking a bit grubby in 'The Dreaming,'" Henry recalls. "And she said, 'Oh, I'm okay with that. So why don't we start "There Goes a Tenner" with me looking a bit grubby?' She ended up with that sort of smudging on her face. She was really excellent in that. I thought her acting skills were terrific."

The production values were upped slightly for "There Goes a Tenner." Kate and the dancers sat on a part-open roof, staring down through the hole at a massive swinging pendulum signifying the ticking time they had to get the "job" done. Then, a mock safe was cracked open by an explosion, fake green pound notes billowing everywhere.

"I'm not sure about the song so much on reflection," Henry says of "There Goes a Tenner." "Actually, my regret was that the songs that we got to make the films for were not the sort of mega hits that other songs had been. So the films didn't really get seen as widely as they might have been if they'd been more successful songs."

Bush would go on to oversee other, more famous videos for far better-known singles. What became obvious at this point, though, was that she was determined to repeat the same ambitious process that now found her in charge at the mixing desk in the studio. She wanted to solely get her hands on her videos and direct them.

"Many artists I worked with would just say, 'Well, what shall we do?' And she was never like that," Henry states. "She would always have an idea of how things should look. She's always had brilliant album covers and I'm sure that was mostly down to her. So I think to say she's a visual auteur is probably quite accurate."

That however didn't stop there being problems on the set of "There Goes a Tenner." Particularly on the floor when Bush's directorial aspirations came alive, causing difficulties for the actual director.

"It's confusing for crew if there are two lots of instructions being passed around," Paul Henry emphasizes. "I just insisted that I had to have a lot more control as the director. The consequence was that the film she shot after that [for 'Suspended in Gaffa'], she had every member of my crew except me (*laughs*)."

23

An "Uncommercial Record"

Reactions to The Dreaming, *1982*

The Dreaming **landed like an alien in September 1982,
the year that synth pop was king and the towering UK
albums were** *Dare* **by the Human League (released
in 1981 but continuing its victory lap),** *The Lexicon of
Love* **by ABC,** *Avalon* **by Roxy Music and the leg-warm-
er-wearing pop of stage school TV drama spin-off
record,** *The Kids from "Fame."*

In this context, it's easy to see why Kate Bush's fourth
long-player—a left-field, art-headed record—might have seemed
truly, deeply weird.

"When I presented it to the record company, they thought it
was unworkable," she recollected. "The phrase that went round
all the [international EMI] record companies, that was spread
from the company in England, was that this was an 'uncommercial record' . . . 'it's not going to be successful.' And I saw that
as a direct result of the fact that I'd produced it and I obviously
hadn't done a successful job."

Bush soon got wind of the fact that, incredibly, even EMI's record pluggers—the very people who were supposed to be pushing *The Dreaming* and the singles lifted from it—were presenting it to radio producers with eye-rolls.

"What was really frustrating for me was I felt the record company had dumped it basically," she admitted. "I had people at the radio stations take me aside and say, 'What's going on, y'know?' They're giving me the record and going like that *(takes sharp intake of breath)*."

"Suddenly, they were perceiving me as being a really difficult artist. I felt that—y'know, for a record company—we'd had quite a good relationship, really. I never had a manager, so I never played the game in the usual way. I always had a slightly different way of dealing with things, I guess. But they gave me a hard time. They really did."

Reviews, meanwhile, tended toward the bemused, as critics struggled to get their heads around *The Dreaming*. *Smash Hits* writer Neil Tennant, at the time beginning to work on his own music with Chris Lowe as the Pet Shop Boys, decided that the album was "very weird. Obviously, she's trying to become less accessible."

Colin Irwin at *Melody Maker* was equally bamboozled, yet more perceptive: "Under the premise that the Great British Public instinctively turns its nose up at anything that's a little unexpected, or which doesn't meet its carefully coiffured preconceptions, then this album will be an overwhelming flop.

"The people'll be guided in their dismissive diagnosis, of course, by the all-wise radio producers who will flick quickly through it for the new 'Man with the Child in His Eyes,' fail to find it, assume Kate's gone off her trolley, and make a grab for the safety of Haircut One Hundred. Initially, it is bewildering and not a little preposterous but try to hang on through the twisted overkill and the histrionic fits and there's much reward, if only in the sense of danger she constantly courts."

Over in the States, reactions were more arch (*Creem*: "Occasionally, her musical ambitions get the better of her, but no one who closes an album braying like a donkey can be accused of being too pretentious, now can they?"). Or piercingly accurate (*Trouser Press*: "A stunning record in more ways than one . . . a triumph of inventive songwriting and unpredictable performances . . . but its sensory overload will drive away the less than dedicated.")

Commercial performances of *The Dreaming*'s singles plotted a downward curve. The title track, released in July 1982, was Bush's first flop single since "Hammer Horror," stalling at UK number forty-eight. "There Goes a Tenner," issued in November, fared even worse, failing to make even the top seventy-five, and getting stuck at number ninety-three.

If Kate Bush had apparently lost her singles audience in Britain, then she remained a buoyant album artist, and *The Dreaming* entered the UK chart at number three. Ultimately, though, it registered as only a silver record, with sixty thousand sales, whereas her previous albums had achieved gold (*Never for Ever*), platinum (*Lionheart*) and triple platinum (*The Kick Inside*).

Reflecting on the performance of *The Dreaming* more than two decades later, Bush clearly still held mixed feelings.

"People's reaction was that they thought the album was weird. It didn't really worry me that it didn't sell loads of records, cause I'd made something that I felt was the best I could do. That's always the way I've approached things—if it's the best you can do, then what more can you do? What was great, I suppose, really, was that they didn't delete it [i.e., pull the album stock from the shops and erase it from the EMI catalog]. I should be grateful that they didn't, really.

"They said it wouldn't be a commercial success and yet the album went straight in at three. For me, that's a successful record. I remember a friend saying to me a few years afterward, 'God, I didn't realize that record went straight in at three. I thought it didn't even chart.' So this was this perception. And, of course, *everything* is perceptions."

But it didn't sell as well as the previous records had done, I pointed out.

"Oh, no no, it didn't. No. But the previous record had been on the back of a successful tour. Whereas with *The Dreaming*, 'Sat in Your Lap' did very well, but unfortunately cause the record took me such a long time, the single was kind of rogue and out on its own for a long time. The album was released after it, so that kind of left it a little bit stranded.

"By the time I got to the end of *The Dreaming*, the people at the record company were going (*mimes slashing her throat*), 'Nutter.'"

24

The Hardest Sell

Promoting The Dreaming, *1982*

Determined to push back against EMI's iffy response to *The Dreaming*, Kate Bush threw herself into promoting the album. Throughout the campaign, she faced increasingly blunt or daft questions from interviewers, who also unhelpfully pointed out the singer's dwindling fortunes in the singles charts.

Here is a diary of the edited highlights of her various appearances and interviews from September and October 1982:

10 September

Radio 1 Roadshow, Covent Garden Piazza, London. Kate is interviewed live on air by DJ Dave Lee Travis aka "The Hairy Cornflake." He starts off by pointing out that she is wearing a T-shirt bearing the legend, "I'm a Prima Donna," a promotional item for Steve Harley's 1976 album, *Love's a Prima Donna*.

"Wonderful stuff," says Travis. "So what about acting out *The Dreaming*? Is there still the old Kate Bush of not too long ago when you used to go on stage wired up for sound and driving yourself bananas in front of the audience? Or have you quietened down?"

"I don't think I've quietened down," says Bush. "I think I've got worse, probably, and I'm dying to get out on the road again and do shows. Really dying. Since the last show, I've been waiting for an opportunity to do it. So I'm just waiting now."

"Are we going to see you out on the road soon?" Travis goes on. "Or is that an awful question to ask?"

"I don't think it will be until next year," says Bush. "But I really want to start getting something together. And, really, I'm just thinking about it at the moment."

September 13

Capital Radio, London. Bush is interviewed by afternoon show DJ Roger Scott, who perceptively notes, on the day of the release of the nearly two-years-in-the-making album, "You [must] have this enormous feeling of relief . . . is there also a tinge of uncertainty there, thinking, 'Well, is this right?'"

Bush laughs and instantly says, "Yes. I think the relief is definitely a big one. Because after having worked on something for so long, you really are glad that it's all finished, especially when it's been hard work. I mean, you could go on doing it forever. But you would actually start making things a little overdone."

"You never have second thoughts?" presses Scott. "And think, 'Maybe I've not done this right? Maybe this isn't going to be . . .'"

"Oh, yeah," Bush cuts in. "I have them all the time, but you just have to pretend they're not happening and say, 'Yes, this is it.' Because . . . well, they're really last-minute paranoias, they just happen all the time. I mean, I've been going through that all last week, just waiting for this album to come out."

September 14

Record-signing personal appearance at the Virgin Megastore, Oxford Street, London. Straight after, Bush takes the train to Manchester for a jovial TV interview with David Hepworth and Mark Ellen on BBC Two's hip music show for "heads," *The Old Grey Whistle Test*. The pair ask her if it's true that she'd hired a guard's van on the train traveling there, so that she'd be able to rehearse a routine with her dancers.

"It is true, yes," she smiles. "They actually cleared it out. They took all the post out and everything. So we just had an empty carriage to work in. At one hundred miles an hour, it's really difficult."

September 21

ITV kids show *Razzmatazz*, Newcastle. Presenter Alistair Pirrie, in voice-over, announces, "Here's little Kate Bush," before she appears, in white TV shirt, red braces and black leather trousers, surrounded by kids, to perform "There Goes a Tenner" with her two robber-masked dancers (Gary Hurst and former Lindsay Kemp trouper Douglas McNicol). In this context, the bouncy routine highlights the song's ska-like groove and possibly previously unappreciated similarity to Madness's 1980 hit, "Baggy Trousers" (a record Bush loved).

October 2

Saturday Superstore, BBC TV Centre, London. Kate is a guest on the launch show of the successor to *Multi-Coloured Swap Shop*, presented by mulleted, tinted-glasses-wearing Radio 1 DJ Mike

Read. From the look in her eyes, Bush would appear to have decided that Read is a twonk.

Read pulls a copy of *The Dreaming* out of a bag of competition prizes and shows it to camera. Referring to the sepia cover image of Kate with a key on her tongue, preparing to pass it via a kiss to Houdini (in fact, Del Palmer photographed from behind), he wonders aloud, "I was gonna say . . . this ring in your mouth, I couldn't quite work that out, Kate. What is it?"

"Oh, you need to look again, if you think it's a ring . . ." she grins.

Somehow, only minutes later, the conversation drifts onto grocery shopping (presumably to tie in with the store-themed show).

Mike Read: Do you have a local store you go to or not?

Kate Bush: Yeah, I do, for vegetables and things like that.

MR: Do you always buy the same things? I find when I go down to the store, I always think, "Mm, what shall I get?" And I always end up getting exactly the same things every week.

KB: Well, I try to get different things. But normally, it's the same thing.

MR: D'you get out to the shop much on Saturdays, or not? You mainly stay in bed after working?

KB: Yeah, I try to sleep as much as I can normally.

[Clearly, then, she will not be tuning in to *Saturday Superstore* next week.]

6 October

Up in Glasgow, Kate makes a record shop appearance, attends a party for regional salespeople and is interviewed by Radio Clyde's Billy Sloan.

Sloan is astute and gently assertive, saying, "Now, you mentioned the fact that ['The Dreaming' single] failed in a chart sense. I mean, I think that you're one of the few artists who seems to suffer through your own incredibly high standards. Do you think that because of the sheer quality of the music that you're making, you're alienating yourself from the charts?"

"I don't know," Bush responds softly. "I've never thought of that. I mean, I think I'm far too subjective, really. I do feel that I'm very out of touch with the singles charts. And also, perhaps my music is moving further away from being single material."

"Yeah, but even when you look in the album charts," Sloan continues, "the top twenty albums this week, there are very few people that you could run parallels with."

"Uh, yes, maybe," says Kate, turning cagey. "Maybe. But I don't know if that matters, in a way. I mean, the fact that it's actually selling, I think, is the most important thing. Although it's been called the most uncommercial album I've done . . ."

After spinning "There Goes a Tenner," Sloan enquires about the heist-themed lyric: "Now everybody like myself probably holds the fantasy of pulling off the perfect crime. Is that really what it's about? And do you hold the same fantasy?"

KB: Well, it's about . . . the opposite of that, really.

BS: Oh.

KB: It's about the idea of people who've planned the perfect crime for months. But when they actually start, they're terrified.

BS: You'd love to do it, though.

KB: (*Clearly taken aback that she's being asked to theoretically plan a bank hit live on Scottish radio*) No, I wouldn't. It doesn't interest me at all. If you look at it realistically, although you have a lot to gain, it's just not worth the effort for the amount you could lose. And I think in this song, I'm really just trying to point out that perhaps in that situation, you'd just be so scared.

BS: Is that not what's just putting you off, though? I mean, if you thought you could do it and get away with it, and nobody would be hurt in the process, surely you would love to have a crack at it?

KB: No, I don't think so. It doesn't actually appeal to me at all. No (*laughs*).

October 8

Personal appearance/signing in Birmingham, and TV studio interview with Paul Gambaccini on BBC One's *Pebble Mill at One*.

"I do notice, of course," Gambaccini ventures, "that we've missed singles from you coming at the rate that they used to. Are you aware when there is a gap? Are you afraid, 'Oh, people might be forgetting me?'"

"Yes, very scared indeed," Bush admits. "And I think there's just this pressure on you that when you're not in the public eye, perhaps they'll forget you. People say how fickle the public are. But I don't think that they really are in a lot of ways. I think if they like something, then they are willing to wait for it . . ."

PG: You do seem to be taking evermore control of the range of your career. You've always had the prime input, but on your current album, you are the writer, the vocalist, the keyboard player, the producer and the arranger.

KB: Yeah. (*Mimes with her hands her "big head" expanding*) Pfff!
[*The show screens the video for "There Goes a Tenner"—the only time it will get an airing on UK TV.*]
PG: "There Goes a Tenner," from the album, *The Dreaming*, and I think that will be a hit actually.
KB: Do you? Do you really? I don't know any more (*laughs*).

October 28

To Paris. Interview with the France Inter public radio station. The unnamed presenter, through an interpreter, asks Bush, "How did you cope with the sex symbol label you had for a long time?"

Bush, amused but understandably nervous about the line of questioning, politely responds by saying, "I think I've always said it's very, very flattering. And I think the only problem it caused was that for a while, perhaps a few people would not take my music so seriously, because there was such an emphasis, perhaps, on the physical side. But I really don't think that is such a problem any more. I think people, as the albums have come along, they take me a little more seriously each time."

Presenter: It was one when you start?
KB: Sorry?
Presenter: It was a problem when you start?
KB: (*Beginning to sound a touch weary*) Uh, never a problem, no. But it worried me that, y'know, people would not take my music seriously, which of course is really important for me. But I don't find it's a problem now.

Postscript

Years later, when I asked Bush if she'd been depressed at the end of *The Dreaming* saga, she said, "I don't actually remember. I remember being very *tired*."

For her, it was becoming clear that trudging around television studios and radio stations was not the way forward. At the end of all of that effort, and even with a number-three album, her future was more uncertain than ever.

"Nobody wanted me to produce the next record," she pointed out.

25

Retreat, Rethink

Hounds of Love, *1983–86*

In the summer of 1983, Kate Bush reached out to her fans to give them an update on her current activities.

"This year has been very positive so far," she wrote. "It doesn't have the same air of doom and gloom that 1981 and 1982 seemed to hold. The problem is that if I don't make an album this year, there will be at least another two-year gap, and the way business and politics are, it would be a negative situation.

"I seem to have hit another quiet period," she added. "I intend just to keep on writing . . . so yet again I slip away from the eyeball of the media to my home."

In fact, she was disappearing to a completely new home. Since the early 1980s, the singer had been living with Del Palmer in a six-bedroomed house in Court Road, Eltham, southeast London. Three years on, however, life in the capital was beginning to wear her down, and so the couple relocated to a seventeenth-century farmhouse tucked away in the leafy calm of Kent.

"I'd moved out of London to a more kind of rural setting, near Sevenoaks," she recalled to me. "It wasn't a big, special house, but it had a lovely view. I just had this little writing room, and I could look out at this lovely view when I was writing.

"It's a quiet space that you create from," she reasoned. "I think of it quite often as being similar to people who write books and stuff. It's disciplined and quite often they do it in the shed in the garden, because they need that quiet space."

Bush, meanwhile, kept the Eltham property as her urban HQ and second workspace. Journalists invited to the house for interviews were typically led upstairs into her dance studio, with its mirrored wall, and an enormous modern art painting that she'd bought a few years before. Titled "The Hogsmill Ophelia," it referenced Millais's pre-Raphaelite masterpiece "Ophelia," replacing Hamlet's drowned heroine with a cracked-faced doll floating beside a sewer pipe, the water polluted with the rainbow colors of an oil slick. It was both beautiful and unsettling and very Kate Bush. "A lot of people find it disturbing, but I don't," she told one writer. "I've lived with it for ages."

Meanwhile, out in Kent, Bush got closer to nature. Her new songs were soon filled with rustic imagery and changing weather patterns, seeing magic in the everyday. One, "The Big Sky," was even part-inspired by her pet.

"I used to have this great cat," she told me. "She was a really big cat, and she was very gentle. She didn't catch mice and birds, and she used to sit on this little wall in the garden, just looking up at the sky. I mean, not that it was about her, but I used to think that that was really cute." More specifically, the song recalled formative memories. "That thing when you're a child," she explained, "and you look at clouds and you try to imagine faces in them."

Bush began demoing songs on her home studio set-up: an eight-track reel-to-reel recorder, her piano, her Fairlight. From now on her songwriting and keen attention to aural detail would work in tandem, with many of the elements of the original sketches for *Hounds of Love* making it all the way to the finished record.

An early breakthrough came with the strident, marching machine beat and Fairlight hookline oddity of a track named, for now, "A Deal with God." "From that moment," Bush noted, "the album 'process' steadily rolled."

⁓

After the difficulties and the dizzying expense that the creation of *The Dreaming* had brought, when it came to begin recording again, it was clearly time for a rethink. Exhausted by the intensive, Stanley Kubrick-esque process of making her fourth album, Bush's next move was both a reassessment and a partial retreat, back to East Wickham Farm. On her father Robert's advice she began to remodel her creative operation as a cottage industry. Even if there was a certain sense of urgency surrounding this fifth album, she had clearly grown tired of watching the studio clock as it ticked off anything up to £100 an hour, and typically more than £1,000 a day.

At East Wickham Farm (an hour's drive north of Sevenoaks), some garages neighboring the barn—the same one where as a child she'd played the pump organ—were cleared out to provide extra recording spaces. Two twenty-four-track tape machines were installed and synced together to give forty-eight-track capabilities.

Inside, the walls were papered in blue, dotted with white clouds. "She loves blue," drummer Stuart Elliott points out. "Sky blue and light blue. It was a lovely atmosphere. A brilliant little studio. The control room was like a very large living room. There were two or three areas for recording, each of which were a good room size."

Bush was now in the position to make records in the same spot where she'd dreamed and experimented as a kid. Rarely would she book a commercial studio again.

"I don't like working in commercial studios," she told me, presumably meaning except for Abbey Road. "For a start, they're so expensive. But also, I don't like the dissipation of the focus. Cause you might be in the middle of doing a vocal and you look through to the control room and you'll see somebody walking in looking for a pair of headphones or something. I think it's very important to get the creative focus and it's very [easy to get] distracted. The creative process is, I think, very much about trying to keep this focus throughout all these things that are trying to destroy it."

Building work on the studio was completed at the start of 1984. The unusual recording set-up at East Wickham Farm meant that there was no traditional "studio glass" arrangement where those working in the control room could watch the per-former. All communication was done via the talkback micro-phone on the mixing desk feeding into headphones in the live rooms. This sense of privacy, lending further creative freedom, was underlined by the fact that Del Palmer engineered the ses-sions (especially the ones involving vocal recordings), before Paul Hardiman and later Haydn Bendall and Brian Tench were brought in to help sift through the takes and record others.

Finally, Bush was utterly freed of distractions as she began to make the album that was to become *Hounds of Love*. Martin

Glover aka Youth, the Killing Joke bassist and record producer who was brought into the sessions to add his low-end rumble to "The Big Sky," was wholly impressed by Bush's skills and discipline in self-producing: "I'd seen other artists self-produce and more often than not, it doesn't come out very well. Occasionally, you can get a masterpiece, and I think *Hounds of Love* is one.

"It made a lot of sense because she was spending so much time in commercial studios, that even with hit albums it didn't make her commercially viable. So, she built her own studio. She had a great team of people around her and it was fascinating watching her work."

One aspect of Bush's modus operandi that didn't change, even when she wasn't renting a costly studio by the hour or the day, was that she worked through lengthy shifts. "Actually, that was one of the things that Andrew Powell [on *The Kick Inside* and *Lionheart*] kind of set out," she said. "We always did work long hours."

But, looking back, and in contrast to the grinding months in the middle of the recording of *The Dreaming*, she remembered being particularly happy when she was making *Hounds of Love*: "Yeah, I really was . . . it was fun."

Tellingly, when a change of location was required to break up the sessions, the unit decamped to Ireland, a country that unarguably favors the slow-lane approach. "I spent quite a lot of time in Ireland," Bush remembered. "A few months, just traveling around, and I think that kind of spirit is in there.

"Of course, I've got quite a lot of family there as well, so I got to catch up with some of [them]. And it's such an incredibly beautiful country. It was really, I suppose, the first time since I was a little girl I'd had a chance to see [it]."

The Irish spirit is very much evident on *Hounds of Love* in the acutely Celtic "Jig of Life," with John Sheahan's sawing fiddles, Liam O'Flynn's intricate uilleann pipe patterns and Donal Lunny's syncopated bodhrán beats. But it's also there in Sheahan's beautifully eerie whistle parts on the reverie-inducing "And Dream of Sheep" and his piped counterpoint on "Hello Earth."

Yet Bush remembered there at first being some resistance coming from some of the musicians during the sessions at Windmill Lane Studios in Dublin, perhaps sceptical of the motives of this English "pop star": "Initially, it was like this (*folds arms guardedly*) and then gradually [the] body language turned into this (*opens arms, relaxes*) and it was just wonderful to feel this lovely response from people. Everybody laughing a lot and just a great team spirit. Obviously Irish music is a big part of my ancestry. It's in my blood."

Most of the lyrics for the album were completed in Ireland, so it's perhaps surprising that in this laidback setting, Kate Bush's head was often burning with thoughts of persecution and possession, of being hunted and haunted. At some points, the atmosphere on *Hounds of Love* is claustrophobic and suffocating. At others, it's manic and euphoric.

Back at East Wickham Farm from June 1984 onward, in what would turn out to be almost an entire year of overdubbing and mixing, Stuart Elliott noted that Bush's work methods were now firmly centred around technology.

"The Fairlight was in full force then," he says. "But we did put a lot on top of that. Sometimes the Fairlight became just like a string for us to hang off, like pearls. There was an awful lot of creativity in the rhythm tracks regarding the sounds. We'd use acoustic and electronic samples. It was just mix and match until something unique came out of it. It's all eureka moments with Kate. There's one brilliant piece of music after another."

Elliott was particularly impressed by the twisty, inventive arrangement of "A Deal with God," which had started life with a tom-tom heavy groove programmed on the LinnDrum, the high-end studio beatbox that powered the 1980s. "I just sort of overdubbed on top of that and did big, explosive electronic drum fills. But the tension in that track is just remarkable. Every step of the way, there's a little twist and turn that's different from the previous verse—an extra line or one line less, or a repeat just in the perfect places. There's absolutely no dead space in that track and it's just so deceptively simple."

"A Deal with God," with its lyric imagining a soul-swap with a lover, so that each can experience the feelings of the opposite gender, was clearly far away from the stuff of the typical pop song. But it also highlighted Bush's stated desire to make music with "male energy." It's worth noting that one of her favorite songs of 1984 was Killing Joke's stomping, muscular and punky single "Eighties." With *Hounds of Love*, Kate Bush would leave any lingering comparisons with fey female singer-songwriters way behind her.

The recording process was at the same time lighter in spirit than it had been on *The Dreaming*. Booking masterly German double bassist Eberhard Weber to play on "Mother Stands for Comfort" and "Hello Earth," Bush was suddenly struck by a left-field notion. "Don't ask me why," she told me, "but I just thought, 'Wouldn't it be great if he did some whistling?' He was out there for a couple of hours whistling. I remember somebody saying, 'God, you've brought this huge star bass-player over and you're making him whistle . . .'"

In terms of her own parts, where on her previous albums the piano had played either ornate and vocal-supporting or rhythmical roles, this time around, she was looking for delicacy in the style of Chopin or Satie. Both "Mother Stands for Comfort" and "And Dream of Sheep" successfully achieved the desired atmosphere, which she evocatively described as being like "the empty ballroom after the party when everyone has gone home." Elsewhere, her method, tested on *Never for Ever* and *The Dreaming*, of bringing in outside players to color her Fairlight sketches was particularly successful with the Medici Sextet's driving, staccato string parts on "Cloudbusting."

If a theme of romantic fear was the undercurrent running through "A Deal with God"—Bush said that the song was "really about two people who are in love and scared about the other person not feeling the same"—then it was brought to the surface in the title track of *Hounds of Love*. In some ways, the narrative reflected Neil Jordan's 1984 gothic horror film, *The Company of Wolves*, with its shapeshifting human-to-lupine fantasies and early scene in which a female character is pursued through a forest by a pack of wolves and killed.

In "Hounds of Love," the singer expresses conflicting feelings—love is pursuing her, and terrifying her, even if she accepts that it may be exactly what she needs. "It's not about wanting the 'Hounds of Love' to catch you and tear you apart," she explained. "That's what you think they're going to do. But they might want to catch you and lick you and play a game and be friendly dogs."

A nightmarish, moonlit chase of a track, the hyperventilating "Hounds of Love" features a stunning vocal performance from Bush: anxious, then intimate, then searing. It was one of the best examples of how her new vocal approach was paying off hand-somely. Recording alone with Del Palmer she said at the time felt "very relaxed and uninhibited, which gives me a head start compared to normal studio situations, where I'm fighting my nerves until I can settle down."

As opposed to the nocturnal vocal sessions for *The Dreaming*, Bush typically recorded in the daytime, which is apparent in the energy of her performances. Although there would be a long procession of musicians through the studio during the album's leisurely recording period, it was perhaps this sense of intimacy that helped the peak-and-trough mood shifts of *Hounds of Love* seem all the more convincing and emotive.

Absolute focus was elsewhere apparent with "The Ninth Wave," the song cycle that swallowed up Side Two of the *Hounds of Love* vinyl. "It's a bit like . . . my first *novelette*," she told me, adopting a faux-lofty tone. "I enjoyed doing that. It was really hard work. But I thought it was the beginning of something really interesting. It's just the idea of taking a piece of music on a journey, which was what opera and classical music used to do all the time."

In the final stretch of the making of *Hounds of Love* in the summer of 1985, the tracks were mixed manually with three or four people moving the faders in what amounted to a final performance. Listening back to the album, on the very rare occasions that she did, Bush told me that she could still hear the humor in it.

"'Hounds of Love' with the backing vocals, the doggy 'Ow, ow, ow,'" she noted, laughing.

I was forced to admit I'd never realized those were meant to be dogs . . .

"Oh, yeah, it's the 'Hounds of Love,' innit?"

~

As an indication of just how fast-moving pop music was in the early- to mid-1980s, in August 1985, Kate Bush was one of the artists to feature in a "Where Are They Now?" story in *NME*. As far as the wider record-buying public was concerned, four years on from when "Sat in Your Lap" had made number eleven in the chart, and more than two years after "There Goes a Tenner" had flopped, the singer was a semi-forgotten figure from yesterday.

Only days after the issue of *NME* had arrived on the newsstands, seasoned Irish broadcaster Terry Wogan addressed the 9-million-plus viewers of his weeknight BBC One chat show, in his characteristically twinkly, avuncular way. He introduced his next guest as "a lady who hasn't graced the turntables with a new record for two years. It's nice to have her back. 'Running Up That Hill,' it's Kate Bush."

Then, after the punchy, rolling beat began and the eerie synth hook crept in over it, Kate, in a fashionable brown duster coat, positioned behind a lectern (all the better to talk to God), started to perform what was essentially her comeback single. Behind her stood six musicians—including Del Palmer on bass and Paddy Bush on balalaika—all wearing similar long coats that when buttoned-up looked like monks' habits. As the song unfolded, they started to inch closer and closer to the front of the stage, moving away from two flag bearers holding billowing standards behind them. It was powerful stuff, with once again something of the ritual about it. Particularly when it came to a song that spoke of a dark magickal act, beamed to the nation in the context of massed, family-time viewing.

Sensing that—at the ripe old age of twenty-seven—the single was likely a make-or-break moment in her career, Bush, for the release of "Running Up That Hill (A Deal with God)," agreed to one of the very few artistic compromises that she would ever make. The word "God" in the title of a song, EMI argued, would be a no-no in certain territories.

"I was told that the radio stations in at least ten countries would refuse to play it," she said at the time. "Spain, Italy, America, lots of them. I thought it was ridiculous. Still, especially after *The Dreaming*, I decided to weigh up the priorities. I had to give the album a chance."

Taking off from this middle ground, the single quickly soared. "Running Up That Hill"—as it appeared on the cover and label of the seven-inch single (although all other versions would bear the full, bracketed title)—entered the chart at number nine, then rose to number three. Not only was it Kate Bush's biggest single since "Wuthering Heights" seven years before, but it also reached the top thirty in the US, becoming her American breakthrough.

The hit single perfectly set up *Hounds of Love*, released the following month on September 16, 1985. It was an album that was to quickly become ubiquitous, entering the album chart at number one and going on to achieve double platinum status in the UK alone, selling more than 600,000 copies. At the same time, the LP's cover featured one of the most iconic images of Kate Bush's career. Taken by John Carder Bush in the East Wickham Farm wash-house, it depicted her reclining on a bed of amethyst-colored chiffon, wrapped in a makeshift blush pink silk dress, with two Weimaraner dogs, Bonnie and Clyde, owned by Kate's parents, nosing into her shoulders.

"Looking through the lens at that exquisite setting for a very elegant Kate, I knew the shots were going to work," her photographer brother noted in his 2015 book, *Kate: Inside the Rainbow*. "You always hope, but sometimes you actually know."

~

Reflecting on the success of *Hounds of Love*, I asked Bush if she'd consciously tried to create pop singles—as unusual as they were—that would help her regain commercial ground?

"There probably was a little bit of that," she admitted. "But I like both ends of the spectrum very much. I like doing tracks with just a piano or maybe an orchestra as well, but something very . . . semi-classical, I guess. And I really love doing the band stuff. And for me, if I didn't do both, I would miss having the other. It's a balance, I think. And I wanted to try to get a really good balance with that record.

"But, yeah, I think there probably was an element to me thinking that the side [of the vinyl record] that had those single tracks, that it would make sense if they were more kind of . . . what's the word? Not commercial. But more . . . I don't know. I can't find a word."

Accessible? Hooky?

"Yeah, I guess hooky. I don't know. I didn't want both sides to be conceptual. I wanted them to have a very different feeling. One side to be very kind of up and band-orientated and rhythmic and the other side to be more this slow, conceptual piece."

For Bush, *Hounds of Love* remained the collection of songs of which she was most proud: "It was something a bit different. That's probably my best album as a whole."

What's more, even if it was some of the most inventive and obtuse pop music to have ever graced a chart rundown, it produced four top-forty hits.

"Were four of them hits?" Bush wondered aloud. "I can only remember three."

I listed them for her: "Running Up That Hill (A Deal with God)" (number three), "Cloudbusting" (number twenty), "Hounds of Love" (number eighteen) and "The Big Sky" (number thirty-seven).

"Oh yeah," she brightly responded. "I don't remember there being four. Oh, that's not bad, is it?"

Most importantly, perhaps, the outstanding commercial performance of *Hounds of Love* closed the decisive battle in her long war with EMI for absolute creative control. Even years later, this victory clearly still tickled her.

"When *Hounds of Love* came out and it was self-produced and it was an enormous hit, it was so fantastic," she beamed. "(*Cups hand to hear*) 'Sorry, what's that you said? Sorry? Didn't want me to produce it?'

"They left me alone from that point. It shut them up."

26

A Night at the Laserium

Hounds of Love *launch party, September 9, 1985*

Hounds of Love **was such an expansive album that EMI decided it deserved to be launched in grand style. And so, on the second Monday of September 1985, seven days before the actual release date, an enormous party was thrown at the Planetarium, next door to Madame Tussauds on the oft-traffic-choked thoroughfare of Marylebone Road in central London.**

Befitting a record designed for total absorption—one, really, for the "heads," as much as a mainstream album-buying audience—the launch of the record was a starry one in terms of the array of constellations beamed up into the building's 60-foot-diameter dome, below which sat three hundred-odd seats in circular formation. Eight years earlier, in 1977, the planetarium had begun staging evening shows featuring whir-ring and zapping lasers, renaming itself the Laserium for these events, including one, "Laserock" featuring a playlist including

"Roundabout" by Yes, "Rhiannon" by Fleetwood Mac and, with a certain inevitability, the futuristic instrumental contours of "Oxygène Part II" by Jean-Michel Jarre.

The *Hounds of Love* bash was notable for being the first time that Kate Bush stepped out into the wider public view with Del Palmer. Those in the music industry were aware of the couple's relationship, but it was a coming-out of sorts: the pair posing for the paparazzi in front of a blown-up cover of the album, all hugs and beaming smiles, she in black suit and wide open-necked white shirt, he in two-tone blue sports jacket and T-shirt, with bushy 'tache and angular sideburns. The next day, syndicated photos of the two would appear in the papers.

The tabloids got a story to accompany the shots, too. Gossip columnists reported that on the night a drunken Youth/Martin Glover had lambasted Palmer by calling him—in that mild and none-more-1980s insult—a "wally." (Glover later sheepishly admitted that this was down to his jealousy of Palmer's relationship with the singer.)

Eventually, the guests wound their way into the auditorium for the grand sonic unveiling of *Hounds of Love*. Among them was drummer Stuart Elliott, who'd played on many of the tracks and remembers, "We all sat back in our seats and then 'The Ninth Wave' comes on. We've got this beautiful visual scape of the stars, and lasers, and it was incredible. An amazing piece of music."

27

"The Ninth Wave"

From Hounds of Love, 1985

A woman is lost at sea and we've no idea how she ended up there.

This is the vivid, disquieting scene that opens "The Ninth Wave," the conceptual second side of *Hounds of Love*. Kate Bush would later refer to the fact that her original notion was that the adrift figure has ended up in the ocean following a storm, but there's no hint of that in the lyric of "And Dream of Sheep." Instead, there are scarce facts: there is a light, most likely one on her lifejacket, that is illuminating her face (giving us the sense that it is night); she feels so alone that she wishes she had a radio to connect her back to the real world.

The rest is all allusive: is her head somehow tuning into BBC Radio 4's shipping forecast? Does she really think she can feel the breath of sheep on her face, or is it the breath of the broadcasters talking through her imagined radio? Is the irresistible tug of sleep almost morphine-like in its heaviness? Is she suffering from the hallucinatory effects of hypothermia? All we really know is that this perhaps hopelessly abandoned character is struggling to stay awake, before she slips into unconsciousness.

If up until now there's been a curious absence of fear in the narrative, it doesn't last. Amid the ominous Fairlight cellos of "Under Ice," the woman finds herself skating over a frozen river, at first dazzled by the beauty of this perfect wintertime scene. Looking down at her blades cutting through the ice, however, she sees a figure scratching at its underbelly, before coming to the scary realisation that, somehow, it's her.

Then the character wakes up—or does she? Intrusive voices appear left, right and center in the stereo spectrum compelling her back to consciousness. Touchingly, among them are the voices of Bush's actual family: Paddy, John, mother Maureen.

"We were asked to say things," Paddy Bush explained at the time of the album's release. "Things put on to telephone answering machines. We were asked to phone people up and say silly things like 'Good morning, dear, this is [your] early morning call.' All this kind of stuff."

It soon becomes clear that the woman hasn't been woken by those attempting to rouse her and is, in fact, deep in another nightmare. A witchfinder appears to her, submitting her to the bizarre seventeenth-century English ritual of dunking suspected sorceresses, tied to a chair, into water. If they floated, it was proof that they had renounced their baptism, and they would be hanged. If they drowned, it was demented post-mortem confirmation of their innocence.

In the shit-scaringly demonic "Waking the Witch," Bush employs a stop-start beat, doomy tolling bells, and extreme vocal tremolo effects (that were a key feature of Eno and Byrne's

My Life in the Bush of Ghosts) to obfuscate her Catholic confession ("Bless me, Father, for I have sinned") and reinforce the fact that anything she says will be twisted and go largely unheard. The spoken word, male-voiced part of the witch-hunter is in fact played by an audibly unrecognizable Bush, her words electronically contorted, via a harmonizer, into deep, threatening basso profundo.

"Yeah, I was a bit disappointed with that," she told me. "I think if I'd had more energy, I would've pursued that with an actor doing the speaking part rather than myself."

The track ends with a coastguard chopper (real or imagined) flying over the hellish proceedings, issuing a warning to get out of the water. It's another wake-up call, but one that leads only to further strangeness.

As another communication-frustrated presence in "Watching You Without Me," the singer enters into the home of a loved one, and sees them fretting, as the time passes without her return. It's an effect rendered in audio via mumbled and slurred lines. Even though the song is a muted ballad—Danny Thompson sailing his elegant double bass-playing over a ticking electronic beat—it's the most unnerving moment yet, conveying the sad exasperation of a spirit who still has a window to the real world.

"It's more of a nightmare than anything so far," Bush noted, "because this is the closest she's been to any kind of comfort, and yet it's the furthest away."

From this point, our protagonist is catapulted into the future in "Jig of Life," witnessing herself as an old woman, who pleads with her younger self not to give up and succumb to the waves: for the sake not only of herself, but of her children to come. There is a reference to the Zen Buddhist riddle of "one hand clapping"; another to a life line on a palm of which the younger woman is just an early part. Though brought to rousing, upbeat life by the Irish musicians recorded in Dublin, it's a sad, desperate and affecting chapter before the story moves on.

Zooming out into space in "Hello Earth"—at over six minutes the longest track in "The Ninth Wave"—Bush takes inspiration from astronaut Neil Armstrong's lunar surface epiphany. "It suddenly struck me," he famously remembered, "that that tiny pea, pretty and blue, was the Earth. I put up my thumb and shut one eye, and my thumb blotted out the planet Earth."

The idea that, from such a great distance, our planet appears to hang in the great expanse of space, beautiful but vulnerable, shapes "Hello Earth." By the second verse, the narrator is witnessing a storm formation over America that begins to move out over the ocean, causing warning messages to flare up in her mind: to sailors, fishermen, rescue boat crews and, finally, to herself, elliptically revealing why she has ended up drifting in the ocean.

It's the big, dramatic moment in the third reel of "The Ninth Wave" and, as such, called for a powerful musical arrangement, which was provided by Michael Kamen, whose skill in writing visualising film scores enabled him to expertly weave orchestral moods around the story: lighter when the singer is tracking a bright object moving through the night sky; darker when she sees that the storms are gathering.

Bush had ambitiously left what she referred to as two enormous "black holes" in the master tape arrangement of "Hello Earth," in the passages where the drums drop out. "People would say, 'What's going to happen in these choruses?'" she recalled, "and I hadn't a clue."

She had a feeling that these should be choral sections and remembered the male choir she'd heard used to such eerie effect in Werner Herzog's artful, Klaus Kinski-starring (or haunting) 1979 horror film, *Nosferatu the Vampyre*. The soundtrack, by German masters of atmosphere Popol Vuh, featured a Georgian traditional choral titled "Zinzkaro," renamed "Der Ruf der Rohrflöte" and sung by the Vocal Ensemble Gordela. Bush approached Herzog and Popol Vuh's Florian Fricke (both are thanked in the *Hounds of Love* credits) to use the piece, which she re-recorded—after forming impressionistic words that imagined what she was hearing on the *Nosferatu* record—using the meditative tones of the Richard Hickox Singers.

Bush explained at the time, "They really are meant to symbolize the great sense of loss, of weakness, at reaching a point where you can accept, at last, that everything can change."

Leaving the ending of the tale tantalizingly open-ended—does she survive and is returned to her family, or does she die and is reborn into some afterlife?—the last track sounds like sunshine burning off "The Morning Fog" of its title. John Williams's bright acoustic guitars work together with Del Palmer's elastic bassline and LinnDrum beat, topped with Bush's joy-filled, madrigal-like vocal layers, to conjure up a mood evoking some kind of unspecified hope and new beginning.

In twenty-six minutes and twenty-one seconds, the story is done. The source inspiration for "The Ninth Wave" may have come from Tennyson's nineteenth-century poem "The Coming of Arthur"—as quoted on the back cover of *Hounds of Love* ("Wave after wave, each mightier than the last / Till last, a ninth one, gathering half the deep . . ."). But, really, this epic tale was all of Kate Bush's own making.

28

Making Rain

The video for "Cloudbusting," 1985

There was a knock on the door of Suite 312 at the Savoy, the luxury London hotel situated between the Strand and the Thames. Canadian film star Donald Sutherland—who had been living in the suite for some months while he was making a movie about the American War of Independence, *Revoluton*, alongside Al Pacino—went to answer it.

"I opened it . . . there was no one there," Sutherland later recalled, with exaggerated comic timing. "I heard a voice saying 'hello,' and I looked down. Standing down there was a very small Kate Bush."

Bush had already approached Sutherland with a view to appearing with her in the video for "Cloudbusting," relaying the request through hairdresser-to-the-stars Barry Richardson, but the actor had offhandedly turned the offer down. Undaunted, she had convinced Richardson to let her know where Sutherland was staying and decided to make the proposal face-to-face.

"What can you do?" Sutherland further reflected. "She wanted to explain what her video was about. I let her in. She sat down, said some stuff. All I heard was 'Wilhelm Reich.'"

"Cloudbusting" was a high-concept song which demanded an ambitious, cinematically minded video. Its inspiration lay in *A Book of Dreams*, the 1973-published memoir of Peter Reich, son of Austrian psychologist Wilhelm Reich. Reich Sr believed that with his invention, the Cloudbuster, he could unlock energy in the atmosphere and create rain on command. Bush had first bought and read Peter Reich's book in 1976 and then re-read it before writing "Cloudbusting."

"If I've got this right," she told *Q*'s Mat Snow, "he believed that sexual energy was positive, usable energy that he tied in with his concept of orgone energy [a theoretical life force, the name of which referred to both 'orgasm' and 'organism']. He upset a lot of people selling orgone boxes, saying they could cure cancer and stuff. He ended up being arrested and put in prison. I knew nothing about Wilhelm when I read the book, which was his son's experience of all this, written from a child's point of view with a tremendous innocence and sadness."

Peter Reich believed that his father's Cloudbuster invention did indeed work, having witnessed him using it in 1953 in Maine on the US East Coast at the invitation of farmers suffering from a drought that was killing their blueberry crops. Reich helped his dad operate the device, and in the early hours of the following morning, it started to rain.

Donald Sutherland, meanwhile, had first become aware of Wilhelm Reich when he read his 1933 book, *The Mass Psychology of Fascism*, as research material for playing the psychopathic Attila Mellanchini in Italian film director Bernardo Bertolucci's five-hour-long 1976 epic, *1900*. At the same time, Kate was a huge fan of Donald Sutherland, after having first seen him in Robert Altman's 1970 Korean War black comedy *M*A*S*H* and then in Nicolas Roeg's creepy, impressionistic 1973 horror, *Don't Look Now*.

"Donald Sutherland I can always watch," she said. "He's got such a wry sense of humor."

~

Plans for the "Cloudbusting" video had first been put into action at Abbey Road Studios, in 1984, when composer Michael Kamen was adding the finishing touches to his score for Terry Gilliam's dystopian sci-fi satire *Brazil*, edited by long-term Monty Python associate Julian Doyle.

Doyle was there in the room at the studio when Bush asked an already deadline-stressed Gilliam if he'd be interested in directing "Cloudbusting." "He said, 'Use Julian,'" he recalls. "We had a coffee, and it was decided I would do the video for her."

When it came to the initial planning meeting, Bush had already drawn up a rough storyboard. "She had some funny ideas," Doyle says, "which I had to try to interpret into something possible. She had the sun being a face that came over the landscape and sang some of the lines. I just thought it wasn't gonna work, that image within it."

Bush also wanted to flip genders and play Peter Reich as a boy, another idea that Doyle wasn't too keen on. Even if it was the 1980s and a time of pop star "gender benders" such as Boy George and Marilyn, the director still felt it might be off-putting to a conservative pop audience. "She wanted to be a boy," he remembers. "I said, 'You can't be a boy. People are not gonna accept that. Let's just be androgynous so that we don't know whether you're a boy or a girl.'"

In the end, Bush appeared as Peter Reich with the aid of a short-cropped, gingery brown wig. To play Wilhelm Reich, Doyle remembers she originally had in mind the second Doctor Who, actor Patrick Troughton ("Who was a lot like her father," he says). Bagging Donald Sutherland for the part was clearly more of a coup. Doyle decided that with such a great actor now attached to the project, they should tell Wilhelm and Peter Reich's rain-making story in a more straightforward fashion.

"I took her storyboard," he says, "and I just shot what was basically the story that she wanted. Y'know, that there's a boy, he's on a hill with his father, and they do cloudbusting and then [his father] gets arrested and the boy goes up the hill and works the machine again. It was a basic storyline, and I just shot that."

The exterior scenes for "Cloudbusting" were filmed, in September 1985, in the Vale of the White Horse in Oxfordshire, which Doyle found by chance when out scouting for locations. "I went around looking," he says, "and we went out west London way. And then we drove around [Oxfordshire] and there was a hill. I think we just found it and didn't know it was where the White Horse is (*laughs*). Then, it was a question of finding places to stay nearby."

Doyle recalls that the crew who arrived to work on "Cloudbusting" seemed completely disinterested at first, having just been working with "wild man of British cinema" Ken Russell on a video for—somewhat incongruously—Cliff Richard's "She's So Beautiful," which featured the Peter Pan of Pop performing footie tricks outdoors with an Earth-painted globe for a ball.

"They actually treated this video as sort of like (*adopts unimpressed tone*), 'Yeah, we've just come off *Ken Russell*,'" Doyle recalls. "And the Ken Russell and Cliff Richard one was awful."

Key to the production was an approximate visual replica of the Cloudbuster machine, built by production designer Ken Hill. Later, a false rumor spread among Kate Bush fans that it had been the work of Swiss artist H. R. Giger, who'd created the terrifyingly brilliant special effects for Ridley Scott's 1979 sci-fi horror, *Alien*. Doyle remembers, however, that some of the same team who'd worked on that film had ended up painting the "Cloudbusting" contraption.

"They'd worked on the legs of the spaceship [in *Alien*]," he explains. "That's where they got that blue shiny glint for the 'Cloudbusting' thing." In contrast to Reich's original machine, the one in the video was much larger and more exaggerated in its features, appearing like a cross between an anti-aircraft gun and a pipe organ.

"I just felt that it had to have these huge funnels that would reach to the sky and could be moved around," Bush said. "And the whole thing should be rotatable. It was trying to design something that would look powerful and possible of doing [the cloudbusting], but that wouldn't be comical. Because we didn't want people to laugh at it. We wanted people to be astounded by the machine."

Thanks to Sutherland's acting skills, his operation of the fake Cloudbuster looked relatively convincing. "Donald made it work," says Doyle. "He turned the wheels like they were doing something (*laughs*). Like any good actor, he made the machine come to life by believing in it."

In the flashback supposedly set in Reich's Maine laboratory (in reality a film studio in Wimbledon), Sutherland fully employed his thespian talents in a scene with Bush where Reich the elder first shows his son—and the viewers—a sketch of the cloudbusting machine. "I said, 'Move into thinking about the past,' and he gave it all to you," Doyle remembers. "He would go from smiling to serious, y'know. He was lovely."

For another scene, in which father and son embrace on a hilltop and Bush pulls a copy of *A Book of Dreams* out of Sutherland's jacket pocket, Doyle wanted the already footlong difference in their heights to be exaggerated to make Bush appear even more childlike.

"I put Donald on a box," the director chuckles. "He said, 'This is the first time I've ever been on a box.' Normally the short actors get boxes to stand on. But he's enormous, so he was never on the box. He was really surprised that I was going to that extent."

~

On location, Doyle says that Bush sometimes felt she was being pushed away from having directorial input: "Kate wanted to learn about directing, and she was with me most of the time." Her frustrations reached a head in the scene where Wilhelm Reich/Sutherland is seen being arrested by government officials and driven off in a car, leaving Peter Reich/Bush stranded in the road. It was mirrored in real life on the day.

"Me and the cameraman got in the front of the car with the driver and Donald sat in the back with the two [arresting officials]," Doyle explains. "I came back, and Kate said, 'You left me here.' But there was no way we could actually fit her in, except for on Donald's lap."

The director meanwhile made sure that he got the most out of every second of Sutherland's available time. The scene where the star is depicted walking down the hill into the sunset in fact caught him leaving the location for the final time: "I said, 'Well, as you walk away, can we get this shot?' I was getting everything I could out of him from the moment he would arrive to the moment he left. He was excellent."

Kate threw herself into her acting role, getting up at 6 a.m. one morning to shoot the scenes where she's tumbling and rolling down the hillside. Elsewhere, the very last image—where she triumphantly pumps her fist into the air after making rain with the Cloudbuster following Reich/Sutherland's arrest—was serendipitous, since the film in the camera was at the very end of the reel, in what was to be the final take.

"We were probably six or seven frames from the last frame of the shoot," Doyle marvels. "It was extraordinary."

When it came to creating the special effects where the Reichs appear to be controling clouds by pointing the machine's funnels at the sky, Doyle had to get inventive.

"There was none of the computer-generated stuff," he points out. "So I did it by shooting some dry ice coming down some stairs. Then we reversed it, so it goes upward, from a narrow bit to a wider bit. Then I got some sped-up cloud effects and we put that on in post-production."

In the editing suite, the director found he had enough material to cut together a seven-minute video and chopped up the five-minute-long audio track to expand it. Screening the result for Bush, Doyle coughed in a vain attempt to cover up the edit. "She said, 'You didn't hide it with the cough,'" he laughs now. "So she wrote another section to go in there."

But, once Bush got fully involved in the cut, Doyle says that the two began to disagree on scene choices. "She would take my word on some things," he recalls, "but the worst thing in the edit room is not being logical and sensible. You really need to be considering the audience all the time, cause you're retelling the story. When you're editing, there's a story on the paper which is the script and then you retell that story. Even in *Python* or with *Brazil*, I'm rearranging scenes because the story is better told. You have to be open to see the material and respond to it and treat it like you're writing a story from scratch."

Ultimately, to solve their differences, Doyle handed the final editing of "Cloudbusting" over to Terry Gilliam. "That way it stopped her messing it up too much," he reckons. "Y'know, she would take his word."

The director meanwhile remembers initially receiving a lukewarm reaction to "Cloudbusting" from the all-powerful programmers at MTV.

"Like everybody, I had been watching MTV and everything was very similar, y'know. You had people singing with some long-legged girls and then you would repeat and repeat. My idea was that you tell a story, so that when you're switching channels, people will stop, because they won't know that it's MTV. They'll go, 'Oh, what's this?' That was my concept, anyway.

"The problem was that when we showed it to MTV, they said, 'Doesn't look like a pop video' (*laughs*). There I was breaking my neck to make it not look like a pop video and the buggers didn't like it because of that. They did show it, of course . . ."

In the end, being the length of a short film, "Cloudbusting" was even screened as a second feature in various UK cinemas.

"I get people still saying, 'It's the greatest video ever made,' and things like this," Doyle remarks. "It's a nice compliment."

Bush even sent Peter Reich a VHS copy of the "Cloudbusting" video, along with a signed copy of the *Hounds of Love* album. Reich watched it with his wife and two small children and said they were all "entranced."

Peter Reich and Kate Bush subsequently met in person. Brilliantly, and poignantly, she gave him a gift of an umbrella.

29

"I Used to Be Kate Bush"

Kate and the comedians, 1978–2020

"'Allo, you remember me," she declared to camera, her voice clearly overdubbed in a cartoon bassy male tone, so that she sounded like a Cockney cab driver. "I used to be Kate Bush."

It was March 5, 1979, and the singer's second appearance on *The Kenny Everett Video Show*, the Capital Radio DJ-turned-surreal comic's ITV pop-cum-sketch show, which saw him inhabit various exaggerated characters including thick punk Sid Snot and triple-chinned French lech Marcel Wave.

On that week's program, ahead of an airing of "Wow," Everett made a sleight-of-hand introduction.

"We're going to have somebody on the show now that we had a few series ago," he began, "and we had so many letters about it because she was so fantastic and what good taste you had with all those letters. It's not often that all the ingredients go together so brilliantly. Perfect songs with beautiful melodies and intelligent words, a unique voice and so sexy, tooooo. Yes, you've guessed it, the wonderful Miss Bush."

As the opening to "Wuthering Heights" played, the camera zoomed in on a weird-looking shrub, which suddenly sprouted arms and opened its red mouth to sing the opening lines to Bush's famous number one. Cue canned laughter.

The year before, leading into a screening of the video for "The Man with the Child in His Eyes," Everett and a giggly Kate had conducted a daft interview in front of a bank of TV screens, in which the gag was that the "impromptu" questions and answers they read from sheets of paper had obviously been mixed up.

Kenny Everett: Well, Kate. How old are you, Kate?

Kate Bush: Manchester.

KE: Funny. You don't look a day over Salford. Do you write all your own songs? And where do you get your ideas?

KB: Well, carbolic soap and then I just leave it messy.

～

Bush had always been a huge comedy fan, naming *Monty Python's Flying Circus* and *Fawlty Towers* among her favorite TV shows. After she'd been propelled into mainstream fame, and luridly caricatured by Pamela Stephenson and Faith Brown, it made sense for her to get in on the joke. But it also provided an unforeseen opportunity to involve herself in the world of comedy, and forge friendships with comedians that would last many years.

Odd, but enticing offers started to come in. In May 1981, three years after becoming a reluctant celebrity, Bush was asked if she'd like to make a guest appearance acting in ITV's kids' show *Worzel Gummidge*, which detailed the adventures of a head-swapping scarecrow played by former Doctor Who, Jon Pertwee. The fact that—dangerous typecasting ahoy—she'd been approached to play the Wicked Witch hadn't dissuaded her. But the fact that she was about to throw herself deeply into the making of *The Dreaming* did.

Five years later, in 1986, Kate was invited to appear in the inaugural benefit shows for Comic Relief, the charity founded by Lenny Henry and *Blackadder* co-writer Richard Curtis. Over three nights, April 4–6, at the Shaftesbury Theatre in London, she performed a solo rendition of "Breathing" at the electric piano, the only time she would play the song live.

But the events were better remembered for Bush's participation in a skit alongside Rowan Atkinson, centred on the Curtis-written duet, "Do Bears . . .?" Bush and Atkinson perched atop barroom stools: he a gold lamé-wearing, crooning lounge lothario; she his suffering paramour, looking acutely mid-'80s in her shoulder-padded suit jacket. One of the biggest laughs came when Bush delivered a punchline where she told the audience "to alleviate the boredom, I sleep with his friends." Overall, it wasn't very funny—especially since it was based upon the weak joke that the singers were avoiding uttering the word "shit" in favor of "sha-la-la-la"—but it was proof that Kate Bush was entirely up for the comedy capers.

From here, she seemed to forge a strong connection to the alternative comedians of the 1980s. Later in 1986, Dawn French and Hugh Laurie—both of whom had been on that same Comic Relief bill—appeared in the video for Kate's latest single "Experiment IV," recorded for inclusion on her first hits collection, *The Whole Story*.

The narrative of "Experiment IV" told a tale of government scientists creating a dangerously powerful sound that they later discover will be weaponized to kill the enemy from a distance. The track itself was a Prince-like mid-paced groover, with *Psycho*-styled violin stabs, echoes of the cut-up vocals of "Waking the Witch" and a chorus melody with a distinctly Celtic bent.

In the video, the scientists' secret laboratory is hidden behind Music for Pleasure, a musical instrument shop. French and Laurie are white-coated technicians who unleash sound via an angelic-looking, blonde Bush, who then shapeshifts into a horror movie monster. The BBC, inevitably, banned the video from *Top of the Pops* for being way too scary for pre-watershed viewing. Like "Cloudbusting," though, it was shown in selected cinemas ahead of the main feature, which was no doubt much more creatively satisfying.

Significantly, the comedy connection seemed to be helping Bush get a taste for the stage again. In 1987, at the Secret Policeman's Third Ball, raising money for Amnesty International at the London Palladium, she appeared alongside David Gilmour and his band for the live debut of "Running Up That Hill (A Deal with God)." She looked edgy initially but grew increasingly confident, her voice loud and strong. It was encouraging evidence for her fans that Kate might not entirely hate singing before an audience after all.

~

Hounds of Love had seen Kate Bush make a respectable dent in the American market—reaching number thirty in the *Billboard* chart—and so, for the first time, Hollywood came calling.

Bush had already contributed the bespoke, strident pop track "Be Kind to My Mistakes" to Nicolas Roeg's Oliver Reed- and Amanda Donohoe-starring desert island true story, *Castaway*. But US director John Hughes (*The Breakfast Club*, *Pretty in Pink*) had her in mind to write a song for a specific scene in his romantic comedy, *She's Having a Baby*.

Bush later admitted that it had been a "very tempting offer," and Hughes duly sent her a rough cut of the clip on video tape. The movie was typically lightsome rom-com fare, but this was to be the climactic scene in which Kevin Bacon (as Jake) was faced with the terrifying prospect of losing his newlywed wife Elizabeth McGovern (as Kristy) and their unborn child due to a traumatic labor.

Kate felt that it was "a very moving piece of film" and, watching the scene on a TV monitor while she sat at the piano in the studio, wrote "This Woman's Work" surprisingly quickly. In capturing the moment of crisis in lines filled with panic and regret, it was a lightning flash epiphany in song and sent out a universal message that was highly relatable. Del Palmer was later instrumental in convincing Bush to include it on her next album, 1989's *The Sensual World*.

Skirting close to mainstream power balladry, "This Woman's Work" proved to be one of her most enduring songs, prickling the emotions of many fans, and many more casual listeners besides. It still regularly features in the top ten of her most-played tracks. Tellingly, however, for the reworked version on 2011's *Director's Cut*, Bush expanded the song to six-and-a-half minutes and played it on a Fender Rhodes piano, adding only boys' choir-like oohs and glacial synth parts, and scaling back the vocal dynamics to a more intimate level. And so, a song born out of comedy inadvertently produced one of her most serious compositions.

At the other end of the scale was "Ken," written for *The Comic Strip*'s fourth series 1990 episode, "GLC: The Carnage Continues"—plotted around a mock "highly controversial new film" starring Robbie Coltrane, as Charles Bronson, ludicrously portraying Greater London Council leader Ken Livingstone. Bush recorded various bits of incidental music for the program, but the song "Ken" was entirely out of character: a thumping dancefloor oddity in which she screamed like James Brown and proclaimed Livingstone to be a "funky sex machine."

Episode six of the same series found Bush further plunging into the comedy world with her first acting role, in "Les Dogs," in which she played a bride on her wedding day, in a series of weird and disconnected dreamlike scenes in which she enraptures Victor, a photographer played by Peter Richardson.

Richardson had recently directed the video for the title track of *The Sensual World*, and he and Bush had become pals. On screen in "Les Dogs," she managed to do a decent job of traversing that wobbly bridge from music to acting that had previously injured the careers of the likes of David Bowie and Mick Jagger.

In an early scene, she sits impassively at the wedding banquet, allowing the groom (Danny Peacock) to kiss her neck while his mouth is full of chocolate, before the families of both tip over the tables for a gunfight. As Richardson the snapper's fantasies become increasingly distorted, his lust for the bride grows and he imagines—or does he?—that she is planning to run away with him.

Even if acting wasn't in the end a parallel career that Bush decided to pursue, her appearance in *The Comic Strip Presents . . .*

was convincing. And, going forward, the comedy connections were maintained. Keeping with her tradition of parachuting in unlikely collaborators onto her albums, Lenny Henry straight-facedly turned in a backing vocal on "Why Should I Love You?" on 1993's *The Red Shoes*, alongside the Trio Bulgarka (the Bulgarian vocal ensemble) and, mind-blowingly for him, Prince.

In a 2016 eulogy to the latter in *The Guardian*, Henry remembered, "When I arrived at the studio, I said, 'It's really weird but the guitar on this sounds so much like Prince—was that what you were going for?' Kate said, 'It sounds like Prince because it *is* him. Do you wanna go in the booth?' I sang my heart out. I couldn't believe it. I was performing on a song with two of my heroes."

∽

In 1999, five years into what would transpire to be Kate Bush's decade-plus of public absence, Steve Coogan as hapless, cheesy broadcaster Alan Partridge worked a farcical medley of her songs into his act, performing it in his theater show and live on Comic Relief on BBC One. In hairsprayed side-flick wig and green blazer, Partridge milked "Wow," "Running Up That Hill" (as a comedy march), "Them Heavy People," "The Man with the Child in His Eyes," "Wuthering Heights" (as pub piano knees-up), "Don't Give Up" and "Babooshka" for maximum laughs.

"It was fun to do," Coogan said. "People laughed and Kate Bush came to the last night of my show to see it when we performed in the West End."

But Coogan wasn't entirely sure if Bush herself was pulling his leg in her response to the medley: "She said, 'It's so nice to hear all those songs again.'"

The two ended up having a phone conversation about live performance. Coogan later let slip that Kate had revealed some of her fears to him about "how terrifying it can be, and how she hadn't done it for a long, long time and she felt just a bit scared by the prospect of going out there again."

Coogan affectionately described Bush's projected persona as being "ripe for satirists." And so it once again proved in 2011 when Noel Fielding appeared on Comic Relief in long tresses, rose in hair, and wearing the now-iconic red dress to act out a wild and flailing interpretation of the dance routine for "Wuthering Heights."

Kate told Keith Cameron in *MOJO* that she'd enjoyed the spoof: "I loved it! I thought it was hilarious and I thought he came across as such a sweet person."

Cameron asked her how she felt about people still taking the piss out of that performance.

"Well, it was taken the piss out of at the time," she pointed out with a laugh. "But it's such a long time ago. It's quite flattering really, isn't it? That it endures enough to keep taking the piss out of."

Later in 2011, the comedy link with Bush remained strong. In the artwork for *Director's Cut*, Monty Python's Terry Jones popped up unannounced, photographed as the eccentric "Professor Need," sitting in an old-fashioned train carriage, mysteriously hooked up to his laptop via a lit-up wired device attached to his hand, and sitting alongside former Python costume designer Hazel Pethig and a barracuda-head-wearing fellow passenger.

Actor/comedian Robbie Coltrane meanwhile—who had been one of the chorus of rousing voices in "Waking the Witch" on *Hounds of Love*—played a hopelessly computer-addicted individual, being catfished by none other than Noel Fielding, in the Bush-directed video for the new version of *The Sensual World*'s "Deeper Understanding," selected as the only single from *Director's Cut*.

When the release of Bush's tenth, winter-themed studio album, *50 Words for Snow*, followed *Director's Cut* with unprecedented swiftness in the November of 2011, the title track featured a spoken-word cameo from another British comedy actor, Stephen Fry, reading out the titular terms in his chocolatey tones.

In the years since, Kate Bush's music has made one key appearance in a US comedy film—2020 sci-fi rom-com *Palm Springs*, with its *Groundhog Day*-indebted plot in which Andy Samberg and Cristin Milioti are forced to relive the same time-looped day. The spell is broken—spoiler alert—thanks to some kind of quantum physics-altering detonation in a cave, as soundtracked by "Cloudbusting."

"I was really thrilled that we got the rights to it," said Samberg, underlining the ongoing affinity the singer has for the world of comedy. "I wrote Kate Bush a letter (*laughs*). She didn't write back, but we got the rights, so either someone who she trusts read it and approved it, or she read it, and even that possibility makes my brain kind of explode."

30

"Under the Ivy"

Performing on **The Tube**, *1986*

Ramshackle and funny, chaotic and controversial, Channel 4's live-to-air music show *The Tube* flew in the face of the glossy pop cultural trends of the 1980s.

Launched on November 5, 1982, three nights after the UK's fourth channel first began broadcasting, the weekly, ninety-minute programme stirred indie rock and pop together with alternative comedy, in a heady cocktail served up by its famously "yeah, whatever" post-punk hosts Paula Yates and Jools Holland.

Filmed by Tyne Tees Television in Newcastle, 250 significant miles northeast of the London record industry, *The Tube* was an untameable beast, which made it all the more thrilling for a generation of British music fans.

As a wide-eyed seventeen-year-old working for a teen mag in Dundee, I was first sent to *The Tube*, to interview Paula Yates, on November 9, 1984. That night, I watched on, only feet away, as comedian Rik Mayall introduced the show to a teatime audience by mock-spewing and announcing, "It's Friday, it's half past five and the pubs are open." It was a live TV moment that quickly prompted outrage. Jools Holland later noted that "one man in Northampton was so appalled he called the police."

The Tube's notoriety—and around 1 million viewers—drew many legendary figures to the northeast. When the inscrutable Miles Davis flew to Newcastle for a strange and stilted onscreen interview with Holland, the awed presenter took him afterward across the street to the Rose and Crown pub. There, the notoriously grumpy landlord Jimmy took one look at Davis and the trumpet case he was carrying and firmly warned Holland, "He's not playing that in here, mind."

Kate Bush, meanwhile, never made the trek up north to appear on *The Tube*. Instead, she contributed a performance to the show's one hundredth episode celebration, aired on April 4, 1986, via a pre-shot, on location film—in the same fashion that both the Smiths and Frankie Goes to Hollywood had previously made striking, star-making debut appearances.

Bush, perhaps unsurprisingly, chose the safe and easily controlled space of Abbey Road Studios for her live, solo rendition of her greatest overlooked song, "Under the Ivy." Quickly written the previous year when she'd needed a B-side for "Running Up That Hill," and uncharacteristically recorded in an afternoon, the piano/vocal ballad was—in keeping with the song's bewitching lyric—a hidden pleasure for those who cared to flip over the single.

For Bush's segment on *The Tube* (fellow guests that evening: the Waterboys, Ronnie James Dio, and Siouxsie and the Banshees), Newcastle instead came to St John's Wood. Ahead of her performance, the Geordie film crew were shown tramping across Abbey

Road's world-famous zebra crossing while badly warbling their way through "Here Comes the Sun."

"Stupid fools," Paula Yates declared, in her introduction filmed as she stood outside the studios. "Actually, the reason we're here at Abbey Road Studios is not to do The Beatles. It's because we're doing Kate Bush.

"She had her first hit when she was nineteen," Yates added, a fact that was mistakenly "corrected" in post-production with an onscreen video flash of the number eighteen. "Since then, she's gone on from strength to strength in breaking completely new territories in music. She has also made her performances into something of an artform, mingling dance and mime and all kinds of theater. In fact, she's a very thespian girl."

(In spite of this slightly piss-taking conclusion to the preamble, Kate later said she found Yates's words, likely due to their highly complimentary nature, "very touching.")

～

"Under the Ivy" was a song about retreating to a special and private space, and so Studio One at Abbey Road was a fitting location for Kate Bush's *The Tube* film. Not least since it was a place where she herself had been known to do some sneaking around and hiding. On more than one occasion in the past when she'd used Studio Two, an engineer had led her through a secret route into the rafters of the larger room. Almost echoing the directions in the lyric of the song she was to perform there, they'd go up over the ceiling, in through a hatch, and crawl along a high beam, to look down at the orchestral players recording below.

"I used to love doing this," she later remembered. "The acoustics were heavenly at that scary height. We used to toy with the idea of bungee jumping from the hatch."

For the "Under the Ivy" performance, Kate faced the Tyne Tees camera from the other end of a grand piano, for a rare showcase of her talents in their stripped-back forms.

The lyric of this alluring ballad found the narrator pining for childhood and slipping away from a party, beckoning a partner into the foliage. There was a clear sense of adults sloping off for furtive fumblings that might have begun, as she revealed, "when they were innocent and when they were children."

As a performance, it was quietly powerful and highly memorable. More so, it has to be said, than Paul McCartney elsewhere in the program banging through a blues riff on an electric guitar while sat in his living room and barking, "One hundred years old! Yeah, *The Tube*'s one hundred. Jools and Paula, they're covered in mold."

Ultimately, the hundredth episode of *The Tube* was to be the first and last time Kate Bush ever performed "Under the Ivy" live. As she hit the song's final notes, she looked up and smiled into the lens, as her piano left behind it a trail of Elgar's "heavenly" Studio One reverb.

31

"Something Good"

Kate goes to the rave, 1992

In the summer of 1988, as Kate Bush turned thirty, halfway through the making of her sixth album, *The Sensual World*, rave was quaking the United Kingdom.

The MDMA headrushes and the doof-doof-doof-doofs of the machine kick drums that soundtracked what the newspapers quickly termed "The Second Summer of Love" might as well have been happening in a universe parallel to the one where Bush was meticulously constructing her new record back at East Wickham Farm.

Up in Yorkshire that same year, DJs Jez Willis and Tim Garbutt were running club nights in Leeds and Harrogate. Like many DJs at the time, they were set to branch out into making their own dance tracks, layering vocal samples borrowed from other records over their own synth riffs and relentless beats.

Flicking through a record shop bargain bin one day, Willis picked out a cut-price £1 copy of the Eurythmics' 1985 single, "There Must Be an Angel (Playing with My Heart)," then took it home and captured in his sampler the first a cappella notes of Annie Lennox's wordless introduction to the song. Mixing it with another snatch of vocal from New Jersey soul singer Gwen Guthrie's "Ain't Nothin' Goin' on But the Rent"—belting out "What can you do for me?"—he added what he describes as "some pretty industrial drums and sequences under it."

Willis took it to Garbutt, who test-played it at a club night where, encouragingly, the dancers proceeded to wig out. The latter then suggested they should get together in the studio and further build up the track. Subsequently released initially in 1991 on their own label, as Utah Saints, with a pressing of one thousand copies on "orange pukey-colored" vinyl, "What Can You Do for Me" quickly took off. After sending a copy to DJ Pete Tong at London Records-affiliated dance label FFRR, hoping to get a play on his radio show, the duo were surprised when Tong instead offered to put the single out via the major label.

"Then, within three months," Willis notes with still-barely-contained amazement, "we were on *Top of the Pops*."

It's an indication of the dizzying speed with which dance records often zoomed up the charts in the early days of rave. From nowhere, "What Can You Do for Me," with its heavy, rock-influenced beats and crowd samples—that earned the respect of the KLF's Bill Drummond, who declared Utah Saints to be "the first true stadium house band"—hit number ten in September 1991.

Now, of course, the pressure was on for the duo to produce a follow-up. In a development that would surprise everyone involved, they turned their attention to Kate Bush.

~

"I can still remember the first time I saw the video for 'Wuthering Heights,'" Jez Willis says. "You have these pivotal moments where stuff just realigns your brain. I was thinking, 'This is almost like an otherworldly being.' The video was using cutting-edge technology, which was probably just a blurry background, but it felt like it was someone in the clouds doing this dance. The soul was coming through the dance as well as the music. That was a really moving thing.

"We were big fans and also a little bit intimidated by that level of artistry and success, to be honest. We had nothing but respect. Just for the fact that she'd broken into the mainstream market from a left-field perspective."

Willis and Garbutt began working their way through a pile of Kate Bush CDs, looking for a likely sample that they could contort into a hook line. It wasn't easy. "It had to tick so many boxes," Willis points out. "The timing, the pitch. But lyrically it couldn't be nonsense. It had to be something that would fit in with our ethos, I guess."

Their ethos being, in common with most rave acts, fling-your-arms-in-the-air with total abandon and sheer positivity. Which is why they came to sample a standout line from the chorus of "Cloudbusting" as the hook for their next single, also appropriating it for its title, "Something Good."

"We just kind of stumbled across that loop, 'I just know that something good is gonna happen,'" Willis remembers. "But we wanted to be respectful as well. We didn't want to make it sound crazy or silly or take the mick out of Kate Bush."

Over the track's sampled, distorted guitars and rolling beats, the pair then tried manipulating Bush's "ooo-aaa" vowel sounds from the beginning of the same "Cloudbusting" line.

"We started messing about with the sample to make it in time," Willis explains. "So the 'ooo-aaa' bit was a pitch bend just to get it to fit. It was never designed as a musical piece. But that became the second hook."

The duo sent the track to FFRR, and one day the label's A&R man Andy Thompson was playing it in his office when London Records' president Tracy Bennett popped his head around the door. "Apparently, he went, 'Who is this?'" says Willis. "Andy said, 'It's the Utahs,' and Tracy Bennett went, 'It's a number one,' and walked off.

"So we didn't know what to do. Pete Tong is a massive Kate Bush fan as well, so he said, 'Yeah, we have to make this work.'"

The band and label were then faced with the gnarly proposition of getting in touch with Bush to request to clear the sample—something she'd never done (or even been asked to do) before.

"We got the impression that everybody thought, 'There's no way this is gonna get cleared.' So then it went quiet. I heard rumors that it had to go to the upper echelons of the music industry, and then back down to her people. It took a few weeks. But it came back that it was cleared."

In some ways, Utah Saints' chopping-up and recontextualising of Kate Bush's vocals in the rave track made her sound all the stranger, which was perhaps bound to appeal to her. (As one YouTube commenter recently posted under the video for "Something Good," "My mother thought I was a devil worshipper when she heard me listening to this.")

Willis says that he and Garbutt weren't particularly shocked when the news came through that they were free to use the

"Cloudbusting" samples. "Because everything was shocking to us at the time," he stresses. "We were already a bit in shock because we'd ended up in this situation of having the first hit. I mean, it was amazing that she'd even heard our track."

~

In the semi-faceless rave band style of the early 1990s, Utah Saints shot a video for "Something Good" at the University of Leeds Refectory (the setting two decades before for the recording of the Who's landmark 1970 album, *Live at Leeds*). But, viewing their performance footage back, they decided that it looked "too staid and sort of run-of-the-mill."

Perhaps pushing their luck, Utah Saints and FFRR then went back to Bush, asking if they could possibly cut some scenes from the "Cloudbusting" video into their own promo. Once again, a surprising response came back: yes. Later, the duo even tried to find out where the cloudbusting contraption from Bush's video had ended up, with a view to using it as part of their stage set-up. "Yeah, we loved that machine," Willis says. "But we couldn't track it down anywhere."

"Something Good" was released as a single on May 25, 1992, and quickly rose to number four in the UK chart. Even by association, it was Kate Bush's biggest hit in Britain (post "Running Up That Hill") for seven years. It also reached number seven in the US *Billboard* Hot Dance Club Play chart, which was of course entirely new territory for the singer.

Ahead of Utah Saints appearing on *Top of the Pops* with the track, Willis remembers there being much anguished discussion about getting a female singer in to mime along to

Bush's vocals on "Something Good," as was the vogue with many dance artists.

"We were going, 'There's no way that's happening.' We were saying, 'Sampling is the future. People need to get their heads around the fact that a sampler is an instrument.' To *Top of the Pops'* credit, they went with it, and it messed up all their camera angles, because they were so used to being focused on the singer."

Soon after, however, reports began to circulate in the press claiming that Utah Saints had illegally sampled "Cloudbusting," and that Bush was planning to sue.

"It was disappointing when that came out," Willis sighs. "Because we didn't want to offend her fans, even. There was already a debate about sampling having no talent to it. About it being just nicking other people's things and riding on the coat-tails of their success. And that just added to it. I suspect the story began because there wasn't a lot to write about us.

"Although, I've heard a rumor," he adds, "and it is just a rumor. But somebody said that they read an interview with Del Palmer, where he'd said that there was talk [with Bush] of us doing something together."

It was no rumor. In a November 1993 interview with short-lived UK music magazine *RCD*, Palmer said: "They [Utah Saints] did a track with a piece of her vocal in it. They were really good about it, went through all the proper channels, asked if they could use it, gave her a royalty. She thought it was absolutely fantastic the way they'd actually used it.

"In fact, one time she thought it would be great to do something with them. It never came to pass, though."

Hearing this confirmation of even the fleeting notion of a Kate Bush/Utah Saints collaboration thirty years on from the release of "Something Good," Jez Willis simply marvels, "Amazing."

~

Having taken Kate Bush to the rave—not her usual habitat—Utah Saints then took her to the stadiums. "Something Good" was a peak moment in the dance outfit's 1993 sets opening for U2 on dates in Portugal, Spain, France, the UK, and Ireland on the Irish megaband's Zooropa tour, exposing the track to hundreds of thousands more people. "That was the beginning of us moving out of raves and into festival line-ups," Willis points out.

In all this time of shared success, though, there was never any direct contact between the duo and Kate Bush.

"We did try to put a message through to her going, 'Thank you. This has been amazing for us,'" Willis recalls. "But nothing ever came back."

From the summer of 1992 on, "Something Good" seemed to be everywhere, particularly since it was used as a recurring soundbed during the BBC's coverage of the Barcelona Olympics that year. These days, its pummeling beats and fractured vocal hooks still feature hugely in Utah Saints' live sets.

"People still love that track," Willis enthuses. "It works in a lot of different environments. We're really proud of the fact that it was an uplifting thing, and it was escapism. People still use it as an optimistic track, and when we play, we can still rely on 'Something Good' to get us out of jail wherever we are."

32

Change the Past and Future

The trials of **The Sensual World** *and* **The Red Shoes** *and the* **Director's Cut** *remake, 1987–2011*

"I think one of my big faults is that I have this real tendency to want to overdo things," Kate Bush told me. "I want to try to be adventurous, I want to try to make things interesting, and sometimes if I'm not careful, I overdo it."

As the late 1980s moved into the early 1990s, for Bush, being completely in charge of her own music had clearly developed its downsides. Both 1989's *The Sensual World* and 1993's *The Red Shoes* were to involve struggles in their own different ways.

I wondered whether achieving total autonomy in the studio had been weird for her sometimes? A lot of bands seem to thrive on creative conflict, I pointed out, which she doesn't have . . .

"Oh no, I do," she argued. "I'm in conflict with myself all the time."

So the battle is internal?

"Yeah, I think so. There's got to be conflict or there is no creative process, don't you think? It's all part of it . . . this struggle with an idea that won't hold still, and you're kind of trying to grapple it onto the floor and hold it down.

"It's all so difficult. It's so difficult to come up with anything that's at all interesting. I mean, I don't think anything's original. Everything has been done before . . . I think it's really true. Nothing is original, it's all built on other people's foundations all the time.

"Even to try to do something remotely interesting that isn't totally derivative, it's really, really hard."

∼

In September 1987, at the start of the recording of *The Sensual World*, Kate Bush sat in her recently updated studio at East Wickham Farm and suddenly felt suffocated by all of the machines surrounding her. As she described it, she found herself "overwhelmed by the amount of equipment around me. It was stifling, and I made a conscious effort to move away from that and treat the song as the song."

At the same time, she was also possessed by a creeping, intangible fear. "Perhaps I was feeling a sense of being scared," she later admitted to Phil Sutcliffe in *Q* magazine. "For the first time, really, I went through a patch where I just couldn't write. I didn't know what I wanted to say."

Turning thirty may also have had an effect, and going through, as she put it at the time, some kind of "mental puberty . . . let's face it, you've got to start growing up when you're thirty. It does make you feel differently."

From the outside, she appeared to have everything she'd wanted and fought for: a state-of-the-art private recording studio, all the time in the world to work in it, a now-pliant EMI and legions of devotees keenly waiting for her next record. But, in some ways, she now seemed to have become disillusioned by—or even disassociated from—the album-making process that she'd been so determined to master down the years.

"Sometimes," she jokily confessed to *Q*, "I think I might as well just be a brain and a big pair of ears on legs, stuck in front of a mixing desk."

It didn't help that the first track Bush worked on, "Love and Anger" (which she later referred to as "that bloody song"), was set to remain a complete stranger to her. Having written it around a fashionable, almost housey piano motif, Bush got Del Palmer to put a beatbox rhythm on it, before bringing Stuart Elliott in to add his syncopated drumming magic. Then the tape sat there, untouched, for more than a year-and-a-half. David Gilmour came to the studio and played a bit of guitar that Bush thought "made some sense." (Gilmour couldn't even remember playing on the track when I reminded him of it years later: "Did I? Oh good.")

But everything else that was thrown at "Love and Anger" Bush felt was "too MOR, or people just couldn't come to terms with it." Various musicians who passed through the studio asked the singer what the lyric was about. She had no idea, really. "It's just me trying to write a song," she laughed.

It was odd, then, that "Love and Anger" sounded so deep. Over a thumping beat that revisited "The Big Sky," Bush turned in a vocal that was determined and powerful and seemed to be encouraging someone (or even the narrator herself?) to confide a deep, powerful secret, whether it be to their sibling or even a priest.

Nonetheless, in the months following the release of *The Sensual World*, she tended in interviews to swerve away from the subject of "Love and Anger." Which made it all the weirder when it was released as a single in the February of 1990. "It's one of the most difficult songs I think I've ever written," she told a DJ on the air at WFNX in Boston. "It was so elusive, and even today I don't like to talk about it, because I never really felt it let me know what it's about."

Back in the studio at the start of the process, though, following the basic construction of "Love and Anger," other songs had started to flow, and the creative pace intensified. Bush colorfully confessed that at this point she'd thought to herself, "piece of piss! Then it all seemed like rubbish, and I had to stop for a while."

~

The breakthrough arrived when she was playing a synthesizer and the phrase "Mm, yes" started looping in her mind. It instantly made her think of the character Molly Bloom's breathless and lustful soliloquy at the end of James Joyce's wild and virtually impenetrable 1922 avant-novel *Ulysses*, which she'd first heard read by Irish actress, Siobhán McKenna on a 1956 spoken word album. Bush went to grab the book, fitted the words over the track and they worked perfectly.

When Stephen James Joyce, the famously protective grandson administrator of James Joyce's estate was sent the track for approval, however, he blocked its release. "Which I felt was a bit ironic," Kate later pointed out to *MOJO*, "considering the piece is totally centred around the word 'yes.'"

Frustrated, she went back and reworked the lyric in a similar metre, still imagining herself to be Molly Bloom, but a version of the character who leapt from the book into the real world. It was perhaps a pointed move: though never named, Bloom was literally escaping from Joyce's pages, and no one could stop her. The resulting track was a slinky slow-groover, with a close-up, intimate vocal of whispered passion, destined to be the opening, title track of *The Sensual World*.

From this point, in Bush's head, and in contrast to the grandly conceptual *Hounds of Love*, her next album would be a set of "ten short stories." But it was an idea that in the end became apparent to the listener only in certain tracks. "Heads We're Dancing" used as its inspiration a conversation she'd had with a friend many years earlier, sat at a dinner alongside "this fascinating, incredibly charming, witty, well-read" man whom they later discovered was J. Robert Oppenheimer, credited with being "the father of the atomic bomb."

In a leap of imagination, Bush then wondered who the absolute worst person might be to have been unwittingly charmed by and instantly decided: Adolf Hitler. "Heads We're Dancing" zapped her back to a German dancehall in 1939, as a woman being wooed by a cocky, coin-tossing Hitler she's later shocked to see on the front page of a newspaper. Following the album's release, Bush became slightly troubled by the idea that she'd somehow turned Hitler into a romantic figure. "It worries me a bit that this song could be received wrongly," she fretted.

"Rocket's Tail," meanwhile, was a track that, ninety seconds in, exploded into a glam-rock Bowie showstopper, as it depicted someone strapping a crude gunpowder-filled missile on their back and lighting its fuse while standing on Waterloo Bridge, before firing themselves briefly into the sky and landing in the Thames. It was easy to read the lyric as a metaphor for mad creative adventure, even fame. Bush cooled speculation in interviews by stating that the song was named after (and dedicated to) her cat.

The track was one of three on the record—along with "Deeper Understanding" and "Never Be Mine"—to feature the complex, keening harmonies of Trio Bulgarka, the Bulgarian vocal ensemble that Bush had first become aware of when her brother Paddy played her one of their albums. The 1986 reissue on 4AD Records of the 1975 compilation, *Le Mystère des Voix Bulgares* (featuring the Trio's leader, Yanka Rupkina) had brought Balkan folk to the attention of a whole new audience of listeners, leading to the release of Trio Bulgarka's own album *The Forest Is Crying* in 1988.

But Kate at first dithered before getting in touch with the Trio, concerned that she'd somehow taint their talents by featuring them on a mainstream album. In the end, contact was made via Joe Boyd of their UK label, Hannibal Records, and in 1988 Bush flew out to Sofia to meet them. It was for her a thrilling, if slightly disorientating experience—all communication was done through a translator or by wordless expression. Incredibly, when the three offered to sing for her, one of them, Eva Georgieva, picked up a phone and hummed along to the dial tone to get her tuning, before the others joined in. Kate was moved to tears by the beauty of their collective voices. The Trio were immediately invited by her to come to London to contribute to the album.

The Bulgarian collective were, however, not responsible for the most unconventional vocal on *The Sensual World*—that honor

went to the "brrrrrooooaaaah!" Captain Beefheart imperson-
ation Bush added to the end of CD bonus track "Walk Straight
Down the Middle" (her mum Hannah, hearing it, thought it was
a peacock). Elsewhere, perhaps the most memorable vocal cameo
came from Bush's father, Robert, on "The Fog," in spoken word
interjections echoing his instructions to her when teaching her to
swim as a child.

But Trio Bulgarka lent a unique emotional depth to the tracks
on which they appeared, not least "Never Be Mine." In the past,
Bush had always preferred to write tangentially about romantic
relationships. On *The Sensual World*, she grew more specific. A
third figure seemed to be in danger of invading a relationship in
"Never Be Mine": one that the singer was clearly daydreaming
about, while acknowledging that the fantasy was more attractive
than the probable reality. The theme returned in "Between a
Man and a Woman," which Bush coyly stated was "about a relationship being a finely balanced thing that can be easily thrown
off by a third party."

Bush herself declared *The Sensual World* to be "definitely my most
personal, honest album" to date, before qualifying the statement
by stressing that not all of the lyrics were written directly from
personal experience. "Although some of it's me," she told *NME*.
"it's this kind of vague mish-mash of other people and yourself."

She did laugh, however, when Phil Sutcliffe in *Q* bravely
pointed out that the idea of a "relationship in deep water" that
was her initial inspiration for "The Fog" sounded "as though it
might be personal about her and Del."

"Well, it does, doesn't it?" Bush averred, before turning evasive. "It's much easier to speak about very personal things to
lots of people through a song than it is to confront the world

with them through someone asking questions. Maybe you worry because it's going to be indirectly reported."

More directly, in her latest fan club newsletter message, she thanked Del Palmer for his determined studio efforts in helping to get *The Sensual World* over the line, writing, "what a long and intense project it was for us."

~

Sometime in the early 1990s, during the creation of her next album, *The Red Shoes*, Bush and Palmer ceased to be romantically involved after being together for around fifteen years (although he was to continue to be her most trusted studio engineer and early ideas confidante). While it's easy to confuse the singer with the song or read lyrics as being purely autobiographical, some of the tracks on the album were incredibly raw in terms of their detailing of emotional turmoil. "And So Is Love" was conflicted and sorrowful. "You're the One" graphically scripted the every-day minutiae of a breakup, as the singer agonized over whether she'd made the right decision, effectively stuck in the moment and afraid to go forward or backward.

Not long after, it became clear to Bush's friends that she'd grown close to Danny McIntosh, one of the guitarists on *The Red Shoes*, who also appeared as a band member in its accompanying short film, *The Line, the Cross and the Curve*. Following the end of the album's promotional campaign, the two officially became an item (although the fact would characteristically remain unknown to the public for some years).

It was likely no coincidence, then, that *The Red Shoes* featured some of the most emotionally charged vocal performances that

Bush had ever committed to record. Often, she would record entirely alone, sitting in the low-lit studio with a microphone while spinning the tape back and forward via remote control.

"It did make it a bit more complicated," she told me. "I was [recording] a lot of the vocals myself, so I would do them when I *felt* like singing a vocal. And I think some of the performances have got an emotional quality cause I did it [that way]. If I wasn't feeling like it was happening, I would go away and come back."

Close to the end of the sessions, a huge shadow fell over the making of *The Red Shoes*, which prevented Bush from working for a long time. Following a cancer diagnosis, her mother Hannah died, aged seventy-three, on February 14, 1992.

She admitted to me that, understandably, she'd lost all impetus to carry on making the album for some time afterward.

"Yeah, I couldn't work for a while. I mean, we were all devastated because she was so loved by so many people. It was a very difficult time, generally. When I could work, I found that it was actually quite helpful. And it was quite late in the album, which in some ways was good because I didn't have that much further to go before finishing it."

She didn't address her mother's death on the record though . . .

"No, no, I didn't. I mean, how would you address it? I don't know how you would address something like that. I think it's a long time before you can go anywhere near it because it hurts too much. I did play her that line in 'Moments of Pleasure'—because she did actually [used to] say, 'Every old sock meets an old shoe.' When I played it to her, she just burst out laughing. She thought it was really funny, and it was lovely that she really liked that."

Still, Bush must have been feeling low emotionally during this period?

"I think I was really tired. I mean, obviously, nobody's going to be in a sort of bouncy, happy state when that kind of thing happens. But, um, I was really tired. The album had been a long slog.

"I've read in a couple of things [written about me] that I was sort of close to having a nervous breakdown. I don't think I was. I mean, obviously, I was very sad at losing my mother. We all were. Our family was just knocked sideways. It's a terrible thing to happen, but it happens to all of us, and that's if we're lucky."

~

As the years passed, and in spite of their commercial successes—*The Sensual World* and *The Red Shoes* both reached number two in the UK and were certified platinum—certain aspects of the albums continued to niggle at Kate Bush.

When I spoke to her in 2005, it was obvious that the latter record in particular still irritated her. She particularly hated the sound of the Sony thirty-two-track digital tape recorder that she'd been talked into buying for the making of *The Red Shoes*.

"Shitty digital tape," she grimaced. "The whole thing's got this edgy sound which drives me *nuts* when I hear it because it's not right. It's terrible. It's so frustrating.

"I was really pleased with some of those tracks," she added. "But I don't like 'Constellation of the Heart.' I don't like 'And So Is Love'—I love Eric [Clapton]'s guitar on that, it's beautiful—but it's a very resignedly sad song, which I think puts almost too much weight into an album that actually has quite a good sense of humor."

Later, for 2011's *Director's Cut*, she would completely rebuild seven of the tracks from *The Red Shoes*, retaining only some of the original features. "I can't think of all the tracks [on *The Red Shoes*]," she claimed in 2005, "but there's quite a few I don't like. And it's just too long. Maybe that should have been a double album."

Instead, it was an album informed by the CD format. Many artists over-stretched themselves from the 1980s on by trying to fill up the seventy-four-minute length that the CD made technically possible. *The Red Shoes* clocked in at fifty-five minutes.

"At the time I'd made it long because I wanted people to feel they were getting their money's worth and [because] CDs were expensive," Bush pointed out, "A forty-minute record—which is what a good vinyl record is—I still think that's a good amount of time. [The CD format] is just too long.

"I feel really strongly about this, actually," she went on. "I think in a lot of ways artists [were] forced into this medium of CDs which is completely against the creative process. It works very well for classical music, that long period of time. But what was always great about vinyl was that you heard the first side and then, even if you went straight into the second side, you had that forced gap where you had to turn the record over. A lot of people would go for a cup of tea or a pee or something and then come back."

After an interval, basically?

"Absolutely. You had this natural space. And I think that's very good. However much you like listening to music, you need that kind of space in-between stuff."

Ironically, then, the reworked versions of the songs from *The Sensual World* and *The Red Shoes* ended up on *Director's Cut*, an album that—at fifty-seven minutes, but befitting its title—was even longer.

It's a fascinating insight into Kate Bush's creative process to track the changes she made to her older songs on *Director's*

Cut. One that she'd expressed her dislike for, "Constellation of the Heart," she didn't even bother with. The other, "And So Is Love," she lightened up, by changing, in her estimation, the "bloody depressing" line "life is sad" to "life is sweet." The original's electronic beats were meanwhile replaced with a more muted rhythm provided by US star sessioneer Steve Gadd (Steely Dan, Paul Simon), who played the drums throughout.

Much of *Director's Cut* involved a decluttering process, which allowed air into the tracks, while replacing the brittle digital sound of *The Red Shoes* with analog warmth. More space and atmosphere are apparent in "Song of Solomon" and "Never Be Mine." At the same time, all of Kate's lead vocals (and many of her inventively layered backing vocals) were entirely re-recorded, sometimes in a lower key to accommodate the changes in vocal range that naturally come with age.

Three of the songs—"This Woman's Work," "Moments of Pleasure" and "Rubberband Girl"—were entirely remade from scratch. The latter, arriving at the end of the running order as an up-tempo jolt to what was generally a slow- or mid-paced album, was the biggest shock to listeners. Where the version on *The Red Shoes* had been a punchy, Prince-like pop track, the *Director's Cut* remake was far looser and loucher, with Danny McIntosh's Keith Richards-aping guitar chops backed by Gadd's brush-played drums and Danny Thompson's woody double bass. Bush sang the words in a twanging voice that stretched and pulled the vowels, as if she was trying to vocally mimic the elasticity of an actual rubber band.

Sometimes, though, it was hard to hear where Bush thought improvements to the tracks had been made: the new version of "The Red Shoes" may have upped the production values, but it lost some of the potent, whirling heat that had been present in the original. In other instances, there was added intensity, particularly with the quiet-loud, verse-chorus dynamics of "Top of the City," with Bush's voice far gutsier in its peaks. Some changes were more prosaic: even with its new vocals, the remix of "Lily" seemed just to offer an opportunity to get rid of the papery thin 1990s beats all too typical of the era.

Another technological advance vastly improved the computer voice effect that Bush had been striving for on "Deeper Understanding." Back in the late 1980s, she'd effected her vocal with a harmonizer and layered it with an overdubbed Trio Bulgarka. Now, with the invention of autotune—created at first to correct the errant pitch of singers, but since used as an extreme manipulation tool by R&B singers—she was able to create chorus passages that convincingly sounded like a computer singing. The fact that the source voice was provided by her son Bertie underlined the fact that her involvement of her family in her music was ongoing.

Absolutely the biggest change, though, came with "The Sensual World," now retitled "Flower of the Mountain" after Stephen James Joyce finally allowed Bush to use the text from *Ulysses*. It came as a result of a bold move on the singer's part: when working on the new version of the track, she'd returned to the vocal using Molly Bloom's words and resubmitted it for approval.

"I couldn't believe it," Bush told Keith Cameron in *MOJO*. "They wanted to have a listen to it. And they said 'yes.' I was just so delighted. To be able to come back to that moment twenty years later and get a positive response was just fantastic.

"From where I stood, it was such a compromise that I'd made at the time. Although I thought [my version] was okay, I was disappointed, because I didn't feel that what I'd done had any-where near the weight that the original piece has. For me, it was just a complete triumph. I didn't feel I was messing with history. I just felt I was being able to put it right."

The latter comments summed up the entire process of *Director's Cut*. Responses to the album were mixed, however, upon its release on May 16, 2011 (the first on Bush's own EMI-distrib-uted label, Fish People). Simon Price highlighted the fact in his review in *The Independent*: "*Director's Cut* was greeted with reac-tions ranging between disappointment, bafflement and ridicule, before anyone had heard a note. On paper, it's true, the pros-pects didn't look promising. Taken on its own merits, however, there's plenty to enjoy."

"These reworked songs don't totally relinquish that unashamed grandiosity that makes Bush such a love-hate proposition," argued Jess Harvell in her review for online music publication *Pitchfork*. "*Director's Cut* provides a unique opportunity to do an A/B comparison between a late-career artist and her younger self. But which you prefer likely depends on whether you favor a more assured artist working within her strengths, or a brash younger artist delighting in the defying of pop conventions."

In the end, it was of course entirely the artist's prerogative to decide what they wanted to do with their songs, and up to the listener to decide what they wanted to hear. As Bush happily pointed out to *MOJO*, "Well, if people don't like this and they like the old ones, then the old ones are still there, aren't they?"

For Kate Bush herself, in revisiting the toughest period of her life and recording career, she'd satisfactorily repaired and smoothed over some lumps and bumps in her album catalog.

33

A Remote Connection

Kate and Prince, 1990–2016

On the surface, Prince and Kate Bush didn't appear to have that much in common. One was a hyperproductive showman who loved the stage, adulation and superstardom; the other someone who didn't crave fame whatsoever and who made vanishingly rare public appearances. Their common language, however, was the recording studio. Both tended to lose themselves, for days, weeks, months and—in Kate's case—years, exploring the possibilities of sound.

Another trait they shared was their striving for control over their music and careers. But whereas Bush didn't achieve creative autonomy until *The Dreaming*, the nineteen-year-old Prince, after signing his deal with Warner Brothers Records in 1977, insisted that he had to produce his own albums, starting with 1978's *For You*, released two months after *The Kick Inside*.

Zoom closer in on their individual stories, and more similarities appear. They were born on different continents, but only seven weeks apart (Prince being the elder). They were two musical prodigies contracted to major record labels in their teens. Each also seemed to be determined to bend the space and time of pop music in the 1980s. Listen back-to-back to "When Doves Cry" (a dance hit that featured no bass) and "Running Up That Hill" and there is common sonic ground: unorthodox Linn-Drum beats, almost cartoony synth lines, ingenious stacking up of the artists' voices as idiosyncratic backing vocal choir.

They had admired one another's work from afar but didn't meet until 1990. Kate went along to Wembley Arena to see Prince perform during his ten-night stint at the northwest London venue during his Nude Tour. Following his Lovesexy Tour extravaganza of 1988/1989—where he'd arrived on stage in a replica Ford Thunderbird to perform in the round on a set featuring a fountain, mini basketball court and brass bed—it was a stripped-back, more cost-effective show that highlighted the hits rather than the gimmicks. Not that the lack of theatrics mattered to Bush. She later declared Prince to be "the most inventive and extraordinary live act I've seen." (Prince—a Kate fan from *Hounds of Love* on—meanwhile told his engineer Michael Koppelman that Bush was his "favorite woman.")

After the show, the two talked backstage and the idea was floated that they should work together. When the tour was completed and Prince was back in the States, the pair spoke on the phone. Bush said that she had a new track with a supporting vocal hook that she'd love Prince to record. Prince said that she should send the tapes over to him in the States.

The near seven-minute-long original version of "Why Should I Love You?" (destined for *The Red Shoes*) that Bush sent to Prince has since leaked online. A mid-paced track with churchy organ and a shape-shifting time signature that moved between "When Doves Cry" syncopation in the verses and straight-ahead balladeering rock in the bridges and choruses, it's easy to hear why Kate thought it might appeal to—and be enhanced by—Prince.

But, going far beyond Bush's request for him to sing a vocal on it, Prince took the track and tore it apart, rebuilding it entirely. Looping a four-bar section from the chorus of the song, he engulfed it with an avalanche of ideas, filling up two twenty-four-track tape reels, adding new drums, playing guitar, bass, keyboards and, almost as an afterthought, singing the actual vocal hook. In the studio, Michael Koppelman was forced to point out to Prince that he'd actually sung the latter wrong: instead of the line "of all the people in the world," he'd recorded it as "all of the people in the world."

Koppelman remembered, "He said, 'No, we had little chat about that,' in his cocky way, as if to say he'd talked with Kate about changing the words to 'all of' instead of 'of all.'"

The next day, Koppelman arrived at the studio to find Prince cutting up his vocal takes and sampling them to rearrange the order of the words. It was highly unusual, the engineer noted, and "something he would normally never do himself. My interpretation? He made a mistake, as humans do, and didn't have the guts to admit it."

Meanwhile, when the original master tapes were sent back to Bush, bafflingly, nothing seemed to have been changed. She called the studio in America and was told that Prince was busy working on the track. A month later, Prince's tapes arrived at East Wickham Farm.

"He'd just smothered forty-eight tracks with everything you could possibly imagine," Del Palmer told *Sound On Sound* magazine. "I sat there and thought, 'Well, this is great, but what are we going to do with it?' So I made a general mix of the whole thing, gave it to Kate, and she puzzled over it for months. We kept going back to it over the course of a couple of years, and eventually, with a lot of editing and work on her part, she turned it back into the song it was."

"We never met while doing the track," Bush explained to *Melody Maker*, "and that appealed to my sense of humor. I sent stuff to him and then he sent it back, and I had to play with whatever he gave me." Talking years later to Matt Everitt on the BBC's Radio 6 Music, she further revealed, "he used to make me laugh because whilst I was working on an album, he would have done two world tours, a couple of albums and a film."

In the end, for fans of both Kate Bush and Prince, "Why Should I Love You?" was a bit of a let down. Though a solidly funky track thanks to the latter's transformation of the original song, it failed to produce the anticipated sparks. Palmer admitted, "It didn't turn out as we'd hoped, I have to be honest. It's still very interesting."

Later, Bush returned the favor, singing backing vocals on "My Computer," which turned up on Prince's messy 1996 triple album, *Emancipation*. Underlining their remote connection, it was a song that examined the burgeoning trend for online relationships. Still, in the final mix, Bush's voice is barely detectable or recognizable. Despite their determined efforts, it seems the two couldn't quite meld their talents. It was almost as if they cancelled one another out.

But, on April 21, 2016, like millions of others, Bush was clearly stunned and saddened when Prince died, aged fifty-seven, of an accidental overdose of the opioid painkiller fentanyl. She penned a tribute to him, which tellingly pointed out the sovereignty he'd maintained over his creative output: "He was the most incredibly talented artist. A man in complete control of his work from writer and musician to producer and director. He was such an inspiration. Playful and mind-blowingly gifted. The world has lost someone truly special. Goodnight, dear Prince."

34

"Moments of Pleasure"

From The Red Shoes, *1993/*Director's Cut, *2011*

Stepping out of the lift at the Royalton, the Philippe Starck-designed New York hotel on Manhattan's W. 44th Street, Kate Bush was delighted to find eighty-four-year-old English film director Michael Powell waiting in the lobby, animatedly waving his walking cane in the air like a silent film swashbuckler, to alert her to his presence.

Bush had long been an enormous fan of the films of Powell, who in partnership with his Hungarian co-director/writer Emeric Pressburger had produced a run of vibrantly original and hugely acclaimed films throughout the 1940s and into the early 1950s. Not least 1948's *The Red Shoes*, their Moira Shearer-starring tale of a ballerina whose actions—and fate—appear mysteriously controlled by the mind-possessing qualities of the titular rouge slippers.

Kate loved the fact that Powell and Pressburger's films had, as she put it, "heart," along with strong female characters and groundbreaking visual effects—the stairway to heaven visions of David Niven in *A Matter of Life and Death*, the vertiginous mountain-side drops of *Black Narcissus*. Bush felt that the pair had brilliantly deployed technology, not for gimmicky effect, but for maximum emotional impact (much like she tried to do in her music).

Powell and Bush had already been in contact, after she'd written to the retired director "to see whether he'd be interested in working with me," as she later told *Time Out*. "He was the most charming man. He wanted to hear my music, so I sent him some cassettes and we exchanged letters occasionally, and I got a chance to meet him not so long before he died.

"He left a really strong impression on me," she went on. "As much as a person as for his work. He was just one of those very special spirits, almost magical in a way."

On the day Powell and Bush met in 1989, snow began to fall on New York, an image that later would be evoked by the songwriter in her elegiac masterpiece "Moments of Pleasure," where in her eyes the Manhattan skyscrapers took on an alpine appearance amid the whiteout. It was clear to Bush, however, that Powell was at the time very ill. The director died of cancer only months later, in February 1990.

At home in England sometime after, Bush was inspired to write a song, using the imagery of the New York trip and detailing her moving meeting with Powell, while revisiting her old method of writing alone at the piano. "I looked up while playing the song through," she later remembered, "and it had started to snow."

In terms of the way it colorfully cuts or dissolves from scene to scene, "Moments of Pleasure" can easily be viewed as a Powell and Pressburger film in song. The action opens on a beach, with the narrator and her partner then diving from rocks into the ocean, leading to a jump-cut into the next scenario.

Many Kate Bush fans have for years speculated about the identity of "George the Wipe" that the singer references in the second verse of the song, whose story she admits to finding unendingly funny. The facts are murky, but he appears to have been an assistant engineer at Town House Studios during the recording of *The Dreaming* (one George Chambers is indeed listed in the credits).

According to some accounts, he was a hapless individual who accidentally erased the master tape of a song. Another version of the tale has Bush and Del Palmer playing a practical joke on him by asking him to wipe a tape that wasn't actually needed, then telling him he'd erased the wrong tape, and only later informing him it was a prank. Either way, like the funniest of in-jokes, it was never explained and added to the mysteries of "Moments of Pleasure."

In some ways, the production of the track also involved a flashback to 1975 and the sixteen-year-old Bush's recording of "The Man with the Child in His Eyes" with a full orchestra at AIR Studios. "Moments of Pleasure" featured her alone at the piano, supported by a stirring and evocative string arrangement by Michael Kamen: swelling with Hollywood-style flourishes when the singer notes Powell's resemblance to Douglas Fairbanks, then turning quieter and evoking pathos when Bush notices the director's ill health.

As a composition which flitted through memories of lost loved ones, "Moments of Pleasure"—in its original form on *The Red Shoes*—required a showstopping chorus. Bush dramatically attacked the notes in the manner of Edith Piaf, expressing the pain of life, but equally the joy of being able to share time and love with others. In her song catalog, it was the moment where she fleetingly transformed into a torch singer.

Writing in a fan club letter, Bush told her fans that "Moments of Pleasure" concerned "my dearest memories . . . with people I love, those things that still make me laugh, the people that have touched me. The song is saying thanks to those friends of mine who were fun to be with, some of whom aren't alive any more—though they are still alive in my memories."

Fittingly, by the end of "Moments of Pleasure," Bush was seeing their spectres. Her aunt Maureen. Her dancer friend (for Tour Of Life and various video and TV appearances), Gary "Bubba" Hurst, who had passed away due to AIDS-related complications in 1990. Her guitarist Alan Murphy, who'd died in similar circumstances in 1989. Then, Michael Powell himself appeared, and at the end, poor Bill Duffield, the lighting technician who'd met his end on the 1979 tour and whom she gently asked to illuminate the close of the song.

~

Returning to "Moments of Pleasure" for 2011's *Director's Cut*, Bush approached the song in a lower key, at a slower pace, and rendered it in a very different tone—someone viewing these reminiscences through the added depth of twenty more years of life experience. The production was further stripped to her piano, voice, and the wordless humming of the chorus melody by the Waynflete Chamber Choir.

In *MOJO*, Keith Cameron was the first to point out to the singer that he'd noticed a couple of names were missing from the end of this new version.

"Um . . ." Bush said, before giggling. "It wasn't deliberate actually. When I went to redo the piano, I didn't quite make it long enough. So, er, there you go. And it seemed all right as it was. It wasn't that I deliberately took people out at all."

It was a very human (and funny) error, for this very human, and most affecting of songs. George the Wipe, whoever he was, would've been proud to know that Kate, too, had made her own recording blunder.

35

The Line, the Cross and the Curve

Kate in the director's chair, 1993

There was already a crowd of fans waiting outside the Odeon West End in London's Leicester Square as Kate Bush and Del Palmer arrived and gently pushed their way through them. Photographers cried out, "Kate!," "Hi Kate!," "Kate!!," in an untypically polite fashion, trying and failing to get the singer's attention.

The occasion was the 37th London Film Festival, and the premiere of Bush's short film, *The Line, the Cross and the Curve*. Directed by and starring herself, alongside Miranda Richardson (famed at the time for her hissy-fitting performance as Queen Elizabeth I in BBC period comedy *Blackadder*), and with a recurring role for her inspirational tutor of old, Lindsay Kemp, the forty-three-minute-long movie was to feature on a bill above Nick Park's claymation caper, *The Wrong Trousers*.

Ahead of the screening, Bush tentatively stepped onto the cinema's stage to make a brief introduction, thanking everyone who'd been involved in the production. "I'd also like to say what a hard act that film will be to follow," she smiled sheepishly, referring to Park's top-notch animation (which the next year won an Academy Award).

The response to *The Line, the Cross and the Curve* that evening, from the largely partisan audience, was wholly enthusiastic. As Bush and Palmer exited the theater and moved with the throng toward the stairs, someone shouted, "Very nice, Kate," and she turned and grinned. Down in the foyer, she was surrounded by autograph hunters, and she scribbled her name for a number of them, before the size of the group grew and began to look worryingly uncontrollable.

Odeon security personnel closed in, and ushered Bush and Palmer out into a waiting car. One fan asked, "Did you enjoy yourself?" There was no time for a response, but as Bush beamed in their direction before the vehicle pulled off, they began cheering and shouting, almost as one, "Goodbye, Kate!!!"

The Line, the Cross and the Curve, it seemed, was a hit.

~

Making a film had been the next logical step on Kate Bush's artistic path. Traditional album promotion was a grind, and although she wasn't set to make a big cinematic statement on the level of other, more ambitious artists, such as Madonna, Prince, or U2, who'd all produced feature-length films in the recent past, the idea of directing a long-form promotional video had appealed to her.

The Line, the Cross and the Curve further riffed on Powell and Pressburger's *The Red Shoes*. Bush cast herself as a frustrated dancer who is pitted against Richardson's Frida Kahlo-resembling villain (listed in the credits only as Mysterious Woman), after she is hood-winked into donning the magical, perma-dancing shoes.

As the synopsis in the London Film Festival program further explained: "[Richardson] tricks Kate into drawing three symbols—a line, a cross, and a curve—and handing over her soul in return for the red shoes. A guide appears (Lindsay Kemp), explaining that the only way to break the spell is to sing back the symbols."

From the outset of the making of the film, however, Bush had felt pressured.

"I was in a real state of exhaustion," she recalled to me. "A few friends said, 'Are you sure you should be doing this? Because it's gonna be really hard.' And I thought, 'Yeah, let's do it now.' Because I thought it was a really interesting idea. But what we should've done was given me a break, put the release date of [*The Red Shoes*] album back and allowed me to work on some proper storylines."

On the set, photographer Guido Harari, who'd worked with Bush on-and-off since 1982, was given full access to roam around and shoot whatever he fancied.

"Since she'd stopped performing in 1979," he remembers, "this was a unique opportunity to capture her in performance and also backstage, during breaks, in a fly-on-the-wall mode. I've never felt so much freedom and complete trust like on that set with Kate. She had a very special way of making everybody feel so comfortable working with her.

"There were so many pressures on Kate, many I had no idea of, like the fact that her mother had just died. Plus, she was not only starring in the movie, but also directing. Not the easiest task, especially while making your first movie."

"It's very difficult," Bush stressed. "One minute you're directing and then you're acting. I felt like I hadn't put enough time
into it. I could feel it at the time . . . it hadn't been thought
through properly and it was making me feel a bit nervous, I suppose. I could feel all these great elements going for it and this
whole load of other stuff that was really going against it."

Not that the singer seemed particularly anxious to the other actors
when it came to directing them. Lindsay Kemp, for one, was wholly
impressed by how his former student had now turned master.

"She was demanding, and rightly so," Kemp recalled in his
foreword to Harari's 2016 book, *The Kate Inside*. "On one occasion she told me off for being too slow, as film directors have
often done in the past. Slowness on stage can be magically
time-warping, but less so on film. Unlike Ken Russell however
[*Kemp appeared in Russell's* Savage Messiah *alongside Helen Mirren in
1972*], Kate didn't accuse me of wasting film."

The shoot for *The Line, the Cross and the Curve* lasted for two
weeks, and was intensive. "She was completely focused on the
project," Harari adds, "and would carry these huge notebooks
filled with very precise notes and sketches. But I remember she
rushed things a bit in order to take the film to the London Film
Festival. She's always been a perfectionist and I don't think she
allowed for much time to shoot and then edit the film."

"It was too rushed," said Kate. "I had no money. I had to be
in it a lot in order to make it cheap."

~

The Line, the Cross and the Curve was not without its charms. The
musical sections were invariably great: Bush and dancer Stew-

art Arnold's pas de deux in "Rubberband Girl"; the singer's solo performance of "And So Is Love" by flickering candlelight and then, arms aloft, spinning and spinning through time in "Moments of Pleasure."

Another highpoint came with "Lily," Bush's song referencing her friend, the self-described "color healing therapist," Lily Cornford, who'd founded the Maitreya School and Healing Centre in London, back in 1974.

"I met her years ago," Bush informed the readers of her newsletter, in a rare insight into her spiritual convictions. "She believes in the power of Angels and taught me to see them in a different light, that they exist to help human beings and are very powerful as well as benevolent forces. She taught me some prayers that I found very useful (particularly in my line of work). She helped me a lot and I guess I wanted to pass on her message about our Angels—we all have them, we only have to ask for help."

In the film, the white-haired Cornford herself appeared as a serenely otherworldly, almost David Lynchian film character, dispensing advice to the singer, who sat at her feet and buried her head in the healer's lap. "I'm scared, Lily," she declared, as the song began and Cornford summoned four white-robed angels—Gabriel, Raphael, Michael, and Uriel—to surround and protect Bush, and drew a circle of fire on the ground with her walking stick. It was deeply strange, yet strangely deep.

Bush's favorite part of *The Line, the Cross and the Curve* was the main section featuring the album's title track (as opposed to its end of film reprise), in which the entrancing Richardson mimes along to the singer's vocal part.

"[That's] the one thing I think works really well in the film," Bush told me, "and that was because I managed to get Miranda, and I was so excited at being able to get such a brilliant actress in on the project."

In contrast, though, as I tentatively ventured, Bush's acting seemed a bit self-conscious.

"I think it's a load of old bollocks, actually," she laughed.

Unfortunately, the reviewer from *Variety* magazine agreed, writing that *The Line, the Cross and the Curve* was "a music promo flick high on whimsy and low on content. Richardson steals the acting stakes as a kind of wicked witch. When not warbling, Bush is colorless."

Hit-and-miss it may have been, but over the years the film has been re-evaluated as a notable curio in the career of Kate Bush. In its mixed review, *Variety* predicted as much, reckoning that the movie would become "a solid bet for special events . . . sure to please Bush aficionados." Released on VHS and Laser Disc, it was later nominated for the Grammy Award for Best Long Form Music Video. Through the subsequent decades, *The Line, the Cross and the Curve* has continued to be screened periodically in arthouse cinemas around the world.

Time, then, has only increased the value of the film. As Prince stated when defending his own, similarly maligned *Purple Rain* sequel, 1990's *Graffiti Bridge*, "Maybe it will take people thirty years to get it. They trashed *The Wizard of Oz* at first, too."

36

Public Image (Further) Limited

Tired of TV, 1989–94

Back to the schlep of promotion. From the 1989 campaign for *The Sensual World* onward, opinions of Kate Bush seemed to begin hardening, her image as a reclusive and mysterious figure becoming cemented in the public perception.

Bush's new label in America, Columbia Records—who she'd signed to after EMI America let her contract lapse—had chosen "Love and Anger" to be the lead single from the album and asked that she make a video for it. The self-directed clip was quite an elegant production: the singer in a black dress, kneeling in darkness, in a white circle of light, was showered with golden confetti and then joined by female ballet dancers, whirling dervishes and, at the end, a band featuring David Gilmour. The video began to pick up plays on MTV, which meant that the all-powerful music station of course requested to interview her.

At the end of 1989, Bush made a short trip to New York. Right from the start, the way that MTV's interviewers approached her seemed a bit odd.

"You did something that was very 'out,'" one offscreen interrogator told her in a segment on their news show, presumably meaning in terms of musical fashions. "And then it came back in again."

"I mean, the music business, and the fashions and fads that go with that, I think in a way are something quite separate [from my music]," Bush offered. "And who can say if it's in or out of fashion? It's just what I do.

"I find it extraordinary the different perceptions that people have of me," she added, smiling. "And I feel for my own sanity, that that's something that is theirs, and not mine (*laughs*). And I think that's quite important. Because, y'know, we all have problems with what other people think of us. But it doesn't really matter, does it?"

Meanwhile, over on MTV's *X-Ray Vision* program, a tone of baffled exasperation seemed to creep into the presenters' voice-overs as they babbled away about Bush over a montage of her video snippets in the introduction to their interview.

Nameless male presenter: She sort of exists only as this magical character you see in videos and hear on records.
Nameless female presenter: But you talked to her, didn't you?
Male presenter: Yeah. She's very guarded.
Female presenter: Guarded?
Male presenter: (*Flatly*) Yeah, guarded.

"I wanted my work to speak," Bush stated, when the edit cut to her. "Not me as a person. Because I feel that's what I want to give to the world . . . is the work that I do. Not really me or what I have to say."

Talk turned, perhaps inevitably, to speculation about a future tour. Bush's response was revealing in that it was one of the rare times when she used the word "reclusive" in terms of describing herself, while explaining her retreat from the public eye as having been a reaction to the bright burn of her early fame.

"After the last tour, I just felt very vulnerable," she said. "I'd been through tremendous public exposure at a young age. And I hadn't really stopped since it had started. And I think really over these years of being in the studio, and being quite reclusive in some ways, I've gained a lot of my strength back that I did lose."

Then, things got a bit bizarre, as the presenters returned to witter on over the "Love and Anger" video.

Male presenter: She definitely wants her videos and records to be this magical place. Can I tell you something weird?
Female presenter: Yeah.
Male presenter: Well, during the whole interview, I was really distracted by this yellow green aura that was surrounding her body. I'm completely serious.

Less unsettling fun was to be had back in England on BBC Two's *Rapido* music show, where Kate was shown arriving at the studio at East Wickham Farm and entering the kitchen, where she exhibited a purposely bad tea-pouring technique, carelessly sloshing it from the pot over the rims of the mugs, then mock-strangling Del Palmer over the mixing desk to display some kind of murderous creative differences. Later, she was filmed pretend-composing "This Woman's Work" at a Bech-stein upright piano and penciling the chords on notation paper.

In the accompanying interview, Bush grinned and marveled at the fact that "people still even bother to ask me if I'm going to tour. I think you're all completely mad (*laughs*). And thank you very much, but . . ."

In France, she appeared, on April 24, 1990, on a national show called *Top 50*, being questioned by the interviewer in the native tongue and replying in English. By now, though smiling and unfailingly polite, she was open about her dislike of the pub-licity game.

"As you know, I don't do a lot of promotion," she stated. "I find it difficult."

~

Three years on, for *The Red Shoes*, Bush made sure her public exposure was even more limited.

"I was *exhausted* after [that] album," she told me in 2005, "In hindsight, really, we should have put the release date back and just given me a chance to catch my breath before it all went off to the promotion. But, y'know, it doesn't always work like that."

The appearances that she did make this time around were selective and targeted. On the high-profile Saturday night ITV chat show *Aspel & Company*, its easy-going, genial host Michael Aspel pointed out that she now had a "Garbo label" attached to her. He then blundered on, telling the singer that their produc-tion office had received many letters sent in by fans, particularly men, ahead of her slot on the show.

"Do you still enjoy being a male fantasy?" Aspel bluntly enquired.

"Em, well, I'm not sure if I've ever really enjoyed it," Bush averred, with a tolerant smile.

"Horrible question," Aspel quickly realized.

"Yes, it is," Bush nodded. "It's a horrible question."

In the December 1993 issue of *Q* magazine, Stuart Maconie insightfully pointed out to the singer, "You are famously uncynical. Or at least, you were. Has all that changed?"

"I think it has," said Bush. "I think it's impossible to move through this business—in fact, it's impossible to move through life without adopting a bit of cynicism. It's a protective and defensive thing. People are going to rip you off, they're going to stitch you up, and if you're cynical, it prepares you for the reality of this. It prepares you for things that, chances are, are going to happen to you (*laughs*)."

Interviewed for Canadian music TV station MuchMusic that same month, Kate seemed to be reaching the end of her patience when it came to being forced to mull over the popular perceptions of herself.

"I think there's always preconceptions about someone who is in the public eye and that's only natural," she reasoned. "But they don't concern me. I am who I am. And people have a lot of conceptions about my image, which is something quite different from what I am.

"I really liked the idea of my work speaking for me. Not *me* speaking for me. I don't feel that what I have to say personally is that interesting, and it's not something that I have enthusiasm about. It's not fun for me. I don't really enjoy it.

"So people's conceptions of what I am . . . in a way, that's their problem, not mine."

~

At the end of the campaign for *The Red Shoes*, the fourth UK single taken from the album, "And So Is Love," slipped out in November 1994. The chart placings of its predecessors had been good-to-fair: "Rubberband Girl" (number twelve), "Moments of Pleasure" (number twenty-six), "The Red Shoes" (number twenty-one).

But Bush admitted to me that she felt she had an image problem come the end of *The Red Shoes*.

"I suppose it was a bit like the way that I felt after *The Dreaming*," she said. "I was viewed as being a weirdo. It was just the same thing again, really."

To push this last single along, Bush surprisingly agreed to return to *Top of the Pops* to perform the track. It was one of her most striking appearances on TV, but not in a great way.

"It's been nine years since she last appeared on the show," yowled *EastEnders* actress-turned-pop star Michelle Gayle over a whooping and clapping crowd. "And I feel proud to welcome . . . Miss . . . Kate . . . Bush!"

The camera swirled around to reveal Bush on stage lined up alongside two anonymous-looking female backing singers. Standing to their right, she wore a black leather designer biker jacket, and looked surprisingly like a power ballad rock chick in the style of Bonnie Tyler or Jennifer "The Power of Love" Rush. This untypically "straight" image seemed to superficially fit with the MOR-ish stylings of "And So Is Love." But—particularly in the context of this peppy pop show—the already mournful song sounded ineffably sadder.

It soon became apparent that the auxiliary singers were miming along to Kate's recorded vocals and that their sole purpose was likely to ensure that she wasn't on the stage alone. She looked plainly knackered and semi-detached from the proceedings.

As the song died away following this strangely listless performance, and the camera pulled back, and the audience once again cheered and hooted, Gayle beamed into the lens and declared, "She . . . is . . . wicked."

And, with that, Kate Bush was gone from her last TV studio appearance, never to return.

37

An Inimitable Artist?

Kate Bush cover versions, 1978–2022

It opens with echoes, piercing feedback guitar and the sound of someone running their finger over a kalimba. Then the rolling bassline and loping beat kick in, and a thick Somerset accent begins to ripely intone the (wrong) opening line: "Out on the winding (*sic*), windy moors . . ."

As the four-minute track progresses there are repeated cries of "Cathy!" and "Heathcliff!" spinning through dub infinity, along with repeated cries of "Ooh arr!" This comedy reggae version of "Wuthering Heights"—equally inspired by PiL and the Wurzels (the novelty "Scrumpy and Western" band whose 1976 hits included "The Combine Harvester" and "I Am a Cider Drinker")—was released in 1979 by one Jah Wurzel on the album *Hybrid Kids—A Collection of Classic Mutants*.

The culprit was Morgan Fisher, onetime keyboardist with rowdy David Bowie-affiliated glam-rock band Mott the Hoople, who'd put together a mock compilation recorded on a four-track in his London bedsit, where he assumed various identities, including the Burtons' Madness-alike Cockney ska take on "MacArthur Park" and Punky and Porky's helium-high, puppet-pig-Sex-Pistols-mashup "God Save the Lean/Pretty Bacon." Fisher's fruity West Country rendering of "Wuthering Heights" was, however, the standout cut, and duly received radio plays from John Peel and Kenny Everett.

It wasn't the first Kate Bush cover version. That honor had gone to British singer and actress Julie Covington, who (with the assistance of John Cale and Richard Thompson) had turned in a smooth folk rock take on "The Kick Inside" for her self-titled album, released in 1978, the same year as the original. Covington was in fact a friend of Bush's brother, John, and considered his sister to be "wonderful . . . she writes such extraordinary songs."

Given Bush's unique vocal and musical character, other artists approaching her material were entering hazardous territory. Attempting to mimic the singer's vocal mannerisms would inevitably sound like parody. Moving too far away from the songs' idiosyncrasies risked allowing their magic to evaporate. Both challenges conspired to sink New York's Pat Benatar, who adopted a faux English accent over a rock power chord backing for her dodgy, musical theater-esque version of "Wuthering Heights" on her 1980 album, *Crimes of Passion* (though it was notably the first American cover version of a Bush composition).

The best interpreters of Kate Bush's songs during her first years of activity tended to be the ones who stamped them with their own indelible vocal imprints. On stage at the Theatre Royal, in London's Drury Lane, in April 1979, Dusty Springfield introduced her next number by stating, "Kate Bush has an immense amount of originality, and I was absolutely staggered by her. And I'd like to sing a song that I think is one of the prettiest ones ever written . . . certainly by her."

Springfield's "The Man with the Child in His Eyes" was faithful, yet slowed for maximum drama, and arranged for piano, synthesizer and brass. Her famously smoky, sultry delivery spun the girlishness of the original into something altogether more mature and knowing. But as she ascended to falsetto in the final chorus, it sounded as if it was with a touch of difficulty. "That's a tough song," she noted at the end.

Others bravely attempted to tackle "The Man with the Child in His Eyes" in very different ways. Pat Kane, singer with Scottish soul duo Hue & Cry, rewrote the lyric in second person and sounded equal parts Stevie Wonder and Frank Sinatra, but in the end marred it with jazz scatting. Natalie Cole—daughter of Nat King Cole—sang it over synth pads, three-quarter swing, and a gospel choir, but it still came across as muzak. Australian singer Tina Arena's 2007 orchestral version maintained the wide-eyed wistfulness for its first half, but similarly ruined it in the second by adding lumpy Indian percussion.

~

On June 25, 2005, mid-afternoon on the Glastonbury Festival's Other Stage, Sunderland's post-punk-inspired quartet the Futureheads split in two the sodden crowd (suffering through a weekend of thunder, lightning and torrential rain). One half, as singer Barry Hyde instructed them, were to sing, "Uh! Oh oh!"; the other half "Ah oh!" The band then launched into their brilliantly fidgety and propulsive version of "Hounds of Love" that they'd released as a single four months earlier.

I was in the audience that day—neither 'uh oh oh'ing or 'ah oh'ing, it has to be said—and it was a marvel to witness an audience of tens of thousands hollering along to one of Kate Bush's biggest hits (particularly at a time when there was no prospect of her ever performing live again).

When I interviewed Bush three months later, I explained what had happened at Glastonbury, telling her that the mass of festival-goers who'd filled the field had virtually exploded with joy.

"Oh, that's great," she beamed. It turned out that she had in fact heard the Futureheads' "Hounds of Love" single, which completely reimagined the song in a new-wave style. "I thought they did a great job," she said. "I was really flattered. It's nice to think that somebody wants to cover your song."

Chicago-born transgender singer Ezra Furman, who in 2018 tweeted, "If you are not listening to the song 'Hounds of Love' by Kate Bush at least once a day, I have serious concerns about your mental health," regularly performed the number on tour that year. While sticking close to the recorded version, she attacked it with absolute, raw-throated passion, to regular crowd uproar.

Few are the artists who have attempted "Cloudbusting." Watford sister trio the Staves offered a delicate acoustic accompaniment and let their harmonies wash all over it. Bath stoner metal band Sergeant Thunderhoof went to the other extreme, with pummeling drums and grinding riffs, stretching it to nearly eight minutes of heaviosity.

Solange—sister of Beyoncé—Knowles meanwhile cited Bush as one of her key "classic" influences in an interview with *Elle* magazine, along with Björk and Erykah Badu, stating that she admired their authenticity and "what they were embodying." In tribute, wowing the audience at the Coachella Festival in California in 2014, Knowles played her live cover of "Cloudbusting" fairly straight, singing it over an electro pulse and synth cellos, and adding soulful trills and a military beat.

Elsewhere, reinforcing the fact that Bush wrote "This Woman's Work" from the perspective of a man in a hospital whose mind is racing with panic at the thought of losing his wife and child, a host of male singers covered the song. British indie folker Luke Sital-Singh sang it over gently played electric guitar and sounded a bit like Jeff Buckley. Californian indie rocker Greg Laswell sang it over gently played piano and sounded a bit like Jackson Browne.

Both 2022 Eurovision runner-up for Britain Sam Ryder and US neo soul singer Maxwell tested their ranges to perform the song in Bush's original key. The latter featured "This Woman's Work" in his 1997 *MTV Unplugged* set and recorded a studio version released as a single in 2002, with an accompanying video storyline that depicted the singer being haunted by his dead partner, tipping the song's sentiment from anxiety over into grief.

Even before the *Stranger Things*-related phenomenon of 2022, "Running Up That Hill" was by far the most covered Kate Bush song. Each artist brought to it different qualities: Placebo (restrained raw power), the Chromatics (icy synths and emotional detachment), Meg Myers (added thump), the Wombats (glitchy beats and tumbling acoustic guitar), Faith and the Muse (goth drumming overload), Car Seat Headrest (lo-fi electronics and funk), Tiffany (karaoke backing and screechy vocal), Wye Oak (warped soul), First Aid Kit (pining folk), and Youth and Durga McBroom's dance duo Blue Pearl (hands-in-the-air rave vibes).

Staying true to the original, on June 11, 2022, American pop star Halsey sang "Running Up That Hill" at the Governors Ball Music Festival at Citi Field in Queens, New York. "I'm sorry, guys, I just had to do it," she exclaimed at the end, as massed, ecstatic shrieking filled the night air. Later, Halsey tweeted, "Truly wish I wrote this song more than anything in the world. I'm soooo happy it's having this resurgence."

Other acts have ventured deeper into the unexplored corners of the Kate Bush songbook. US alternative rock outfit Nada Surf refracted "Love and Anger" through a prism of skippy beats and chiming guitars. Scroobius Pip remade "Feel It" as woofer-pumping trip hop. Tracey Thorn treated "Under the Ivy" with tenderness and respect. The Waterboys rocked up "Why Should I Love You?" Jane Birkin quickened the pulse of "Mother Stands for Comfort." Swedish mezzo-soprano Anne Sofie von Otter and string quartet Brooklyn Rider performed *Aerial*'s "Pi" with muted chamber orchestral intensity.

One artist who didn't dare go near a Kate Bush song until half a decade into her career, was Tori Amos, dismissed by some as a Bush copyist in her early days. During an interview conducted on a long train journey from London's Paddington to her Cornwall home in 1998, I delicately pointed out that it seemed as if no review of her 1992 debut album, *Little Earthquakes*, had failed to mention Kate Bush.

"I'll never forget the first time I heard about Kate," Amos told me. "I was playing in a club. I was, like, eighteen or nineteen and somebody came up to me, pointed their finger and said 'Kate Bush.' I went, 'Who's that?' This was 1981 and I wasn't really familiar. Kate didn't really happen in the States until *Hounds of Love*.

"I was kind of shocked because the last thing you want to hear is that you sound like someone else. Then handfuls of people kept mentioning her name to me when they heard me sing, to the point where I finally went and got her records. When I first heard her, I went, 'Wow, she does things that I've never heard anybody do, much less me.' But I could hear a resonance in the voice where you'd think we were distantly related or something."

I asked Amos if she was ever directly influenced.

"Well . . . I must tell you that, when I heard her, I was blown away by her. There's no question."

Did she sing along with the records?

"Absolutely. I knew though that I had to be careful, so I did not voraciously learn her catalog. I left the records with my boyfriend at the time because I didn't want to copy her. People were already saying that I reminded them of her."

As time passed, Amos learned to embrace the comparison. In the summer of 1996, she'd sung a few lines of "Running Up That Hill" during a show in Denver, Colorado. But, by 2005, on stage she was bookending a piano/vocal version of her song "God" (from her second, 1994 album, *Under the Pink*) with repeats of Bush's "R.U.T.H." chorus hook.

In June 2022, during performances in Los Angeles, Phoenix, and Oakland, acknowledging the *Stranger Things* effect, she sandwiched a full band "Running Up That Hill" in the middle of "Bliss" from her 1999 long-player *To Venus and Back*.

Eight years earlier, on July 18, 2014, at a gig in Portland, Oregon, Amos had performed another Bush song, "And Dream of Sheep," twirling on her stool from Bösendorfer piano to eerie-sounding synthesizer and back again.

"This is in honor of all the ladies here tonight, and the great lady who wrote this song," she announced, before adding, perhaps to highlight the fact that she didn't harbor the slightest trace of rivalry, "who we all love very much."

38

"Ooh, I've Just Come!"

Kate at the Q Awards, 2001

**As he walked into the dining hall at London's world-fa-
mous Harrods department store, just after noon on
a late October day in 2001, *Q* magazine writer John
Aizlewood was worried that he might not be able to
recognize the woman he was here to meet. After all,
she hadn't really been seen in public for seven years.**

"I was petrified about going up to some strange woman in
Harrods," he remembers, "and saying, 'Are you Kate Bush?'"

Aizlewood needn't have worried. Upon his arrival, the singer
was clearly identifiable, though, the writer remembers, "not to
look like 'Kate Bush' or stand out in any way." She was dressed
down in jacket and trousers, her hair long and with a side-parted
fringe. Having spotted the journalist obviously scanning around
looking for someone, she'd waved in his direction. As he sat
down with her and they ordered a pot of tea, he was struck by
how easily Bush was able to hide in plain sight.

"Not because she was in disguise," he stresses. "But because she hadn't allowed herself to be recognized for so long. So she could sit in public, in Harrods, with me, and no one would bother her."

The year before, in 2000, Bush's friend Peter Gabriel had let slip in an interview that she was now a mother: the birth of Albert McIntosh, two years old by this point, had gone unannounced. The only reason Kate was resurfacing now in 2001 was because she'd been tipped off she was to win a Q Award at the magazine's annual ceremony the following week. Consequently, she'd not only agreed to attend, but also to give her first interview since 1994.

"I didn't get the impression at all that she was doing it under duress," Aizlewood says. "I think she just wanted to put her head above the parapet. I think it was an interview which bought her time with EMI to make music."

The writer had briefly been introduced to Danny McIntosh and the now three-year-old Bertie, when father and son (in pushchair) hovered around ahead of the interview, before going off shopping for an hour. It was obvious that Bush adored being a mum, and she explained that she'd happily put her music career on the back burner.

"Although I hadn't *always* wanted children," she said, "I had for a long time. People say that magic doesn't exist, but I look at him, think, 'I gave birth to him,' and I know magic does exist. I don't want to miss a second of him."

During their chat, Bush admitted to Aizlewood that she'd suffered from deep fatigue after *The Red Shoes*, and that "the batteries were completely run out and I needed to re-stimulate again." In the immediate aftermath, she'd spent her time sleeping, or watching "really bad quiz programs or really bad sitcoms," none of which she cared to name.

"It just seems that I needed to be in a position where there were no demands," she reflected. "I saw friends occasionally and I was very quiet. I was just trying to recuperate." In the intervening years before the birth of Bertie, she'd lived for a time in a flat in central London (she told Aizlewood exactly where, but politely requested he didn't print the location) and had been busy doing normal things: visiting museums, going on holidays.

Bush did reveal, however, that she was working on new music. Aizlewood advanced a theory that she was in fact the Stanley Kubrick of the music world (mystically reclusive, unwilling to surrender creative control, wholly original, obsessively perfectionist) and Kate didn't entirely disagree.

"I admire Kubrick," she said of the revered film director, who'd died two years previously, in 1999, aged seventy. "He really was a genius, and he took himself away. I'm privileged to have creative control. That to me is everything. I wouldn't dare compare myself to him, but I know what you mean."

As to giving the readers of *Q* a progress report on her eighth studio album, Bush was cagey.

"There's quite a lot of it done," she offered, "but I can't really talk about something that's not finished. It's like talking about an event that hasn't happened."

~

The following Monday, October 29, 2001, Kate Bush arrived early at the Park Lane Hotel ahead of the ceremony. Misunderstanding the protocol, she walked quickly up the red carpet, failing to stop and pose for the waiting photographers, who proceeded to loudly boo her.

Once inside, Bush worried that it had actually been the members of the public waiting on the pavement outside who'd been booing. John Aizlewood reassured her but noted that she seemed instantly deflated. It wasn't a great start to the proceedings.

As other artists and bands—among them Brian Eno, Donovan, Cher, Liam Gallagher, Damon Albarn, members of Radiohead, the Prodigy and the Manic Street Preachers—started to enter the room, word began to filter out that Kate Bush was in attendance. Elvis Costello wandered over to the singer's table and offered her his phone number, hoping that they could work together in the future.

Aizlewood says he witnessed Costello turn utterly deferential in Bush's presence: "Obviously, he's a very collaborative artist, but he was absolutely fanboy-ish. There was a bit of desperation. Like, 'This is my chance to speak to Kate Bush and ask her to work with me.'"

It seemed as if Bush was entirely taken aback by being the focus of such intense attention. "Because in the same way that she hadn't grasped the etiquette for the red carpet," says Aizlewood, "she hadn't grasped the notion of just how pleased her peers would be to see her, and how they'd come and say hello all the time, and how they only had praise for her."

As the ceremony got underway and progressed to the point in the running order when it was time for the Classic Songwriter Award, guest presenter Midge Ure stepped up to the podium. He began by recalling the first time he'd met the recipient of the next honor.

"It was in the late 1970s and I was in the Rich Kids, and we were appearing on a TV show together," he said, before adding, "I was desperately trying to get off with her and get a lift back in her limo." In his increasingly jokey speech, he went on to reference the time he and Kate had shared the stage at the Prince's Trust benefit show in 1982, when she'd suffered her wardrobe calamity and, as he put it, "almost got her tits out for Prince Charles."

When Ure announced Kate Bush as the winner, the assembled musicians in the audience rose to their feet and gave her a standing ovation as she walked onto the stage. Her first words—gobsmacking everyone—repeated a catchphrase from the BBC's quickfire comedy sketch show, *The Fast Show*: "Ooh, I've just come!"

"Which was obviously the least Kate Bush thing you could imagine her saying," Aizlewood points out.

Afterward, Kate chatted to Donovan, and was then invited upstairs to have her photograph taken with John Lydon. Earlier, Lydon, along with his wife, Nora, his dad, John Sr, and his notoriously screw-faced pal/minder John Rambo had made a dramatic arrival at the Park Lane Hotel, pulling up in a horse-drawn rag-and-bone cart. On stage, collecting his Inspiration Award, Lydon had loudly declared, "Kate Bush, I love you. Your music is brilliant."

Interviewed after he'd left the stage, Lydon ranted further in praise of the singer, "Kate Bush is a true original. It's not nice that she's been imitated—Torrid Aimless, sorry, Tori Amos. But Kate Bush is a genuine talent. She went through the same shit I did when she started: 'Oh, that's not singing.' Who the fuck wrote the rules about music? Why follow this slavish idiocy?"

Similar to Elvis Costello earlier, as Bush arrived in the photo room, Lydon immediately transformed, dropping his cocky act. "The power changed *instantly*," Aizlewood recalls. "John Lydon, the man who'd taken over the awards ceremony, and who is so intimidating, suddenly turned into this pussycat. He wasn't trying to work with her like Elvis Costello was. But he was very, very polite."

Back down in the main room, Radiohead/Beck producer Nigel Godrich was another individual unashamedly seeking an opportunity to get creatively involved with Kate. "I'm in awe of her," he said. "Her records fundamentally enforced what I am as a person. When you listen to stuff as a teenager, you identify with elements in the music. There's a real hidden wisdom there. It's beautifully written. If she needs anyone to mix her new album, I'm after the job."

John Aizlewood, meanwhile, grabbed a few last words from Bush. She told him that her proudest achievement of 2001 had been "giving up smoking." She confessed that the last record she'd bought had been for Bertie: "Bob the Builder. Not the Mambo thing, the one before that—whatever it's called [*'Can We Fix It?'*]." She said that "a few of us" were now heading off for "a little drink," but she wouldn't say where.

Ultimately, for all of its rollercoasting emotional effects upon her, John Aizlewood felt that, in the end, Bush very much enjoyed her day at the *Q* Awards.

"The situation spiraled out of control—first badly, and then amazingly well," he concludes. "So she was totally out of her comfort zone.

"But she was the absolute star of the show, by simply being there, and by simply being Kate Bush. And she absolutely loved it. I think it was a really big thing for her to be seen and to interact in public. But there is also no way she could have left that building feeling unloved or unappreciated. And I think, too, without any evidence whatsoever, that it was something that did help her creative process. Because she did feel that her work was loved and that she could go on.

"She understood, I think, that people were excited about whatever she was going to do next."

39

A Sea and Sky of Honey

Aerial, *1996–2005*

"Would you like to see the studio?" Kate Bush wondered, before leading me outside and a couple of minutes' walk along her driveway, into the building where she'd just—finally—completed her first double album, *Aerial*.

As creative inner sanctums go, Bush's recording facility was an unfussy and compact set-up. Far from flashy, it was a modest, cozy, and private environment. In the blue/grey-walled control room lay the SSL mixing desk she'd used to record all of her albums from *The Sensual World* on. In the live room sat her grand piano, alongside a Celtic harp with half the strings missing, under an old poster for Lindsay Kemp's inspirational *Flowers* production lopsidedly pinned to the wall.

Other than Abbey Road, she hadn't used any commercial studios since she'd embarked upon the early-1980s odyssey that took her through London's top-flight recording rooms while making *The Dreaming*. At the same time, being closeted away since *Hounds of Love* had perhaps had its disadvantages.

Bush still remembered how anxious she'd felt when in 1985 she'd been asked by Peter Gabriel to sing alongside him on "Don't Give Up," his 1986 hit (and *So* album cut). Recorded at the latter's barn studio at his then-home, Ashcombe House in Somerset, its session had involved Kate apprehensively moving out of her safe zone.

"It was a gift to be given that song to sing," she emphasized to me. "But because I don't sing a lot in the presence of other people, I get really nervous. And I was really nervous when I did that. See, it's alright when I'm in my situation, my environment, I feel very relaxed."

It was clear why Bush felt at ease in her home studio in Berkshire. Despite being filled with state-of-the-art gear (some of it relocated from East Wickham Farm), it retained the feel of being a converted garage in her garden. She'd spoken earlier of the "quiet space" that authors often need "in the shed" to focus on their work. And here we were in Kate Bush's shed, effectively, where she'd ensconced herself for the past few years.

Aerial was conceived, Bush said, very much as an extended *Hounds of Love*, the album of which she was most proud. But while that record, released twenty years earlier, had run to forty-seven minutes, this latest record was only two seconds shy of eighty minutes long. She'd resolved to split *Aerial* into two discs, the first seven songs under the banner of "A Sea of Honey," followed by the conceptual piece, "A Sky of Honey."

"I thought, 'Wouldn't it be nice? Double album . . .' It gives people something to really get their teeth into. And also, I used to really like the double albums I bought of artists that I loved.

It was somehow more of an artistic statement. I wanted it to feel like a nice object, something that had pictures and a story."

If there was perhaps less mystery to Kate Bush than might have been expected, her music remained a curious alchemy of the humdrum and the otherworldly. *Aerial* found Bush marveling in the magic of the everyday: the wind animating a shirt hanging on a clothes line, the trace of footprints leading into the sea, the indecipherable codes of birdsong.

Work on the album had picked up pace from 2002 onward when her son Bertie had started school and Bush regained some of her daytime hours. I asked her if she'd accelerated creatively by the end?

"'Accelerate' . . . that's a bit too strong a word," she grinned. "Once I'd really made the decision that a double album was what I wanted to do, I thought I needed to contact the record company to see that they felt that it was something that they could go with from [their] point of view. Which normally I wouldn't do. Normally I would only present the finished work to them.

"But what I didn't want to happen was to [start making] a double album, which obviously meant a lot more work, and then either them turn around and say, 'Sorry, we can't put out a double album,' or say, 'Okay, it's a double album,' but then put it in the shops at some really extortionate price. I didn't want people to have to pay a lot for it."

EMI were, of course, more than amenable to releasing a Kate Bush double album. And so, work began in earnest. But making an album at home didn't prove any easier than it had been on her past records.

"Some of these tracks, they were so difficult," she admitted. "What I wanted to try to get right this time was the basic arrangements of the tracks, to get the actual bones right before building on top of it. Some of them we redid three or four times."

Once again, the main problems stemmed from communication: explaining to the musicians exactly how she sonically imagined the tracks.

"It gets difficult when you think, 'Oh God, is it me? Is it that I'm not communicating what I want properly? Or is it that they don't get it?' Of course, you're full of self-doubt and then you think, 'Oh, maybe the track's not any good.' I mean, like, 'Sunset' was really, really difficult to get the basic track together. We did it loads of times. And even now, although it's okay, it's still not really what I heard in my head. But it *kind of* did it."

For *Aerial*, Bush reassembled familiar cast members from her previous albums: drummer Stuart Elliott, who by this stage had played on every one of her records since *The Kick Inside* ("He's a bit like my lucky mascot now," she said), her brother Paddy on backing vocals, Del Palmer engineering and playing bass, Danny McIntosh providing guitar parts.

There were some new faces—Lol Creme (10cc/Godley & Creme) sang with her on "π" and "Nocturn," Gary Brooker (Procol Harum) played organ or sang on three tracks, including the duet chorus of "Somewhere in Between." But nevertheless the core of her creative operation involved people long-known to her.

"I think with musicians, y'know, trying to communicate something to somebody, you have to use sort of silly terminology sometimes in order to get them to know what you mean," she explained. "What's nice, say, for instance, working with Stuart is there's a communication there and we have a laugh. There's a sense of being at play as well as at work. I think that's very important because it is so hard and so frustrating trying to get an idea to materialize. I really like working with people that are old friends."

But could she—if she was forced to—make an album with an entirely new team?

"Well, I suppose if I had to," she responded. "I mean, I do work with new musicians, and I think that's important too because you've got to keep moving and changing, haven't you? You can't just work with the same people all the time, or it gets a bit stagnant, I guess. Potentially, anyway."

Being aware that any enquiries into her and Del Palmer's separation of more than ten years previous would likely prompt her use of the "too personal" card, I instead asked her if she'd had to think twice about maintaining their working relationship?

"Um, I don't know, really," she replied, warily. "No, I don't think so because he's just like an old friend, y'know. Working with Del, there's a very relaxed feeling. I don't feel self-conscious with him there and in some ways it's almost like he's not there. Now, I mean, that could sound rude, but that's not how I mean it. He doesn't interfere with what is a very vulnerable process. I feel confident, I suppose, is the big thing. And for somebody who's so headstrong, I'm actually quite self-conscious about a lot of my process."

Was it a bit like when a couple divorce and they both see the kids? They both saw the music?

"I don't know," she laughed. "I've never really thought about it that way. To me, he's just an old friend and we work together. What's good is I'm not surrounded by people who are sycophants. Danny is very critical of my work and Del is very critical . . . supportive but critical . . . and I think that's fantastic.

"I mean, it's utter hell sometimes, but you need people who are challenging and questioning what you're doing. A lot of people who become successful are just totally surrounded by people who say yes to them all the time. Which I mean, for me, would be like a living nightmare.

"But you almost can't rely on what other people say," she further reflected. "You can't please other people. You have to go with an internal voice."

~

Aerial began with "King of the Mountain," the first song Kate had written for the album. Its lyric explored the idea that Elvis Presley was alive and well and living in some remote, snowy, elevated location. More significantly, it was someone who'd had myths built around her, writing about another individual who'd had even greater myths built around him. It was essentially a song about fame.

"There's only three or four people who've been as famous as Elvis," Bush reckoned. "You've got Elvis, you've got Frank Sinatra . . . even Marilyn Monroe, I think it probably happened more after she died. But Sinatra and Elvis lived these lives that . . . I mean . . . I can't imagine what it must have been like.

"What a horrible nightmare. Particularly for somebody like Elvis. Because the impression I get was that he was fun-loving and just happened to be really gorgeous and sexy and talented. And I think, y'know, partly why people respond to him the way they do—and I really feel strongly about this—is that people [sense] an *intention* from somebody, whether it's an actor or a singer. People felt that Elvis was a really genuinely sweet person and that's why everybody loves him so much. Not that I know a great deal about Elvis, but I thought he was a very beautiful-looking man with a fantastic voice and this fun-loving quality where you see he's up there kind of taking the piss out of himself."

I said I'd recently re-watched Presley's 1970 Vegas-era documentary, *That's the Way It Is*, and it had struck me that it often must have been a real laugh being Elvis.

"Well, I hope it was. What I see is somebody who was a sweetheart in the truest sense, just being eaten alive. To be as famous as he was . . . how could anybody survive that and still be a human being? I see him as being destroyed really by the fact that he was so famous. So I just love the idea of him being alive somewhere, away from all the people and the greed and the wanting to take him over."

Next in the *Aerial* track list came "π," in which she sang whole segments of the infinite mathematical constant, investing such passages as "5-0-2-8-8-4-1-9 . . ." with genuine emotion and going some way to proving that Kate Bush could indeed probably sing the phonebook.

"I thought, 'Wouldn't it be fun to see if I could sing numbers as if you *really* mean it,'" she said. "Just the idea of, like, *nine* being something that has a tremendous amount of feeling about it."

Then, in the madrigal-flavored "Bertie," with its Renaissance instrumentation, Bush had produced likely the most unusual outpouring of unconditional love toward a child ever recorded. "Oh, do you think?" she said, genuinely surprised. "Oh well, that's nice. I wouldn't have wanted it to be sort of over-sentimental."

Elsewhere, being an album made at home, *Aerial* was a record very much informed in parts by domesticity. The haunting piano balladry of "Mrs. Bartolozzi" was the one track that best bridged the divide between Bush's domestic and creative existences. In it, the housewife character of the title drifted off into a nostalgic reverie while watching her and her absent partner's clothes entwining through the porthole of her washer-dryer.

But it was also the song set to polarize opinion among listeners, with its sparse, eerie, slightly unhinged chorus repeating the words "washing machine." Bush anticipated as much.

"A couple of people who heard it early on, they either really liked it, or they found it very uncomfortable. I liked the idea of it being a very small subject. Clothes are such a strong part of who a human being is. Y'know, skin cells, the smell. In a way you could kind of (*gesturing to the floor*) put out a T-shirt, a pair of jeans and a pair of socks and you've almost got a person there, haven't you?"

There also seemed to be an intangible air of grief about "Mrs. Bartolozzi."

"That's interesting too because at no point is it saying there's a bereavement," Bush smiled. "Somebody thought that maybe there'd been this murder going on. I thought that was great. I love the ambiguity.

"I suppose one reason people found it personal is because it's so raw, and it's just a piano and a voice, done at the same time. It's a live performance. It's not something that's been cut around, like you would normally to get the best pieces. It's a bit brave, because there're [parts of the vocal] in there I don't like— (*laughs*) which, for me, is being brave."

How many times did she have to record it?

"I can't remember really. I don't think that many because, quite often, I'm up against time limitations. When you're doing something like that, you're thinking, 'How long is the piano going to stay in tune?' I know some people keep piano tuners on site, so that every three or four goes, the piano tuner comes in and tightens it up a bit. Which I don't do. So I could only go for as long as the piano didn't sound like an old pub piano."

In "How to Be Invisible"—the track that was later adopted by Bush as the title of her 2018 book of collected lyrics—she constructed a tongue-in-cheek incantation over a skipping beat and chopped-up art rock guitars. At the song's close, she uncannily transformed her layered voices into the sound of an eerie wind blowing.

Remembering the story that Bush had first found Peter Reich's "Cloudbusting"-inspiring *A Book of Dreams* in 1976 when rooting around in Watkins, the occult book shop off London's Charing Cross Road, I jokily wondered if she'd maybe also found an actual dusty old tome called *How to Be Invisible* there?

"You'll never know, will you?" she laughed.

Where did that idea come from then?

"Y'know, that was funny, that one," she said. "I had this old keyboard idea that I'd put down, (*sings*) 'Du du du dah dah dah.' We were getting a bit short of [material] for the single song disc and I was looking around to see if I could find anything. And I came across that and I thought, 'Well, actually, that's quite interesting. Maybe I should try to do something with that.' Then I just went out and tried some ideas lyrically and vocally and it just kind of came. I sort of worry that that track's a little bit obvious . . . I dunno . . ."

I said I thought it could be a single, actually.

"Do you? Mmn."

She clearly wasn't convinced. I told her I suddenly felt like some dude from EMI, getting "the look."

"(*Laughs*) No, I love the guitars on that. I think they're fantastic."

Was it fair, I ventured, to describe the next track, "Joanni," as an electronic folk song?

"I don't know," Bush said. "I mean, I dumped that. Again, we were short of a track—this was much later in the process—and I was thinking, 'Was there something?' And it just suddenly came into my mind. One morning, I thought, 'Oh! I never did anything with that track.' We put it up and I thought, 'Actually that's not bad.'"

What was the attraction for her to the song's subject, Joan of Arc?

"I'm not quite sure, because it wasn't really her initially, and it sort of turned into Joan. I think she's a fascinating idea, isn't she? And so tragic. Again, you get the sense of this real sweetheart among it all, basically just being . . . well, murdered.

"I suppose [it's] the idea that she's married to God. She thought she was there to do God's work. Which, again, I find very touching. And so brave. I mean, in some ways, not that I'm saying she was like Jesus, but you almost get that sense of that Garden of Gethsemane image, where she's asking, 'Look, get me out of here.'"

She was also, I pointed out, a woman apparently filled with visions leading an army of men. Did that sound familiar? Or was that taking it too far?

"Yeah, it probably is a bit . . ."

~

Aerial's second disc, the forty-two-minute-long "A Sky of Honey," was themed around light and color and charted the progress of one day, from late afternoon, through to the sunrise of the next. While I called it a song suite, Bush struggled for a term to describe the lengthy piece.

"I don't know what you'd call it. We used to call it the concept. Because as a working title, what do you say? You can't keep saying, Oh, the *suite*. What do you call it? My rock opera! It's so naff, isn't it?"

One of the standout features of "A Sky of Honey" was birdsong, much of which had been recorded in the garden outside. Bush had then listened to the results and "transcribed" them in her own voice, for the bird and human duets in "Aerial Tal" and the closing title track.

"I've always liked wood pigeons," she said. "That was quite easy because that's quite simplistic actually, isn't it? It's an easy shape. But the blackbird, that was tricky. Because it is intricate. It was trying to think, 'What in our language is in any way comparable to birdsong?' I thought about that a lot and the only thing that seemed to have a sort of natural connection is the way we laugh. There is something strangely connected in the shapes.

"I have a great association with times of day being connected to birdsong," she added. "For instance, the obvious thing, like the dawn chorus. And whenever I hear wood pigeons, I just think of a sunny afternoon. Then there're the songs that blackbirds sing when it's sunset as the light's starting to go down.

"It's like they're keyed into the light. It's almost like they're kind of vocalizing light. And it's just the idea that it obviously is a language which we don't understand. But there is a language there because they're communicating to each other. Obviously, a lot of it is, like, (*Cockney tone*), 'Fuck off! This is my spot.' We presume. I mean, we don't really know. But, there's a bit of an assumption about that. And obviously, 'Cor, you're a bit of alright!'"

In "An Architect's Dream," Bush depicted a pavement artist trying to capture an image before the light changed, or the rain washed his creation away. "Yeah, we're all working against that one, aren't we?" she laughed.

(On the original version of *Aerial*, the role of the painter in the spoken word introduction of the song, and in "The Painter's Link," was played by Rolf Harris. Following his 2014 conviction for indecent assault, however, the part was re-recorded, without any explanation necessary, by Bertie McIntosh for the 2018 remastered release.)

"A Sky of Honey" was a meditative work designed to gently hypnotize the listener. But in its final run of songs—the shadowy unknowns of the crepuscular hilltop views in "Somewhere in Between"; the sheer delight of swimming in the ocean, under a blanket of stars, conveyed in "Nocturn"—it became increasingly groove-driven. By its ending, with the four-to-the-floor bass drum punch of "Aerial," it turned decidedly rave-like, as the sun rose, in the most ecstatic of Kate Bush's songs.

～

The day before we met, Bush, Danny McIntosh, and a few unnamed friends had stood around a radio, waiting to hear the BBC Radio 2 debut airing of "King of the Mountain," her first single release in eleven years.

"Just to see what it sounded like as much as anything," she explained. "Sometimes [tracks] sound really bad on the radio. They might sound a bit quiet, which is always the worst thing because that means people will perceive it as being weak against the track before and after. So it's nice to hear what it sounds like."

Did she feel proud, then, hearing a new song of hers beaming over the airwaves after all this time?

"I don't know if I was proud," she averred, "but it was exciting to think that there was something being played on the radio. It's been a long time and really hard work making the record and it feels like that's the completion of the puzzle almost. The last piece of the jigsaw puzzle is it going out into the airways. The response was really genuinely touching.

"Obviously, the big worry is that people are going to go, 'Oh, is that it?' I was very worried that people would think it was an anticlimax."

Ultimately, with its release on November 7, 2005, *Aerial* was assessed by critics and fans alike as one of the great creative peaks of Kate Bush's career: second only, perhaps, in most minds, to *Hounds of Love*. Reviewers were generally effusive with praise (even if some admitted to being a touch baffled at points by its quirkier elements).

The Observer stated that *Aerial* was the work of "an artist supremely articulate in the language of experimental pop music . . . who because she is sincere and can communicate her odd and unpredictable vision in both words and through sumptuous music, occupies a cherished and indulged position in the culture."

The Independent declared, "Kate Bush [is] still operating at the cutting-edge of intelligent adult pop, every bit as relevant now as at any point in her career. Just a bit weirder, thank heavens."

The *Sunday Times* proclaimed, "*Aerial* is extraordinary: baffling, uncategorisable, monumental, exhilarating."

Alongside the reviews, various contemporary pop stars or more left-field artists were vox-popped for their opinions of Bush—which ranged from hilariously banal to insightful—and her relevancy to the music scene of 2005.

"I think she is still relevant," said Mutya Buena from the Sugababes. "It's nice to see people reinvent themselves. She was a great performer and a great singer. I like that song, you know the one, 'It's me, I'm Cathy . . .' I think our older fans like her music."

"Of course she's still relevant," argued Katie Melua. "Y'know, she's a musician."

"I think she's a genius," said Alison Goldfrapp. "I love her because she is nothing to do with fashion . . . she's so self-contained. My favorite album is *Hounds of Love*. It's the ultimate concept album. I took a lot of drugs listening to that album, mainly E. So much so that when I listen to it now, I can start to feel sick very quickly."

"Her music sounds religious to me," said Tricky. "She should be treasured more in this country than The Beatles. She can and does walk away from everything, and not make albums, and I respect her for that. Just to live your life and not play the game . . . to me, that's success."

～

As the noise surrounding Kate Bush continued to rise in pitch and volume once again, she insisted to me, six weeks ahead of the album's release, that—even though she'd been slightly nervous about hearing how "King of the Mountain" sounded on the radio—she wasn't worried whatsoever about the commercial performance of *Aerial* (which, in the end, reached UK number three).

"No, I don't think that's ever really mattered to me too much," she offered, genuinely. "The most important thing for me is that it's interesting from a creative point of view. And the reaction that I've had to particularly the second disc, already that's been enough to have made it all worthwhile.

"Someone said to me the other day—I mean, it is a sort of friend, so I suppose they've got to say something nice anyway—but they said, 'Oh, it's not like listening to a record. It's like watching a film.' And I thought, 'Oh, that's great, I love that.' And if it doesn't sell and it bombs, just *that* is enough. What a great thing to say. I feel totally fulfilled as an artist and I can now move on *(laughs)*."

40

"A Coral Room"

From **Aerial,** *2005*

For someone who'd gained a reputation for taking an age to make albums, some of Kate Bush's greatest recordings were achieved in a single take. "Wuthering Heights" was one. Another was the beautiful, mysterious and moving "A Coral Room."

The spine-tingling stand-out track on *Aerial* came at the end of its first disc, "A Sea of Honey." "A Coral Room" was a piano-and-vocal ballad that Bush admitted she'd first considered too personal for release, dealing as it did with the death of her mother. But by returning to what she called "an old process" of writing alone at the piano (rather than building up a track with beatboxes and keyboards), the reflections in the song were all the more affecting, given that they employed the very adult song-writing skills first developed by the teenage Cathy Bush.

It felt as if the listener was eavesdropping on an extremely private moment, as Kate summoned memories of her mother and her family life, walking in her mind back into the kitchen at East Wickman Farm years before, as she'd previously done in the lyric of "Warm and Soothing."

"It wasn't intentional at the time," she told me of the similar scenes that featured in both songs. "But it's exactly the same sentiment being revisited."

"A Coral Room," however, opens on the image of a drowned city: the tops of its skyscrapers covered in fishing nets, whose sub-aquatic movement Bush seems to mimic in the second half of the first verse, as she slides between the notes and slurs her words, as if they're being swept along by the undertow.

Clearly some kind of cataclysmic event has taken place. The flooding was apparently sudden, causing planes to nose-dive into this new ocean.

But it soon became apparent that this was really a song about the passing of time, imagining a future world, centuries on. People still existed on the water above the sunken city, zipping around on fast boats that might appear in the wider picture to be in flight over the submerged towers.

In many ways, "A Coral Room" could be viewed as almost a sequel to, or a continuation of the ideas explored in "Moments of Pleasure." The hills of time metaphor in "Moments . . ." has transmuted into the spider of time, depicted by Bush to be crawling over the underwater buildings, their fishing net-covered peaks appearing web-like. The singer places the listener on a boat and instructs them to dip their fingers into the water and then asks them what they feel (both physically and emotion-ally, it has to be assumed, although it's never made explicit).

"I suppose really the image I had in my head," Bush said, "was this idea of somebody putting their hand over the side of this boat and down into the water and feeling the top of this city. It's this connection with somebody from the future reaching down and touching the past."

But it's the almost filmic transition from this widescreen scene into Bush's domestic image of her mother, laughing and holding a brown jug in their kitchen, that precedes the most powerful moment. Before it arrives, her mother sings—via Kate's vocal and then that of classical tenor Michael Wood—the old nineteenth-century American drinking ditty "Little Brown Jug," which it's easy to imagine once resounding through the air of the folky Bush household: a song originally about alcoholism that had become through the years something more joyful and childlike.

But then the jug falls from her mother's hands in slow-motion, and as the piano chords tumble down along with it, the singer's voice turns hopelessly sad.

"I suppose it's that whole Zen thing of the broken glass," she said. "If you have an object, it will break. It's got to at some point, hasn't it? How can it not? So it was just playing with this idea of putting this little spider of time and this object together."

As the song nears its conclusion, the spider returns and crawls out of the shattered jug and keeps moving. The years rush by and the house is sunk underwater, and the coral takes over.

"That's what life is, isn't it? Change," Bush reasoned. "Life is change and it's just moving, and we come and go, and it keeps moving.

"I mean, everything's gonna change. We're all gonna die. (*Laughs and mock-screams*) We're all gonna die!!

"And I suppose that's the spiritual thing, isn't it? Appreciating living now and what you've got because, y'know, it's not going to be there forever."

I admitted to Bush that "A Coral Room" gave me the shivers.

"Oh well, that's nice . . . I *think*," she smiled. "Nice shivers or . . .?"

Spooked a bit as well.

"Spooky shivers . . ." she said, in a thoughtful tone that made you think that this was not a bad reaction to have to "A Coral Room" at all.

41

Guest Testimony

Guido Harari

"I first met Kate in 1982. She appeared so self-assured and fearless on stage and in her videos, yet off stage she was this quiet creature, all big, heart-warming smiles and soft-spoken. But you could tell she had balls of steel.

"I'd just completed a photo book with her mentor, Lindsay Kemp. When I showed it to her, she was totally enthralled by it and agreed to be photographed by me. At the time, she was promoting "The Dreaming" at a TV show in Italy along with dancers Douglas McNicol and Gary Hurst. Gary had collaborated with her since the Tour of Life, and Douglas I knew very well since he was one of the most creative members of Kemp's company.

"After the show, they came back to the hotel in their ship-wrecked astronaut gear and accepted not only to pose for me, but to actually improvise statuesque positions. Working with Lindsay had really spoiled me, and it seemed I was taking for granted that

Kate and the others would 'perform' for my camera as easily as he had done, but luckily, they did, and ever so wildly.

"Then, three years later, Kate called me to shoot her official press pictures for *Hounds of Love* and that's when our collaboration really took off. When we first gathered at her house in Kent before the shoot, I expected some kind of brief. But curiously enough she was always very open to my ideas. She'd give me the space and the time to create in a very organic way.

"I felt very much challenged because of the wild imagery of her concerts and videos. I wondered how I could raise the bar and create something different, but Kate immediately made it clear that she didn't want to work with dark concepts or elaborate sets. She simply said, 'Please do what you did with Lindsay.' That was to be the rule and the aim for our shoots.

"She'd done it all with Gered Mankowitz over the first two albums with the dancing, the leotards and the glamorous Hollywood clichés. Gered's images were more structured as he drew from elements in her early videos and concerts. He really defined Kate's identity in the early days and brilliantly so. She wanted to move away from that. We didn't have props or wild outfits at hand, just a bunch of backdrops, studio lights, and plenty of time.

"Kate's very loose approach to our photos made for some kind of instant complicity. We didn't have much verbal communication during the shoots. I don't recall lunch breaks and there was no music playing in the background to create any kind of mood. We were, so to speak, psychically hooked on the creative process, and she never vetoed any of my suggestions. Mind you, we knew these photographs would be disposable, fed to the press by her record company, so the aim was to come up with 'beautiful' photos with no major concepts. But here and there I managed to sneak in a few pre-Photoshop 'tricks' [*multi-exposure effects, sub-aquatic-looking backgrounds*] that made some of the images more interesting and certainly unusual, and she loved it. I think her strong sense of visual identity may have to do with having been photographed by her brother John since she was a child.

"Me, I was very much a devoted fan of Kate since day one and was over the moon for having this incredible opportunity not only to photograph her, but to collaborate on her official images. Photography for me is about establishing and deepening a relationship and having the camera record its dynamics. But what's most important is the relationship. Kate trusted me and that was enough to put me at ease and be in the moment. It was very much a 'feel' process.

"Kate didn't put on any 'mask' during our shoots. She may have slipped into a 'Kate Bush' pose or expression, but it all felt spontaneous and direct, and lots of fun too. It had to be real, and it had to be fun. This is why in my *The Kate Inside* book [*published by Wall of Sound Gallery, 2016*], I decided to present my photos in sequences that could give an idea of the dynamics of the shoots. Something that not many photographers like to show. They'd rather go for their iconic images. But during a shoot there's so much going on that will show the real person and also tell a lot about who the photographer is. Those are the images I love the best.

"Our photo shoots were twelve- or fifteen-hour-long marathons. It's impossible to sustain your subject's interest for such a long time, but we had quite a few very inspired moments that I'm very fond of. The only thing I can say is that when I look at my pictures of Kate, I see the person, not the icon."

42

"I Obviously Have a Very Recognizable Nose"

A conversation about the past twenty years, 2006

In 2006, the now-sadly-defunct *Q* magazine celebrated its twentieth anniversary. To mark the occasion, a special issue was put together involving twenty individual covers featuring twenty different artists.

As well as being a bit of a marketing gimmick, it was an opportunity for *Q* to demonstrate its pulling power at the time, since the issue featured new interviews with, among others, Paul McCartney, Madonna, U2, Keith Richards, David Bowie, Pete Townshend, David Gilmour, Paul Weller, Beyoncé, Dave Grohl, Britney Spears, and Jimmy Page.

Most of these chats were presented as light-hearted question and answer sessions, often posing the same (or similar) queries to all of the artists, and generally focusing on the past twenty years. Kate agreed to get involved, and so on May 28, 2006, we had a chat on the phone.

How are you?

"I'm very well, thank you."

Where are you right now?

"I'm at home, near London, in my front room, having a cup of tea."

At the _Q_ Awards in 2001, you received a standing ovation from the likes of Elvis Costello, Brian Eno and Radiohead. Did it take you aback?

"Yeah. I was knocked out. It was just a fantastic moment for me, it really was. You're standing in a room of your peers, but there's something about that that is so much more touching somehow. I suppose because a lot of artists, like myself, are musical snobs. I think we're quite hard on each other in this country as well and the feeling that was coming off everybody was so warm. It blew me away.

"It was a fantastic thing for me too because at that point I was still struggling away with making this album [_Aerial_] that was supposedly meant to be coming out and had already taken far too long. I knew it was still going to be quite a long while before it was finished. And it was almost like I felt people were sort of saying, y'know, 'Yeah, stick with it.' That really helped me feel good about the fact that I knew I was going to have to be working on this album for so much longer. It does make you feel confident.

"There is always this worry when things take such a long time, which they always do with me. I start hitting this point about . . . ooh . . . it's normally about two or three years in, but with this one it was probably about (_laughs_) seven or eight. You're thinking, 'God, everybody's just going to forget me.' So it really meant a lot to me. It was fabulous. Magic, really."

You and John Lydon seemed very happy to see each other. Some people were surprised that you got on quite so well.

"Well, we already knew each other. We're friends, really. I don't see a lot of John, but we've known each from the sort of early- to mid-1980s. He used to come round, and we'd go out for dinner with him and [his wife] Nora. We were quite pally for a while. I don't think we're that different, really. I think John is one of those people who's a brilliant actor and I mean that with the greatest of respect. He's a true showman. Everybody loves John and he's a very intelligent man."

What were you doing twenty years ago?

"Oh my God! 1986? That would've been when I was asked by the guy at the record company to put out a greatest hits album [*The Whole Story*]. Which I thought was completely naff. I thought it was such a crap idea and I said, 'No, no way.' He went away and came back with all this research he'd done and presented it to me again and he just completely won me over. So I said, 'Oh, okay then, let's do it.' And, of course, it ended up being my biggest-selling record. It went back up to number one twice. I just thought, 'How brilliant that he persuaded me to do it, because I was so against it.'"

***Hounds of Love* had also gone top thirty in the US album chart the previous year. Most artists would have toured and promoted it endlessly, but you didn't. Why?**

"Well, it's typical sort of me really, isn't it? I suppose America and I have never really seen eye to eye. Even still I would love to be a big, well-known act in America. But I'm not and I'm not really prepared to do the touring and TV shows. I suppose in some ways I've always been worried that it would take my soul away. It's very important to me that I'm a little person who works and I'm not like a big star.

"The reason that went in [at number thirty] was because of the twelve-inch version that we did of 'Running Up That Hill,' which was very popular in the clubs. I did go over to the States at that time and did my version of what I considered 'pushing it.' But I suppose sitting in a hotel room with a cup of tea talking to some journalists probably didn't quite do what they'd expected."

That was maybe the first real indication that international success wasn't top of your agenda . . .
"Well, I had had opportunities to go to the States before that. We did the tour in 1979, [and] when it was all over, it was then mooted [that I] go to the States with it. But by that point I was too exhausted to pick it all up and go off with it again. And I've been incredibly lucky to have a fantastically loyal audience across Europe, so I can manage to keep working without needing to break places like the States."

What car were you driving twenty years ago?
"A little red convertible Golf, if I remember rightly."

Did you own a mobile?
"Yes, I did and it was the size of a fridge. I remember everybody just taking the piss out of me continually."

What's your high point of the past twenty years?
"Well, it's got to be having my son, Bertie."

And the low point?

"My mum dying. In a way, that's not a low point. That was like the end of the world."

Which song of the past twenty years do you wish you'd written?

"'The Boy in the Bubble.' I like a lot of Paul Simon's stuff, really. He's got a fabulous voice, but really his forte is poetry."

Who's your favorite artist of the past twenty years?

"I like Antony [*now Anohni*] of Antony and the Johnsons. I think [she's] brave and I like that. And I like . . . um . . ."

Tori Amos?

(*Silence*)

Just joking.

"(*Laughs*) As you could hear, I took a deep breath there. Who else? Mr. Boombastic, I liked him."

Shaggy?

"Yeah, Shaggy! I liked him! (*Dissolves into giggles*)."

What's your biggest fashion disaster of the past twenty years?

"Oh my God! The binbag I wore last Sunday."

What's the single biggest thing that's changed in your life?

"It's got to be Bertie. It's one of those clichés, but it's really changed my life. All for the better. And more."

Is fame a pain in the arse?

"I think it's a double-edged sword, really, isn't it? Purely from my personal point of view, without it, I wouldn't have been able to do what I wanted creatively. So that's been incredibly important to me because it is such a big part of who I am. It does make my life a bit difficult, but I think I'm extremely privileged to have such a loyal audience who still want to buy my stuff. I have a nice life. I feel really lucky."

How often are you recognized in the street?

"Well, I find it surprising because it's always when you don't think people might recognize you that they do. Like, if I'm wrapped up and all that's showing is maybe just my nose or something. I obviously have a very recognizable nose."

Do people still come up to you in the supermarket?

"Yes, they do, but not as much as they used to. They sort of smile from a distance now, whereas before they would actually come up and put their hands on you . . . a touchy feely sort of thing. I tell you what I do feel sometimes is I feel really moved. Sometimes people's reactions in shops and stuff can be quite overwhelming. But that's not *me*, that's my music. Years ago, when I was in the supermarket, this young black girl came up and said, 'You wrote that song that Maxwell sang [*"This Woman's Work"*],' and I thought that was so great."

Your favorite drug of the past twenty years?

"Oh, definitely caffeine. I drink so much tea. Some days I must probably drink about twenty cups."

Have you tried decaf?

"Yes. It doesn't do it for me."

Your best and worst haircut?

"I've had the same haircut since I was about five, I think. One of the best letters I got in the big void when I was making *Aerial* was from an irate fan who was saying, 'Why does it take you so long to make albums? And you haven't changed your image for twenty years . . . get your hair cut!'"

The *Q* review of *Aerial* imagined you "in a cobwebbed stately home, brandishing a candelabra, looking for fairies." Sound like your typical day?

"They've got a camera in here, haven't they? Most of the time now my typical day is school run, violin homework . . . I'm coming back into the real world again, having got the album behind me. I've got more free time now than I have had for quite a long time. Just the past couple of months, really. I've watched more films in the past couple of months than I have for years. I'm catching up. *Life Is Beautiful, King Kong* . . ."

What have you been up to post-*Aerial*?

"Well, because I'm very hands-on with what I do, it wasn't really until post-Christmas that everything quietened down. I was really exhausted, actually, and I felt quite run down. Now I'm at a really great point again and though I'm not actively doing anything about it yet, I'm thinking about ideas for projects. As we all know, that's a slow process [for me]. But the thought of actually going in and doing something that's not a track on *Aerial* is so exciting."

Were you disappointed that Il Divo's *Ancora* and Westlife's *Face to Face* kept *Aerial* off number one?
"How can I compete with an audience like they've got? They're so mainstream. But if you think that I was away for . . . oh, I've forgotten how long now. . ."

It had been twelve years since *The Red Shoes* . . .
"So, for it to go straight in at three, I think that's absolutely bloody brilliant. And a number-four hit single [with 'King of the Mountain']. I think a lot of people had totally written me off as being a singles artist. I was really chuffed with that."

What's the best thing you've bought in the past two decades?
"I bought that lovely painting that went in the *Aerial* cover ['Fishermen and Boat' by James Southall]. I saw it in London in a window as we were driving past. Just in a flash it caught my eye and I got Danny to drive back so I could jump out and see what it was. I was besotted."

You've only released three new albums in the past twenty years. Do you wish you'd made more?
"Oh, don't! That's not true, is it? I think of *Aerial* as a double, though. It takes me four years on average. I sort of wish I'd made more, but it is what it is, isn't it? It's not so much I wish I'd made more . . . I wish they hadn't taken so long to make. Then I could have had lots of holidays in the Bahamas in-between them. Every time I start an album I think, 'Right, this one I'm going to make really quickly and I'm going to just shock everybody.' Then something just seems to happen in my life and

before I know it, it's taken me so much longer than I would ever have dreamt of. Sometimes that is a bit depressing, really."

Can we realistically expect to wait twelve years for another album?
"Oh, God. I hope not. I'm *sure* I can make the next one in six weeks."

Where will you be in twenty minutes?
"Probably in the toilet cause of all the tea."

43

"Among Angels"

Into the mystic, 1978–2011

On her tenth studio album, *50 Words for Snow*, released in 2011, Kate Bush in a sense circled back to the beginning of her career. It was a record with a deep focus on her piano playing, more so than on any long-player she'd made since *The Kick Inside*. At the same time, her sound had, of course, moved on, involving further elements of neoclassical and atmospheric jazz.

It was also an album filled with some of the most haunting— and haunted—characters she'd ever created, or investigated. The angular grooves and Asian keyboard figures of "Wildman" explored the Himalayan legend of the Yeti (also known, in keeping with the record's winter theme, as the Abominable Snowman): tracking sightings, feeling sympathy for the hunted creature, and even brushing away its footprints to protect it. "Snowed in at Wheeler Street" was a story of frustrated romance, as two characters slipped together through time and met at key points in history (Rome burning, London during WWII, New

York on 9/11), continually being torn apart by circumstances beyond their control. In addition, in a development that would likely have been inconceivable to the teenage Cathy Bush, ". . . Wheeler Street" saw her duetting with Elton John.

"Lake Tahoe," meanwhile, comprised eleven minutes of spectral scenes and choral eeriness. Aided by the classically trained voices of Stefan Roberts and Michael Wood, Kate returned to the unearthly preoccupations of "Wuthering Heights," her voice deepened with age, in this slowly unfurling piano ballad. Here a Victorian female ghost surfaced from the titular lake, looking like a water-damaged porcelain doll, and was reunited with her dog Snowflake in what might be an apparition of their former home. Free of any electronic interference, it provided a close-up of Bush's innate musicianship, while sounding like a far more experienced take on her debut album. It was as if, after all of the adventures in sound with drum machines and synths and effects, she'd reconnected with the Kate Bush of 1978.

Most intensely mysterious was "Among Angels," a stripped-back, piano, strings and vocal message of deep empathy, directed at an unnamed someone, that spoke of knowing the doubt and pain of everyday existence. The singer then appeared to gaze through the veil of reality and see shimmering angels around her friend, in a visual echo of the protective figures of "Lily." These unseen presences, she promised, would act as guides on life's ongoing journey. "Among Angels" was one of Bush's greatest songs and a beautiful expression of transcendence—a spiritual (but secular) hymn revealing deep beliefs.

But Kate was always reluctant or unwilling to talk about these elements of her writing, likely because she feared them being reduced to two-dimensional spookery.

"Do you believe in the paranormal?" Stuart Maconie asked her in Q magazine in 1993.

"Yes, I do," she replied.

"Is that it?" Maconie responded, surprised that that was all Bush wanted to say on the matter.

"Yes," she smiled.

Earlier in her career, the singer was a touch less guarded. In December 1978, on a promo stopover in Wellington, she was interviewed by David Young of the *New Zealand Listener*. Young picked up on what he felt were the "frequent references to the occult in her music," citing the mention of Beelzebub in "Kite" and even Cathy's desire to steal Heathcliff's soul in "Wuthering Heights."

"That's really interesting," she said. "That's an amazing thing about interviews, they really make you think. I am interested in the occult but not the negative side of it. I really don't know much about it. I believe we are controlled by forces . . . the moon and the stars."

~

The one arcane namecheck that was frequently picked up by fans and interviewers in Kate Bush's early days was that of George Gurdjieff in "Them Heavy People" on *The Kick Inside*. Gurdjieff was a philosopher, spiritual teacher and composer, born in Alexandropol at some indeterminate point between 1866 and 1877 (and dying in France in 1949). His Fourth Way doctrine combined the traditional religious beliefs of yogis (dedicated study), monks (ascetic devotion) and fakirs (physical endurance) to form a Westernized path to self-development and higher states of human consciousness.

The Russian mystic was much loved by a whole generation of 1960s and 1970s musicians, drawn to him during their search for something deeper than drug-induced mind expansion. It helped that Gurdjieff was himself a musician who believed in "inner octave" drones that were felt by humans at their emotional core. Some who discovered his writings, such as Richard Thompson (Fairport Convention) or Martin Stone (Mighty Baby) went on to dedicate themselves to Sufism (or Islamic mysticism). For others, it sparked a fascination with the esoteric. For King Crimson guitarist Robert Fripp—who in 1975 dropped out of music entirely for ten months to live at Sherborne House in Gloucestershire and enrol at J. G. Bennett's International Academy for Continuous Education, studying among others, Gurdjieff—his teachings represented discipline.

Kate was characteristically coy about her own interest in Gurdjieff. This was made uncomfortably clear on one occasion, when she was asked by a phone-in caller to explain more about him during a live radio interview with Gloria Hunniford, on BBC Radio 2, in September 1982:

> Gloria Hunniford: Jonathan Jenkins is on the line from Cornwall, from St Austell. Hello, Jonathan.
>
> Jonathan Jenkins: Hello, Gloria.
>
> GH: And what's your question to Kate Bush?
>
> JJ: Oh, hello, Kate.
>
> KB: Hello!
>
> JJ: Um, a couple of times you mentioned in your songs a person called Gurdjieff [*only once, actually, in "Them Heavy People"*]. I know a little about him. But I wonder if you could

explain what his beliefs are and how he influences you when you're making music?

KB: Well, Gurdjieff was really an influence in that I've just read some of his books. Really no more than that. I just found a lot of what he said interesting. That's really as far as it goes.

GH: Maybe we should elaborate a little bit about who the gentleman is?

KB: Yes, well, Gurdjieff was . . . well, he was considered a leader of a religious movement, I think. But as far as I know, he just had a lot of ideas about creating a way that would make people stronger and more together. And it's just a different way of doing it. And it was also trying to go for a more Western way of doing it. But I do know very little about it. So I really wouldn't like to say very much, because it's a subject that I feel, if I'm going to speak about, I should know what I'm talking about.

GH: It's obviously something you've cottoned on to, Jonathan?

KB: Yes (*laughs*).

GH: Are you interested in that side of it?

JJ: Well, a friend of mine mentioned him to me and I'd heard basically nothing about him, and I went to the local library and there was nothing there about him. Of course, Kate mentioned him in a few songs (*sic*). So I just wondered if she could inform me any more.

GH: (*Sounding keen to close down this line of enquiry*) Well, the influence was minimal by the sound of it.

KB: Yes, yes, it was. Yes.

GH: Tough luck, Jonathan, you picked out the wrong one.
(*Bush laughs*)
JJ: Not to worry. Thanks a lot.
GH: Thank you very much indeed for your call. Bye bye.
KB: Bye.

~

Later, in 1994, Bush was more engaging when she was interviewed by David Lynch-associated actress Laura Dern (*Blue Velvet, Wild at Heart*) for a *SPIN* magazine feature promoting *The Red Shoes*. It was at a time when celebrity head-to-heads were in vogue. Dern led the singer onto the subject of psychoanalysis.

"I've always wanted to ask you," she said, "if you have interests in the shadow side, in understanding the repressed self— things we are in denial about?"

"Creative art is an awfully positive way of channeling the shadow side," Bush offered, "and I think it's much more healthy to explore it and have fun with it within the boundaries of art. I'm not sure that it's something terribly good to go looking for. Do you know what I mean? I think it's actually something that ends up coming to you anyway."

~

In my experience of talking to Kate Bush, it was only when attempting to coax her toward a discussion about her interest in the otherworldly that she seemed to turn uncomfortable.

"Well, otherworldly, I don't know," she sighed. "What does that sum up? I'm not very comfortable with that actual term in a way. I think there is a lot more than the physical, material world. And I think we all live inside our heads. Although you have to live in the physical world . . . you can't escape that. We all live in here (*taps temple*), really, don't we?

"It's all to do with how we perceive things," she added. "There's all kinds of things that we pick up on and we might not recognize it. But we are very feeling, instinctive, intuitive creatures. And a lot of people feel uncomfortable with their intuitive side. And a lot of people feel very in tune with it. But I think we work on these different levels all the time. A lot of communication is not verbal . . . it's about feelings you get from people."

As much as there were intriguing mystical elements to her work, it was obvious that she didn't want them drawn into the cold light of an interview.

It wasn't difficult to understand why. Online, there's much in the way of speculation and deep discussion among her fans about the hidden significances of certain aspects of her output, not least her artwork. One theory has the honeyed sea-and-sky *Aerial* cover art as depicting a "golden dawn" (alluding to the late nineteenth-century and early twentieth-century occultist Golden Dawn sect). Another even views the seven-inch label design of "Breathing," where Bush's dancing figure is repeated in a circular pattern of connected limbs, as a direct reference to the Black Sun symbol associated with Nazi mysticism. Both of these examples show how it's dangerously easy to read too much into all of this stuff.

Appreciating that Bush clearly wasn't going to go into any great depth when it came to esoterica, I tried to carefully reverse out of the cul-de-sac of uneasy subject matter that we'd found ourselves in by mentioning I'd just been reading (or at least trying to get my head around) theoretical physicist Brian Greene's 1999 book, *The Elegant Universe,* about the "hidden dimensions" of string theory.

"They're up to eleven dimensions at the moment, aren't they?" she said, instantly proving herself to be no stranger to the subject. "But it's lateral and it's so *not* how we think that it's almost impossible to get a grasp of it, isn't it? But I think actually a lot of things are like that. We only think from a very narrow little corner."

44

Before and Beyond the Dawn

The view from Row T, Seat 34, 2014

As I emerged from Hammersmith underground station, my phone pinged with a text. I immediately had a choice—smoke the joint I'd pre-rolled or prepare myself to take copious notes for the four-page magazine live review I'd just been offered. In the end, I did both.

The previous evening, in a night filled with ovations, Bush had returned to live performance after a thirty-five-year absence. Ahead of this second show, internet froth had spilled many of the production secrets of Before the Dawn. Now, I felt, it was somehow my duty to try to go deeper.

After the jaw-dropping announcement on March 21, 2014, that Bush was to return to live performance, after the demented online scramble for tickets, after the social media whoops of delight and howls of despair from the lucky and not-so-lucky ticket baggers, after the months of brouhaha and build-up, after the hastily typed glowing opening-night reviews, there was this . . . Wednesday, August 27, the second night of the singer's staggeringly long twenty-two-show run at the Eventim Apollo.

Much had already been made, by fans and reviewers, of the absence of key early Kate Bush hits from the Before the Dawn show. You had to wonder if some presumed that she had been preserved in aspic since her last shows in 1979 and would appear pirouetting her way through "Wuthering Heights" or "Wow," as if time had never moved on.

But, in truth, very few were disappointed. Before the end of the almost three-hour show on the opening night, musician Anna Calvi and actress Gemma Arterton were whisked away to comment live on BBC Two's *Newsnight*.

"I think everyone that was there was so appreciative of how special this night was," said Arterton.

"It felt," said Calvi, "like being inside her mind."

The lavish £15 program on sale in the lobby of the Apollo—cover line: "The KT Fellowship Presents Before the Dawn"—revealed certain details previously hidden. It was the now-sixteen-year-old Bertie who'd encouraged his mother to stage Before the Dawn in the first place. The rehearsals were held in a "retired" school in an undisclosed rural location while set designers and costumiers and puppeteers worked in surrounding outbuildings.

Later, Kate would reveal to *MOJO* that her decision to commit to the shows came as a result of the fact that she'd released two albums in 2011 (*Director's Cut, 50 Words for Snow*). She hadn't then wanted to make another straight away, and suddenly "felt a real desire to have contact with the audience that still liked my work."

The former Hammersmith Odeon, setting for the final three dates of 1979's Tour of Life, was clearly something of a performance safe space for Bush. But, in the Before the Dawn programme, she detailed how she'd first considered putting this show on in a "really beautiful space . . . similar in size to an aircraft hangar." But ultimately—after seeing a small human figurine placed within a scale model of the huge venue—the idea of performing in such an expanse had made her feel "physically sick." And so the project had shifted to the medium-sized west London theater, made all the more intimate by the fact that the elaborate production—eighteen months in the planning—required the first four rows of seats to be removed to make way for an enlarged stage.

Two nights before the first show, on Sunday, August 24, there had been a full dress rehearsal at the Apollo, before a crowd of family, friends, kids and music industry personnel. Bush had reportedly appeared visibly nervous. There were stops and starts as some of the film projections refused to work. Only at the end was there the fulsome applause that would erupt time and time again on the opening night.

No details leaked from the dress rehearsal. But immediately after the curtain fell on the first night, the internet was awash with details or spoilers, depending on your perspective. In terms of songs, there was nothing from the four albums before *Hounds of Love*, and nothing from *The Sensual World* ("Never Be Mine" from the latter had been rehearsed but cut from the set due to an overlong running time; it would be reinstated on the 2016 *Before the Dawn* live album).

Outside the Eventim Apollo as I arrived on the second night, brilliantly and pointedly—since this was viewed by its creator as a theatrical presentation rather than a run of gigs—there was no evidence whatsoever to suggest that Kate Bush was actually performing there that evening. Instead, the marquee's signage was lit up with the red-lettered words "Before the Dawn" followed by "Sold Out." Fans milled around, some of them holding signs pleading for spare tickets.

Inside the auditorium, the stage was bathed in blue light as the audience took to their seats for the prompt 7.45 kick-off. If the reappearance of Kate Bush on stage the evening before had been greeted as something close to the Second Coming, then tonight in the 3,600-capacity theater there was a more muted atmosphere, a hushed air of anticipation.

There were likely some here who'd witnessed her last appearances at this venue, three-and-a-half decades before. There were perhaps some who had been there for her storming one-off performance of "Running Up That Hill" with David Gilmour at the Secret Policeman's Ball at the London Palladium in 1987, or even for her tentative surprise guest rendition of "Comfortably Numb" at the Pink Floyd guitarist's Royal Festival Hall gig in 2002. But chances were that this was the very first time most people here would have the opportunity to see and hear Kate Bush singing live and in the flesh.

The mood of quiet reverence was made explicit by the fact that even the male-voiced-message that came over the PA, asking us to turn off our phones, was met with an understanding cheer.

~

The next voice to be heard was that of Lily Cornford, Bush's late friend and spiritual healer, intoning the ancient Gayatri mantra that includes the words: "Unveil to us the face of the true spiritual sun / Hidden by a disc of golden light." As the band launched into the song "Lily," its arrangement closer to the 2011

Director's Cut remake than the 1993 original on *The Red Shoes*, a grinning Bush entered from stage left, with a procession of her backing vocalists. She then began singing, to reveal a voice that age and time had not withered in the slightest.

"Lily" was a bold and provocative opener. Its arcane lyrical qualities—the frightened, psychically damaged singer performing a protective, angel-summoning ritual within a "circle of fire"—led you to believe that it had been carefully chosen, and not just for its cooking groove. While she has always been reluctant to discuss her more esoteric interests, Kate Bush clearly believed she was making this space her own, on levels seen and unseen. ("I wanted the whole thing to begin with this prayer of protection that would go out into the theater," she later carefully told *MOJO*.)

From here, we were off and into more familiar territory, with a charged and impassioned reading of "Hounds of Love," after which Bush seemed to be temporarily flummoxed. The band launched into the opening of "Joanni" as she stepped to the side of the stage, gulped down bottled water, returned to the spotlight, closed her eyes, composed herself, then delivered a note-perfect performance. It was the only blip of apparent nervousness all evening from this fifty-six-year-old woman who hadn't performed a full show since she was twenty. Sometimes, as any seasoned luvvie will likely tell you, second nights are harder than the first.

But then, standing with a hand-held microphone in front of her seven-piece group, it was perhaps amazing how quickly Bush seemed to become entirely relaxed, her still-startling voice belting it out, as she likely called upon her teenage experiences fronting the KT Bush Band in pubs and clubs in the 1970s. The opening six-song run continued with a verse-tender, chorus-gutsy "Top of the City," a strident "Running Up That Hill" and a punchy "King of the Mountain," the ending of which was dramatically tweaked. Where the recorded version ended with the words, "The wind it blows the door closed," here Bush added, "There's a storm rising . . . can't you feel it?"

This ushered us—via dreadlocked percussionist Mino Cinélu whirling a bullroarer above his head on a suddenly darkened stage lit by lightning flashes—into Act II, "The Ninth Wave," the *Hounds of Love* song cycle that was to be the first extended theatrical staging of the night.

A short film followed involving an astronomer, played by actor Kevin Doyle (delivering words scripted by Bush and novelist David Mitchell). While out observing a meteor shower in a place named Church Rock, he'd received a broken SOS radio transmission from a stricken ship called the Celtic Deep, which he was now desperately relaying in a phone call to the coastguard.

Bush then appeared on screen, floating in what appeared to be the ocean at night: the victim of an unexplained shipwreck, singing the evocative lullaby-to-self, "And Dream of Sheep." It was a dramatic moment that took the ambitious and immersive staging of Pink Floyd's shows one key step further, since the vocal had in fact been recorded live as the singer bobbed in a water tank at Pinewood Studios.

Bush explained in the program that this recurring vision of her onscreen as the water-marooned woman was the "reality" of the piece and that everything that appeared on stage was the "dream." But, in keeping with the negatively rendered *Alice in Wonderland* theme of the 1985 recorded version (girl descends into world of utter terror), it was more nightmare than dream: the scarily claustrophobic "Under Ice," the horrific "Waking the

Witch," wherein Bush was physically pushed and pulled around by a threatening inquisitor.

Then the auditorium was thrown into pitch-blackness as a smoke-belching "helicopter" rotored above our heads, picking out audience members with a searching beam. In any other production this might have been a diverting, costume changing moment. But here it seemed to go on. And on. And on. No one in a crowd ever feels comfortable being spot lit and so the longer it lasted, the more it became clear that it was a great, psychologically intimidatory tactic.

As the stage lights faded back up, a set spun into view: a surreal, slanted living room that was also part-shipwreck. Here, Bertie McIntosh and backing singer Bob Harms as "Dad" enacted a domestic sketch that might have seemed a bit too cosy if it hadn't suddenly turned so dark. "Mum's late," said Bertie, before a door swung back to reveal a hidden Kate, to audible gasps in the audience. A vexed, virtually mute ghost in her own living room, she launched into "Watching You Without Me"—always (even with some stiff competition) the creepiest song in "The Ninth Wave." By its close, with backward and cut-up voices swirling around, young Bertie had been physically paralyzed by unknown forces.

In "Jig of Life," hellish spirits tussled over Bush's soul. Surrounded as she was by dancers in fish masks, the effect was like bearing witness to some occultist ceremony. In "Hello Earth," the fish people then picked the singer up and carried her horizontally, as if stealing her away, soundtracked by the haunting Popol Vuh-inspired Georgian choral of the recorded version. They moved with deliberate slowness to the lip of the stage, as Bush lay on her back atop their hands (as if passed out or worse), down a set of steps, into the stalls and up the aisle, making for a side door to a roar of astonished cheers.

It was heavy, headspinning stuff. The stage then brightened to reveal the band stepping toward the audience, playing "The Morning Fog" acoustically in the style of a Parisian street band. Bush walked back through the crowd and on stage to deafening applause. After half an hour of such shadowy intensity, the post-near-death-experience revelations of the song were made all the more joyful and uplifting. "I tell my mother . . . I tell my father . . . I tell my son," she sang, gesturing toward Bertie, "how much I love them."

It was time, then, for a slightly dazed twenty-minute interval.

~

When the curtain lifted for part two, the stage had been rearranged and divided into two areas: left for musicians, right for drama. The recording of the primary school-aged Bertie on *Aerial* could be heard narrating the introduction to "A Sky of Honey."

Throughout the first half of the show, most of the time the focus had been entirely on Bush. But at the beginning of this third act, where the audience's eyes were drawn to a child-sized faceless wooden puppet walking through a Moorish doorway (animated by black-clad puppeteer Ben Thompson), it took a minute or two to realize that she was actually back on the stage, performing nimble arpeggios behind a grand piano amid the band. This, you felt, was entirely the point: to divert attention away from her and onto the theatrical marvel of the whole affair.

Bush played the opening of "Prologue," as enormous slo-mo birds winged across a vast screen backdrop and cirrus clouds were projected onto the stage floor, making the band appear as if they were floating above the clouds. Next, the teenage Bertie stood in front of a framed image of a perceptibly moving sky painting, in the role of the Painter, as we moved into "An Architect's Dream." The curious puppet wandered over to see what he was doing. "Piss off," McIntosh exclaimed. "I'm trying to work here."

If by this point, there may have been some feeling that there was too much in the way of motherly indulgence going on with her son's continued presence, then it was to forget how much Bush has always involved her family in her music and artwork. Throughout the production, McIntosh pulled off his parts with no little confidence, too, not least when singing "Tawny Moon," a brooding new composition written by Bush specifically for the show. "I feel so privileged to be able to work on this project," he noted in the program, "and have tried to earn my place."

Less dramatic than "The Ninth Wave" act of the show, "A Sky of Honey" was a gentler production that marveled at the wonders of nature, particularly bird song, which Bush vocally mimicked with as much enthusiasm as she had done on *Aerial*. While more ruminative, it was filled with stunning set-pieces: the gloaming light of "Sunset" the hypnotic beats of "Somewhere in Between," in which the stage grew even murkier. As "night-time" fell, a projected moon hung over the proceedings, with geese flying across it, for the trancey dancefloor shapes of "Nocturn."

As spellbinding as all of this was, the show took a turn for the gobsmacking once again with the pumping, club-like "Aerial." Where in the album version, Bush's ecstatic cries of "I've gotta be up on the roof" could be heard as simply a celebration of the rising sun, here it was translated as an intense desire to *become* a bird, as Kate appeared to grow a wing in place of her right arm, the band appeared in beaky, avian masks, and silver birch trees descended from the roof of the stage. Then, piece by feathery costume piece, Bush's body fully mutated and, for a brief moment, she rose into the air and took flight, before the lights were killed. Once again, there were audience gasps followed by the uproarious applause of a standing ovation.

Returning for the encore, the singer was—for the only time in the whole show—entirely alone. At the piano, highlighting just how special her musicianly skills were even without the theatrics, she performed "Among Angels." Not for the first time, you could sense the heightened emotions in the crowd.

All through the evening, the audience had been a touch over-policed by security personnel—who scoured the rows for phone-snappers or filmers, and nearly prevented two girls from placing a bouquet of flowers on the stage ahead of the encore. By this point, the assembled were itching to dance. And so, with the string-stabbing introduction of "Cloudbusting" they were up on their feet, before joining in with a beaming Bush on its wordless chant for a triumphant finish.

As she took her bows, you sensed that the singer was truly affected by the fervent response and, perhaps, a touch relieved that the second night had gone without a hitch.

○⁀

As we filed back into the foyer afterward, I heard one or two dissenting mutters that the second half had relied too heavily on "A Sky of Honey," leaving less potential time for more hits. This was to miss the point though. As an artist, Kate Bush has always followed her muse entirely and so to expect anything less from her first shows in three decades-plus was perhaps to not really understand what motivates her as an artist.

A night filled with magic and mystery, Before the Dawn was an undisputed triumph. By no means a straightforward gig, or even comparable to what had ever gone before in terms of the theatrical rock show, this was a soaring and uncompromising flight of imagination; an outpouring of surprises as rich and strange as the arkful of creatures that had spilled from Bush's dress on the cover of *Never for Ever*.

Whispers among the crowd spoke of Madonna, Björk and even David Bowie being in attendance that night (none were confirmed, though David Gilmour and, later, at another date, Paul McCartney were spotted in the aisles).

As Kate Bush's Hammersmith residency progressed, it was perhaps to be expected there might be a production hiccup or two. On September 3, the filmed astronomer vignette introducing "The Ninth Wave" packed up, prompting a twenty-minute interruption. On September 26, due to electrical problems, the whole show was delayed for over an hour-and-a-half, resulting in some unsporting slow-handclapping and a larger intake at the bars.

Nevertheless, the atmosphere inside and outside the Apollo bristled with excitement every night, with ticketless fans queuing earlier and longer with each show for the few returns, and others simply hanging around on the pavement, absorbing the atmosphere. Those devotees who coughed up £414 for the VIP package—as opposed to the top-level £135 ticket price—were treated to a hamper meal in a church across the road, involving "allotment vegetables and edible soil" and "spatchcock slow roast poussin" along with a drop of 2012 Château Haut-Piquat.

By the end of the run, everyone seemed to have a Kate Bush gig story. This writer has one friend who daringly sneaked in—twice—emboldened by hash brownies. *MOJO*'s art director, Mark "Wag" Wagstaff meanwhile had the cheek to "high-five" the singer as she was carried through the crowd during "Hello Earth."

Those who attended more than one show all agreed that the performances got better and better as the weeks went on, Bush understandably appearing more relaxed, to the point where, by the closing shows, she was entirely in her element.

What this all meant in terms of future live performances was, of course, impossible to speculate upon. As for the singer herself, her parting words on the final night of October 1 were typically tantalising. "This is our last night," she offered, grinning. "For a while anyway . . ."

Two performances (September 17 and 18) were filmed, but despite expectations, no footage—aside from the "And Dream of Sheep" film, released to promote the *Before the Dawn* live album—was released. Later, unsubstantiated stories circulated claiming that Bush wasn't happy with the live footage (due to technical difficulties), or even perhaps with how she appeared in it.

"It has been archived," she told Jim Irvin in *MOJO* in 2016. "But there are no current plans to bring out a DVD. I think that the CD is, in a way, much more representative of being at the shows than a DVD. When you're at a live show it's the whole experience of sitting there in an audience. You can scan the stage, choose where to look, it's completely different from the film."

Beyond the dawn, it seemed—no matter how teeth-grindingly frustrating it must be for her fans the world over who didn't manage to make the pilgrimage to the Eventim Apollo—Bush wanted the show to exist only as photographs and audio and in the collective memories of those who were there.

45

"Bigger Fucking Waves"

The video for "And Dream of Sheep," 2014

The most powerful and lasting images of Kate Bush onscreen were often the most simple and direct: red dress and rose-in-hair ("Wuthering Heights"), sword-wielding warrior queen ("Babooshka"), white robe and dunce cap ("Sat in Your Lap").

Sometimes, a strong, yet simple look that might have become equally indelible in the public's memory was lost along the way. In the spring of 1980, in the unlikely setting of a BBC TV special focusing on piratical New Jersey soft rock band Dr. Hook, a guesting Kate performed "Delius" as a taster for the release of *Never for Ever*. In a white ballgown, with a head-dress of matching feathers, she became a lesser-spotted dove, rhythmically flap-flap-flapping her silken winged sleeves to the song's staccato beats. Even if it was performed in that instance in a BBC set cheaply approximating a magical summer garden, it was a routine that really only required a costume brought to life with deft dance moves. Just the same, it was never seen again.

More immediate in terms of its impact was the video for "Running Up That Hill." Bush ignored lip-syncing pop traditions by featuring in it a choreographed routine involving herself and her dance partner, Michael Hervieu. It showed the two wearing grey Japanese hakamas, locked together in complex moves that seemed both embracing and combative, and filmed in a way that was untypically non-flashy for the mid-1980s.

"Over the past couple of years," Bush said at the time, "[in] all the videos I've seen, dance has become a very exploited thing and hasn't really been treated seriously. We thought it would be nice to do almost a classical piece of dance, filmed as well as possible."

It was additional proof that robust ideas, straightforwardly rendered, always seemed to produce the best results. And so, more than twenty-five years after they'd last worked together, Kate called up "Running Up That Hill" video director David Garfath with a view to collaborating on the short film for "And Dream of Sheep" to be used in Before the Dawn shows.

Bush liked the idea of floating on her back in the "sea" for the film, and so a plan quickly came together to shoot it in the 20-foot-deep tank—named the "Underwater Stage" and used for scenes in *James Bond* and *Star Wars* movies—at Pinewood Studios in Buckinghamshire. It was a notion that appealed to Kate on more than one level. If she put herself in such a testing situation, she may, as she put it, "transmit a sense of the very difficult environment that the woman finds herself in." In other words, if she sang the song live while undergoing the experience of actually floating in deep water, she might well capture the convincing emotional qualities that she was always searching for in her vocals.

But, if she'd initially been drawn to depicting the character's "struggle," the actual filming was to make it all too real.

On the first day of the shoot, underlining her dedication, Bush spent six hours in the Pinewood tank, staring up at the camera, and performing the song, her face and hair dripping wet. Two microphones on her life jacket were disguised as inflation tubes (while a third boom stand mic hung overhead and had to be erased from the shots using digital trickery). The flashing red light on her vest was itself modeled on a Second World War original made by the Easco Electrical company. (One believed to date from around 1940 had been given to Kate by her brother Paddy not long after the release of *Hounds of Love*.)

Tasked with recording the singer's vocals on set was Before the Dawn's sound designer Greg Walsh, who had enjoyed a career as a record producer in the 1980s for the likes of Tina Turner, Heaven 17, and the Associates. (Coincidentally, his brother Peter, also a producer, for Simple Minds and Pulp, had recently and similarly ventured into difficult sonic terrain when working with the late-career Scott Walker. He'd fulfilled the increasingly avant-garde Walker's requests for Walsh to record the sounds of illegal machetes being sharpened, or a side of pork being punched.)

But the difficulties of recording vocals in a water tank immediately presented themselves. Garfath called for the waves to be enlarged and, as they flooded over Walsh's mics, Bush turned "incredibly grumpy."

"You can't have bigger fucking waves," she recalled herself ranting, in the Before the Dawn program. "They go all over the fucking live vocal, and they sound like a fucking bathroom, not the fucking ocean!"

On her return home after day one of the shoot, Bush felt her temperature rising. The next morning, she was fever-ish and couldn't get out of bed and was forced to leave the crew to shoot auxiliary scenes at Pinewood. Her GP diagnosed her with mild hypothermia and advised that when she returned to Pinewood to complete the filming she only perform in the water for stretches of no longer than two hours. (Bush would have known only too well the tale of Millais' muse Elizabeth Siddal, who'd ended up with pneumonia after posing in a bath filled with cold water for his pre-Raphaelite "Ophelia" masterpiece.)

In the end, the striking visual effect of the "And Dream of Sheep" film was worth all of the trials of its shoot. Entirely black and white, save for Bush's orange life vest and red flashing light, it perfectly captured her in a dreamlike/night terror setting, her vocal swirling over her pre-recorded piano parts, before she finally submerged under the oily black water.

Still, it was clearly not an experience that she was keen to ever repeat.

"It was the first time in all my years of nutty ideas that I questioned my sanity," she admitted. "It really was my most challenging performance yet."

46

Tory Furore

Kate in the echo chamber, 2016–19

For someone who had never seemed to want to get involved in any kind of political debate, Kate Bush was to learn to her horror how in the modern age a sound-bite can instantly echo around the world.

Endorsement of any one political party was clearly not Kate's bag. Even when she'd been photographed back in 1979 in a Manchester hotel, during the Tour of Life, with Labour Prime Minister James Callaghan, it had been more of a desperate move on the part of the latter in his failing campaign against Margaret Thatcher.

Ten years later, in 1989, the singer revealed her own shrugging indifference when it came to the subject in a filmed, EMI-released interview for *The Sensual World*.

"I don't think I'm politically minded at all," she stated. "Politics are something that . . . they're just not a part of me. I don't understand politics. I don't like what I see of politics. I don't see politics doing any good for people, really. It seems a very intellectual pre-occupation, y'know. It's kind of action, isn't it, that does things for people . . ."

But then, in November 2016, after she'd committed to a small number of phone interviews to promote the *Before the Dawn* live album, she spoke to Elio Iannacci of Canadian news magazine, *Maclean's*. Iannacci was interested in talking to the singer about what he viewed as the "gender equality" theme of "Running Up That Hill" and her possible concerns for the next generation's struggles in this area.

"My God, the world is continually changing," she responded. "I think in some ways it's changing in a very positive way. You have to try to embrace it all and everyone who represents that change, because it is happening."

The writer then pulled out an old quote of Bush's in which she'd said that "Waking the Witch" was about "the fear of women's power." In the wake of the vicious political campaign that had resulted in Hillary Clinton's presidential defeat to Donald Trump earlier that month, had that fear intensified?

"We have a female prime minister here in the UK," Bush pointed out, meaning Theresa May. "I actually really like her, and I think she's wonderful. I think she's the best thing that's happened to us in a long time. She's a very intelligent woman but I don't see much to fear. I will say it is great to have a woman in charge of the country. She's very sensible and I think that's a good thing at this point in time."

Although clearly more a statement of pride in the growth of female power than a ringing endorsement of the Conservative Party, Bush's comments instantly sparked an explosion of dismay, outrage, fury, and abuse on social media that carried on throughout 2017 and into 2018, only rising in volume and hardening in its absolute certainty that Kate was—to quote one post—"a rabid Tory."

When the singer released her remastered album catalog and *How to Be Invisible* lyric book in the latter half of 2018, the *Maclean's* quote began to do the rounds again, seemingly offering "proof" that she was a dyed-in-the-wool Tory, and proud to shout it from the rooftops.

One of the main issues seemingly was that she'd never said anything even vaguely political before. There were, of course, anti-war sentiments at the core of some of her key early songs ("Breathing," "Army Dreamers," "Pull Out the Pin"). She'd also been involved down the years with the Amnesty International and War Child charities. Other than that, she'd chosen to remain mute in terms of any particular affiliations.

By January 2019, however, she'd decided enough was enough and put out a statement via her official website.

"I was very disappointed that the use of a quote out of context was timed with the release of the live album," she wrote, "and it seemed as if the focus went onto the quote rather than the work. It was deeply frustrating. At the time I discussed the idea of responding to it with close friends and we all agreed it was best to let it go. It seems the quote keeps being used, and so I'd like to present my side of the story.

"Over the years, I have avoided making political comments in interviews. My response to the interviewer was not meant to be political but rather was in the defence of women in power. I felt he was putting a really negative slant on powerful women, referring to a witch hunt involving Hillary Clinton. In response, I said that we had a woman in charge of our country, and that

I felt it was a good thing to have women in power. I should have been clearer when I then said it was the best thing that had happened to us for a long time—because I greatly disliked the behavior of the previous PM [*David Cameron*], who at that point I felt had abandoned us [*i.e., by resigning in June 2016 following the Brexit referendum*] and everybody felt angry and let down.

"Again, with no response from me to the latest resurfacing of this article, it could make it seem like I am a Tory supporter, which I want to make clear I am not."

Let's have a rewind and a word rejiggle for absolute clarity here: "I am not . . . a Tory supporter."

And so there it was. The tactic worked, too, in terms of grabbing the desired corrective headlines.

"Kate Bush rejects rumor she is a Tory supporter" —*Irish Times*

"I'm not a Tory supporter" —*BBC News*

"Kate Bush wants everyone to know she's not a Tory!" —*Evening Standard*

~

If the controversy taught Kate Bush anything, it was probably—sadly—to say even less in the media in the future and to absolutely avoid any "hot button" topics. For someone who was already deeply ambivalent about interviews, it had doubtless been a bruising experience.

In the aftermath, it didn't help that when blundering Tory Prime Minister Boris Johnson was interviewed by *Grazia* magazine in

March 2020, in relation to International Women's Day, he named Bush as one of the "five women who have shaped my life," along-side Malala Yousafzai (Pakistani female education activist), Munira Mirza (the Director of the Number 10 policy unit), Boudicca (queen of the British Iceni tribe who led an uprising against the Roman army, circa 60 AD) and his own grandmother, Yvonne Eileen Irene Williams AKA "Granny Butter."

Johnson suggestively claimed that in his adolescence, Kate Bush had "stirred" his "emotions." He stated that with "Wuthering Heights" she had written "what is surely one of the world's greatest ever pop songs," although further added that he couldn't understand all of the words or why the singer "hopped around in a red chiffon thing."

Bush herself, unsurprisingly, wasn't available for comment. But still it provoked more in the way of online hubbub, although it was Johnson, rather than Bush, who was the target of the attacks.

～

In a weird addendum, in 2020, a government paper newly released to the public after thirty years revealed that Kate Bush had narrowly dodged another Tory bullet back in 1990. In her final, flagging year as Prime Minster, Margaret Thatcher had expressed an interest in meeting a "pop star," with Bush being one of the names thrown around, along with Roger Daltrey of the Who.

The Iron Lady had tried to perform this youth-appealing trick once before, granting an interview to *Smash Hits* magazine in 1987. Thatcher was even briefed ahead of the interrogation in a memo written on February 26 ,1987 by Christine Wall of the Number 10 press office.

"You may not *enjoy* the interview," Thatcher was warned. "Mr. [Tom] Hibbert may ask superficial questions which betray a lack of understanding. The challenge of the interview will be for you to demonstrate that just because you are not part of the pop scene, you are still in touch with youngsters and understand their needs."

But, knowing little of the magazine's irreverent approach and even less of the masterful skills of interviewer Tom Hibbert (who'd bought a suit from cut-price high-street menswear chain Mister Byrite especially for the occasion—"£19.99 . . . a snip!" he noted), the PM managed to make herself look ridiculous. Her favorite record, she said, was Lita Roza's 1953 rendition of novelty ditty "(How Much Is) That Doggie in the Window." Elton John she meanwhile blandly praised for being "highly professional," while also singling out Cliff Richard for having "done wonders."

Apparently undeterred by the *Smash Hits* encounter, in 1990, Number 10 planned an official visit to Abbey Road Studios for the PM. Thatcher even walked in the footsteps of The Beatles when she posed on the famous zebra crossing outside the studio (although cluelessly walking in the opposite direction from the Fabs in the *Abbey Road* album shot).

Inside the building, there was indeed a pop star ready and waiting and eager to guide Margaret Thatcher on her tour around Abbey Road. Not Kate Bush, not even Roger Daltrey, but Mike Batt of the Wombles.

47

The Ultimate Kate Bush Experience...

...And The Most Wuthering Heights Day Ever, 2013–22

It was quite the jaw-dropping sight. On July 16, 2016, close to four thousand people—women, kids, burly blokes with beards—gathered en masse in Melbourne's Fitzroy Gardens. Donning red dresses, tying scarf belts around their waists, popping a rose or two into their hair (or long, flowing brown wigs), together they twirled and waved their way through a very familiar dance routine.

The event was The Most Wuthering Heights Day Ever, an affectionately jokey celebration of Kate Bush's most famous choreography. As the sound of the singer's debut 1978 hit single filled the air—or more accurately, the 1986 version on *The Whole Story* with its re-recorded vocal—the amateur performers worked their way through a series of moves variously dubbed "the zombie walk," "horror hands" and "the backward pterodactyl."

While the bizarre 2016 happening staged in the southern coastal Australian city was to date the largest attendance for a

"Wuthering Heights" celebration, it was by no means the only one that year. Others were held in fifteen different locations around the globe, including Tel Aviv, Montreal, Atlanta, Berlin, Amsterdam, and Copenhagen.

The origins of The Most Wuthering Heights Day Ever can be traced back to the Brighton Fringe arts festival in 2013, when English performance group Shambush created The Ultimate Kate Bush Experience. Originally an attempt to set a Guinness World Record for the greatest amount of people dressed as Kate Bush grouped together in one setting, it was an idea rebuffed by the Guinness committee.

"That was a bit controversial," states Shambush's Georgie Sworder. "They said that the 'Wuthering Heights' video wasn't iconic enough."

"Which is absolutely not true," adds Imogen Miller Porter of the group. "Because even if you had two or three of us dressed as Kate Bush in that red dress outfit, people knew exactly who we were . . . they knew exactly what we were doing."

The four members of Shambush (Sworder and Porter, along with Annie Whelan and Anne Litobarski—their name a cut-and-shut abbreviation of "Shambolic Ambush") first started dressing up as the singer when attending music festivals back in 2007. One of their skits involved rousing bleary-eyed campers in the mornings by coaxing them to join in with their "Kate Bush Aerobics" sessions.

"We'd all dress in Lycra," says Porter, "and it'd be like, 'Big hands, big *hands*, big eyes, big *eyes*.'"

Sworder stresses that these Bush-centric capers, while done in jest, reflect the group's love of all things Kate: "I think she's got a really great sense of humor. She's very outlandish in her storytelling, and she doesn't hold back."

While the 2013 Brighton event was disappointingly not to be recorded as an official world record, it developed into its own Kate Bush festival tribute, attracting around four hundred people, via radio publicity and social media, to the city's Stanmer Park.

"Everyone turned up just wearing things they found in charity shops," says Sworder. "We had whole families come down in red dresses. Dogs turning up in red dresses as well."

"It wasn't just the dance either," says Whelan. "We had four hours of warm-up—Kate Bush aerobics, Kate Bush karaoke, a Kate Bush quiz."

Key to teaching the routine to such a large number of people was an instructional video that Shambush made, breaking the "Wuthering Heights" step sequence down into moves given daft descriptive terms, such as "serve the plates," "chained to the master," "he was *this* high, officer," and, for the end of the song, the stamina-requiring "endless wave."

The toughest move, all agree, was the one where in the outdoors-shot version of the "Wuthering Heights" video Bush bent backward and touched the ground. "Kate Bush was much bendier than us," Porter admits. "You've got seventy-year-olds there, and everybody's trying to do this sort of bend-over-backward crab move. Kids were obviously great at that one. But, anyway, by the time we did the big one, four hundred people were rehearsed."

Filmed on the day and subsequently uploaded to YouTube, The Ultimate Kate Bush Experience clip began to incrementally attract viewers over the next three years, until in 2016 people began to get in touch with Shambush, asking if they could organize their own copycat events in other cities. "We sort of stumbled into a community of Kate Bush fans who took us on," says Porter. "They call us their 'Wuthermothers' (*laughs*)."

Georgie Sworder, who had by this time moved to Australia, helped to orchestrate the massive 4,000-strong Melbourne gathering. "I think it was really popular in Australia because it attracted a demographic of mainly older women," she says. "I guess this was like their having-fun-at-a-festival type feeling that they hadn't had for a very long time, or maybe ever."

Shambush were collectively amazed to watch the "Wuthering Heights" phenomenon take off internationally. While the worldwide assemblies generally retained the original's tongue-in-cheek attitude, many took the dance steps far more seriously. "It was like, 'Good luck to you,'" Sworder says. "Because they're very hard moves."

So popular were the "Wuthering Heights" rallies becoming that in the UK the producers of ITV's *Britain's Got Talent* show got in touch with Shambush, inviting them to come on the program and "audition" for the Simon Cowell-led celebrity panel of judges.

"They said they could accommodate one hundred Kate Bushes," Porter explains. "I suggested, 'What about if it's a big reveal? So we're sat there in the audience wearing coats. And then one hundred people stand up as Kate Bush and then go and perform it on the stage.' The producers were all over this. They absolutely loved it. I organized all these people from our network, they were all practising at home, and then the producers called up and just said, 'Oh, we've decided to go in a different direction.' What can you do?"

During the first British COVID-19 pandemic lockdown of spring 2020, Shambush organized a "Wuthering Heights" event over Zoom, involving hundreds of participants. Particularly during a period of uncertainty and isolation, it provided a moment of much-needed fun and togetherness.

"Just for that hour, it was really, really lovely," says Porter. "It was just so touching to see everyone dressed up as Kate Bush on a Sunday in their own houses."

Given the runaway success of their cast-of-hundreds-and-thousands "Wuthering Heights" jamborees, Shambush have considered branching out into other Kate Bush songs and routines.

"We did talk about a mass 'Babooshka,'" says Sworder. "You'd have to bring your own double bass. Maybe you'd do it with a friend, and you'd take it in turns . . . one could be the kind of Xena Warrior Princess version, and then the other one could be in the black veil. 'Running Up That Hill' would be amazing. It's one of my favorite videos of her dancing. But I definitely think there'd be a lot of broken bones if we tried to do that."

Meanwhile, The Most Wuthering Heights Day Ever has now become an annual occurrence and grown even further in its international reach. The year 2022 saw more than forty similar get-togethers take place as far afield as Edinburgh and Christchurch, Sofia and Chattanooga, Adelaide and Uppsala. Many of these were held on July 30, to celebrate Kate Bush's sixty-fourth birthday.

Meanwhile, for originators Shambush, there's one lingering ambition left to possibly achieve.

"We're still obsessed with the idea of having a Guinness World Record," says Annie Whelan.

"I think we should do it," says Georgie Sworder. "I really can't see Guinness still saying it's not iconic or recognizable enough. Because it definitely is. It would be an amazing thing to do. Maybe even Kate Bush would come down . . ."

48

"KT"

The real hidden symbols, 1978–2018

In a tradition that is likely more playful than deeply meaningful, every Kate Bush album has had a "KT" symbol—which actually looks like a "T" with the limbs of a "K" sprouting from its body—hidden somewhere in its artwork.

Obviously, this has provided something of a treasure hunt for her fans through the years. Some symbols have been easy to spot; others required a magnifying glass or digital zooming.

"The original 'KT' was discovered by my brother, Jay, on the door of an old church in deepest, darkest Wales," Bush explained. "The commercially used KT symbol was designed by Del Palmer to be used on the first album and it has been with us ever since."

For the listeners of BBC Radio 1's Personal Call in 1979, Bush talked a bit more about the origins of, and her attraction to, the KT symbol, after being asked a question about it by a listener.

"It's sort of two things," she said. "That actual sign is an old Knights Templar sign, and round the countryside you'll find it scattered on the doorways of churches and things, and it was just very fitting because I used to be in a band called the KT Bush Band. Katie, KT. It's just a theme we've kept running."

And so here, for your scrutinizing pleasure, is a list of where the symbols can be found:

The Kick Inside (1978)
It's on the back cover: the little kite-flown character has a clear "KT" on their left wing.

Lionheart (1978)
Really obvious on this one. The letters have been written on the left side of the wooden box upon which Kate throws her leonine pose.

Never for Ever (1980)
This is where it gets trickier. Inside the gatefold vinyl, where the lyrics are printed, there's a drawing of a pink rose. Right at the very bottom of its stem there is a tiny "KT."

The Dreaming (1982)
Minuscule again; the location being just below the second black stripe on the sleeve of Bush's checked jacket.

Hounds of Love (1985)
Spin the back cover around 90 degrees to the right. In the black and white photograph of Kate, it's faintly scratched in grey on the puffy section of her dress.

The Whole Story (1986)

Inscribed into the run-out groove of the vinyl.

The Sensual World (1989)

Super hard to find. Trace a line below the "H" of her surname on the front cover, and amid the blackness, there's a ghostly "KT" imprint.

This Woman's Work: Anthology 1978–90 (1990)

Easy. It's on the top of the CD box set (and redesigned to feature a head, to complete a figure in which the "KT" becomes arms, body and legs). Also on the front of the accompanying booklet and the covers of the two *This Woman's Work* rarities collections.

The Red Shoes (1993)

Just to the left of the red en pointe toe.

Aerial (2005)

Tougher to locate. Draw your eye to the middle soundwave, move it along almost to the next one, scan down to the bottom of the image and the "KT" is there in the golden sea.

Director's Cut (2011)

Hard again. Look at the central image on the tangled film stock. To the right—in-between two of the sprocket holes—the "KT" has been printed.

50 Words for Snow (2011)

Front cover, snowman's head, just to the left of his nose, hidden inside the icy "veins" of his temple.

Before the Dawn (2016)

The easiest one: found within the design of the words "The KT Fellowship." Some keen-eyed fans reckon it's also written on the stage floor, in black, between the puppeteer's legs. Partly obscured, but definitely appears to be.

The Other Sides (2018)

The "I" of the first word of the "Running Up That Hill" lyric painted up and down her arms in the cover image has been transformed into a "KT." Also, in the portrait where Bush is covering her mouth with her coat lapel, used for the cut-down streaming compilation *Selection from the Other Sides*, it's under her fringe. Have a look. Hours of fun for all the family.

49

The End of the Day

A secret garden, a tub of slime, and a lost tape,
2005

**Nearing the end of my day spent at Kate Bush's house,
I'd returned from a loo break and wandered back into
her living room. The singer was staring absently into
the late afternoon light leaking through her window,
momentarily lost in thought, face frozen in a profile
familiar from probably a dozen of her videos and hundreds of her photographs that—daft as it sounds—
made me think, "Wow, that's Kate Bush."**

As opposed, that was, to the highly amused mum who was
the very next minute delightedly demoing her kid's favorite new
toy: a disembodied hand—like Thing from the Addams Family—that crept its way across the carpet.

Earlier, as a clock somewhere chimed two, the chipper,
ever-attentive Danny McIntosh had arrived with lunch for us:
tea, pizza, avocado drizzled with balsamic vinegar, and cream

cake for dessert, only to be playfully admonished by his partner. "I can't eat all this shit!" she'd protested.

Being aware that the one-to-one interview process can be knackering (for both parties), I'd suggested taking frequent breaks, involving more cups of tea, and cigs (me . . . she'd given up). We'd sat at a table outside and had a natter, and later she even let me light up a rollie while in her kitchen, explaining that Danny sometimes still smoked indoors. (All the same, I felt a bit bad about it and stood by a window, blowing the smoke out.)

It had all in all been a very pleasant and entertaining way to spend a sunny autumn day. At one point earlier, after we'd been in the studio, Bush had taken me on a tour around the grounds: down to the end of the property where an old weir regulated the flow of the nearby river; into a walled-off space enclosed on all four sides by tall hedging, surrounding a central plinth, upon which sat a statue of two dancing (or boxing) hares.

"It's like a secret garden," I said.

"That's what everyone says," she grinned.

It also occurred to me that there was possibly no setting that was more Kate Bush. It was as if we'd wandered into one of her songs.

$\sim$

Back in the sitting room, Bush picked up a tub of Bertie's toy slime, tipped the goo out into her hand, and started squeezing it back into the container, to make fart noises.

"I'm sorry," she laughed. "I'm starting to get bored now."

Fair enough, I thought. I'd been there for over five hours, more than four of them spent interviewing her, which was an incredible amount of access to be given to such a high-profile artist—especially one who was, for many reasons previously explored, acutely press-shy. There wasn't a publicist on hand, either, to wind down the interview, as is the norm. Still, I was suddenly aware that I'd better start swiftly wrapping up the loose ends of the conversation.

I said that, when talking to her today, I'd been surprised by just how intensely hypercritical she was of her own work. She seemed to somehow view her back catalog as a series of let-downs.

"Well, I felt for a long time that my records were really disappointing, but each one was less disappointing than the one before," she smiled. "And that was my way of gauging that they were getting better. It's not that they were great, but they were less disappointing."

At the same time, she was quite obviously proud of the success she'd achieved in what was, in 2005, still a very male-dominated music industry.

"You feel as a woman you do have to fight quite hard," she admitted. "But I think I've been really lucky to get a lot of the breaks that I had. I know a lot of people who've worked hard and they haven't had the kind of privileges that I've had. So I really do feel privileged."

I mentioned one thing that had struck me about being there with her in her home—there were no records or CDs (other than the CDRs she'd brought over from the studio) anywhere to be seen. Did she never these days play other artists' albums just for pleasure?

"Well, I *don't* really listen to music and part of that is quite conscious," she said. "I always used to think it was totally cool that Steely Dan always said that they didn't listen to other people's music. And I really loved *Aja* [*1977*] and *Gaucho* [*1980*]. I just thought they were very unusual . . . they were coming from a different place somehow. And I don't know if there was any connection . . . but I connected that with the fact that they weren't listening [to anyone else's records] . . . maybe I got the wrong end of the stick (*laughs*)."

As a result, though, the only music that she'd been listening to in recent years had been *Aerial*.

"Just checking the progress of the record," she explained. "This is my listening room as opposed to the control room [in the studio], so a lot of my work is listening to check stuff to do for the next day because I'm working in such short little spurts. So I'm very out of touch with a lot of contemporary music."

What's more, she felt that the omnipresence of music in everyday modern life was hugely reducing its value.

"I think that's a terrible thing, the dissipation of music, because it's everywhere," she bemoaned. "It's complete overkill. Even when they give traffic news and weather reports on the radio, they put music behind it . . ."

Away from music, there was one other thing I'd wondered— in the early 1980s, there had been talk that Bush was considering writing her autobiography. She'd even given it a very fitting title: *Leaving My Tracks*. Publishers Sidgwick & Jackson had mocked up a dust jacket design and it looked like the presses were ready to roll. Then, in 1984, the singer abandoned the project. What happened?

"That was something that I was being put under pressure enormously to do because other people were writing books about me," she said. "Everybody was saying, 'Look, you should write one.' I started to toy with the idea and I thought, 'No, I don't want to write an autobiography.' The whole point is to try to do what feels right for me and not do what other people say I should do. I don't know about autobiographies. I think I'm (*assuming super-posh tone*) far too young, luvvie."

~

Time has a tendency to fly, as Kate Bush knew only too well. Before the end of today, she still had to get on with proofreading the lyrics and credits in the artwork of *Aerial*.

She began to tidy up our plates and cups and get ready for Bertie's arrival home from school with his dad. The initial air of tension when I first arrived had been replaced with an atmosphere of post-interview relief (for her) and the lingering thought (for me) that, today, I may have just caught a glimpse of the warm, funny, if gently controlling woman the singer's friends might recognize (although, in a phone call to me a couple of days later, she fretted that she'd perhaps relaxed *too* much).

As she led me to her front door and out to a waiting car, there was probably only one more question left to ask. Was there any chance of her next album a bit sooner, please?

"Yeah, I thought I'd do two next year," she laughed. "Two in one year. That would really surprise them, wouldn't it?"

And with that, the door very delicately closed on Kate Bush once again.

~

Except that wasn't quite the end of it. As I got into the car, I unzipped the front pocket of my bag to check that I definitely had the three C90 cassettes I'd recorded the interview on. There were only two. I thought, *Shit shit shit.*

So I had to get back out of the car and knock again on Bush's front door. When she opened it, I sheepishly said, "Really sorry, Kate. I think I've left one of my tapes in the living room."

"Oh, well, I didn't see anything . . ." she replied, and we wandered back through. There was no cassette lying anywhere obvious. Next thing, we were both lifting the cushions up off the chairs and sofa. Nothing.

"Maybe it's gone under one of them?" she suggested, and both of us ended up on our knees, poking around under her furniture. Her Irish wolfhound, Ted, who'd been lolling around the room all day, suddenly became interested in this activity and began nosing around and licking our faces.

Still no tape. I felt like a total arse. It was a complete mystery. I'd massively fucked up, somehow.

Then, I thought to check the back pocket on my bag, though I never, ever used it normally. I opened it, and there it was, the missing cassette.

I apologized for being an idiot, we had a laugh about it, and headed back toward the front door. But as I walked to the car, Ted followed, and Kate suddenly began panicking because the front gates had been left open as the driver waited for us. Frantically, she chased after the excited dog and managed to grab his collar.

And it had all been going so well . . .

Still, we smiled and waved our goodbyes as the car pulled away.

~

A few weeks after the fourteen-page feature appeared in *MOJO* magazine, following an extract in *The Guardian*, Bush sent me a great letter. In it, she wrote: "It's the first interview where I feel it actually sounds like me and not some strange woman."

For years, I kept it tucked away inside a book. Eventually, I got around to framing it.

50

Strange Phenomena

"The whole world's gone mad!," 2022

No one could have envisaged what would happen in 2022. On May 27, Netflix released internationally the first seven installments of the nine-episode fourth season of the Duffer Brothers' 1980s retro sci-fi horror drama, *Stranger Things*. Over multiple episodes, "Running Up That Hill" featured heavily: less as a mere soundtrack inclusion and more as an essential narrative device.

Set in March 1986, the plotline for the series involved the beleaguered group of teenagers from the fictional midwestern US town of Hawkins—who had in previous seasons done battle with supernatural creatures from parallel reality netherworld the Upside Down—facing a new and dangerous threat in the shape of a serial-killing entity named Vecna.

One of the central characters, Max Mayfield (played by Sadie Sink), has become a Kate Bush fan, and repeatedly plays "Running Up That Hill" on a cassette of the *Hounds of Love* album, through the headphones of her Walkman. In the fourth episode, "Dear Billy," she is possessed by Vecna, whose perilously entrancing spell is broken only when her friends press "play" on Mayfield's tape machine, and she escapes back to the real world. From here, "Running Up That Hill" becomes a protective sonic totem for the character.

Stranger Things music supervisor Nora Felder had approached Bush for potential clearance of the track to be used in the series, unaware that the singer was already a fan of the show. In some ways, this was no surprise: for instance, the secret government facility in *Stranger Things* (in which CIA scientists conduct tests on children who appear to have extrasensory and telekinetic powers) was very similar in its appearance to the sound-weaponising laboratory in her 1986 video for "Experiment IV." This was storytelling of the kind that Kate Bush could fully appreciate.

"Actually, we watched it right from the word go, from the first series onward," Bush told presenter Emma Barnett on BBC Radio 4's *Woman's Hour* on June 22, 2022. "So I was already familiar with the series. And I thought, 'What a lovely way for the song to be used in such a positive way, y'know, as a kind of talisman almost, really, for Max.'"

Introduced to an entirely new generation of listeners, "Running Up That Hill" provided an example of how inventive, empowering, and plainly weird pop music could be in the 1980s, and sent the track skyrocketing back up international charts.

The statistics were staggering. Throughout June 2022, on Spotify alone, "Running Up That Hill" was achieving 6 million streams daily. Over the summer, it became the most-played track in the world, twice topping *Billboard*'s Global 200 chart. In the UK, it reached number one and stayed there for three weeks, eclipsing its initial 1985 chart placing of number three. The song also hit the top spot in Australia, Ireland, Belgium, Lithuania, Luxembourg, New Zealand, Switzerland, and Sweden.

In America, streaming activity for "Running Up That Hill" increased by 9,990 percent. Where the song had previously been Bush's biggest hit in the US at number thirty, *Stranger Things* catapulted it to number three. Music sales data company Luminate calculated that in 2022 alone, the track had earned Bush upward of $2.3 million.

At the same time, she broke no fewer than three Guinness World Records: longest period taken for a track to reach the top of the charts in the UK (thirty-seven years), biggest gap between British number ones (forty-four years since "Wuthering Heights"), and oldest female artist to reach number one (at the age of sixty-three). The previous holder of the latter record, Cher—who was fifty-two when her club hit "Believe" reached UK number one in 1998—immediately tweeted her support for Bush's achievement.

"Bravo Kate," she wrote. "Records are meant 2 be broken!! Remember back in the day when women had short sell-by dates!? We had 2 fight our way through the testosterone curtain, & we did it so the girls who came after us could sing as long as they want to. With mega respect . . ."

As a shining example of how "Running Up That Hill" had captured the imagination of a younger generation, when *Vanity Fair* magazine interviewed *Stranger Things*' Sadie Sink, she revealed that she herself hadn't previously been aware of Kate Bush. Since listening through the singer's back catalog, she had then become "increasingly obsessed" with it. What's more, Sink had employed an almost method actorly approach to her role as Max Mayfield by playing the track over and over.

"I cannot even tell you how many times I've listened to 'Running Up That Hill,'" she said. "It's been a lot, but I'm still not sick of it, which is good (*laughs*). Knowing [Max's] emotional connection to that song, and how it's kind of her anthem, played into it. It's something about the energy of the song, the synth and the lyrics and everything. It's so perfect. They could not have picked a more perfect song."

For her part, Kate released a series of statements, via her website, reacting to the surprise success of "Running Up That Hill," and becoming more and more enthused with each missive. On June 15, 2022, she wrote, "'Running Up That Hill' is being given a whole new lease of life by the young fans who love the show—I love it too!"

Two days later, when the song had reached UK number one, she posted another comment under the heading "On Top of that Hill." "I'm overwhelmed by the scale of affection and support the song is receiving and it's all happening really fast, as if it's being driven along by a kind of elemental force. I have to admit I feel really moved by it all."

The following week, Bush posted, "It's so exciting! RUTH is at No. 1 in the UK for the second week running and is now No. 1 in Ireland. My mother was Irish and would've really loved this." On July 1, under a banner heading of "Still up on that Hill," she was brimming over with excitement: "Whoooo Hoooo everybody! I just can't believe it—No.1 for the third week. We're all so excited! In fact, it's all starting to feel a bit surreal."

On July 8, Bush was even magnanimous in defeat when 'Running Up That Hill" was knocked off the top spot by Scottish dance duo LF System's soul-house track, "Afraid to Feel."

"Many, many congratulations on the UK No.1 single for LF System," she wrote. "Thank you everyone for supporting RUTH with such positivity. It's lovely to see the song continuing to do so well around the world—it's just boomeranged back to No.1 in Australia!"

On *Woman's Hour*, Bush had described her feelings even more succinctly when expressing her shock and delight at the "Running Up That Hill" phenomenon.

"The whole world's gone mad!" she exclaimed.

~

Meanwhile, the internet virtually exploded. Kate Bush memes started appearing everywhere. One featured Dutch photographer Claude Vanheye's 1979 image of Kate posing on the back of a fake dolphin, now captioned, "If there is indeed an afterlife, then God is Kate Bush riding a dolphin." Another adapted the "two guys on a bus" meme—one on the left staring miserably out of a window onto a dark stone wall; the other on the right smiling beatifically over sunlit mountaintops—to have the first labeled as "a Kate Bush fan," the second "doesn't know who Kate Bush is."

There was, of course, some kickback, particularly from "real" fans getting in a sulk with "fake" fans.

"Kate Bush did not go through 'Wuthering Heights,' run all the way up that hill to make a deal with God & shout 'Babooshka' for y'all to be finding out about her in 2022!" carped one affronted tweeter.

In the end, though, it was hard to hear much of this criticism through the noise of the endless social media cover versions of

"Running Up That Hill." There were many a cappella renditions performed by singers looping up their vocal layers to represent all of the complex parts in the song. Spanish-speaking singer Gabriel Merez uncannily performed it in the style of South Yorkshireman Alex Turner of the Arctic Monkeys, while elsewhere a thirty-something American chap played the "Running Up That Hill" chorus melody on a trumpet for his Cactus Choir of dancing novelty cacti toys. Said toys then recorded the audio into their tinny-sounding 8-bit chips and replayed it out of time, all the while wobbling along with fuzzy felt grins glued to their faces.

Most visible on the socials were an entire army of teen and twenty-something female Kate Bush lookalikes, or "Copy Kates" as they were dubbed in the press. TikTok and Instagram were their domains, as they filmed themselves miming to "Running Up That Hill" and—second most popular, even more so than "Wuthering Heights"—"Babooshka."

Some, like Danimay Palmer aka the Head of the Tempest, performed meticulous routines, replete with 1970s visual effects, for "Them Heavy People" or slightly deeper cuts such as "In Search of Peter Pan" (from *Lionheart*). Sydney Golding, posting as syd_not_so_vicious, lip-synced to various snippets of Kate Bush tracks while ranking her albums (*Hounds of Love* top, *50 Words for Snow* bottom).

In other areas, Bush was approvingly assessed by the new younger fans for having been an early advocate of vegetarianism, or for dealing with a same-sex theme in 1978's "Kashka from Baghdad." Others even adopted the gender-swapping lyric of "Running Up That Hill" as a trans anthem.

Bush once again became a fashion icon, particularly for her 1970s and 1980s looks ("She was really iconic with her layering," commented one online influencer). In a different corner of the internet, some wag even mucked around with "Wuthering Heights," using digital technology to wildly and erratically pitch-alter Bush's vocal to the point where it sounded deranged.

"You are not allowed to maim this perfect creation!" screamed a commenter.

Kate was herself moved once again to write a note of appreciation in mid-July when Brisbane's Pub Choir filmed their rendition of "Running Up That Hill," featuring a string quartet, guitarist, electronic drummer and 1,600 singers. The choir's founder and director Astrid Jorgensen told *The Guardian*, "My manager called me and said, 'You've got to get home, Kate Bush has emailed.' I ran straight back—I was literally running up that hill."

"Dear Brisbane Pub Choir," Bush wrote, "I've been so busy that I've only just had the chance to watch you all singing RUTH. It's utterly, utterly wonderful! I love it so much! Thank you everyone. You sing it really beautifully. I'm incredibly touched by your warmth and all your smiling faces."

All in all, Kate Bush's reputation achieved vertical take-off in 2022, soaring to new and uncharted heights. And it was no one-song fad, either; new devotees excitedly discovered and explored various different corners of her work.

But in terms of "Running Up That Hill" itself, the intervening near-four decades had done nothing to date the track, in fact underlining its timelessness and unique qualities. Thirty-seven years on from its original release, in "The Nina Project," episode five of *Stranger Things* 4, Sadie Sink as Max Mayfield fretted that over-playing "Running Up That Hill" might rob the song of its safeguarding potency.

"Will it still work?" she wondered. "Or will Kate Bush lose her magic power or something?"

"Kate Bush?" responded her co-star Caleb McLaughlin aka Lucas Sinclair. "Never."

~

From her quiet, normal everyday life, living in the English countryside, the clamor of appreciation for Kate Bush in 2022 likely sounded to her like a distant rumble coming from somewhere over the horizon.

Far from Bush losing her magic power, it has manifestly increased. If it wasn't already, her legendary status among the pantheon of the all-time musical greats has been assured and cemented in place for the generations to come.

For someone who never wanted to be famous—and still really doesn't want to be any kind of celebrity—the continual and vast outpouring of love for her work must be enormously gratifying. It's all a far cry, a different world entirely, from the barn where that young girl determinedly pedaled out hymns on her family's clapped-out old pump organ. Or from her teenage bedroom where David Bowie and Elton John gazed down at her from the posters on her wall.

Just as a casual compliment in regard to her music from someone close to her would sometimes provide all the creative fulfilment that Bush needed, the fact that Elton John has become a collaborator, friend, and fan must seem utterly surreal to her. More than that, as he admitted in 2014, when recalling the lows of his 1980s cocaine addiction, Bush's reassuring voice in her 1986 Peter Gabriel duet, "Don't Give Up," gave him the strength to go on.

"This was one record that saved my life," he said in BBC Four's 2014 documentary *The Kate Bush Story*. "That record helped me get sober. So she played a big part in my rebirth. I never told her that, but it did."

At the same time, Elton managed to sum up exactly what makes Kate Bush and her music so special.

"I mean, they're not normal songs . . . none of her songs have been normal," he stated. "She's unique. She's the most beautiful mystery.

"Let me tell you a story," he went on. "When I had my civil partnership, nine years ago, in 2005, we invited Kate. We didn't think she'd come. But she then came with Danny. And there were a lot of very famous people in that room. There were, like, 600 people. And [everybody] wanted to meet Kate Bush. I mean, musicians, anybody, they couldn't believe Kate Bush was there.

"She's kind of an enigma. I mean, when has the next Kate Bush come along, after Kate Bush? There hasn't been one."

Most remarkable of all, perhaps, Kate Bush's towering (and enduring) status as an artist has been built upon only ten studio albums, released over a span of thirty-three years.

At one point when talking to her, I wondered if she ever wished that she'd made more records?

"Well, I dunno, really," she smiled. "I mean I could've made more records. That would have been an easy choice. So I had that choice, and I chose not to. I chose to go through this incredibly sort of masochistic way of making records, which take a long time and obviously there's fewer of them.

"But I think what's nice is, although there aren't many records out there, they've all really been made with a lot of care. So I suppose I'm quite proud of that, really."

So concluded Catherine Bush, unequaled purveyor of lovingly made artisan albums since 1978. Still very much in business.

Acknowledgments

For their generous interview time and for quotes (in conversations with the author) that made their way into this book, thanks to Kate Bush, John Carder Bush, David Gilmour, Paul McCartney, Ian Rankin, Guido Harari, Tony Wadsworth, Brian Bath, Stuart Elliott, Youth, Nick Launay, Tori Amos, Paul Henry, Julian Doyle, Jez Willis, Annie Whelan, Imogen Miller Porter, Georgie Sworder, and John Aizlewood (whose Q Awards recollections brought the whole chapter to life).

Massive thanks to my agent, Matthew Hamilton, for providing the spark of inspiration and to the brilliant Pete Selby at Nine Eight Books for seeing the visions. For all their ongoing help, thanks also to Melissa Bond, Francesca Eades, Karen Stretch, and Isabel Smith and to Lora Findlay for her cover-design magic.

Special thanks to Danny Eccleston for commissioning the original 2005 interview for *MOJO* (and for his great Gurdjieff theory). Big up too to the rest of the *MOJO* Wrecking Krew: John Mulvey, Ian Harrison, Jenny Bulley, Mark "Wag" Wagstaff (high-five), David "Hutchie" Hutcheon, Stevie Chick, Andrew Male, Jim Irvin, Phil Sutcliffe, Phil Alexander, Mark Blake, and Keith Cameron. Thanks also to all those who did their very best to keep the good ship *Q* afloat: Ted Kessler, Chris Catchpole, Niall Doherty, Simon McEwen, and Dave Everley (who commissioned the 2006 Q&A with Kate).

For direct or indirect assistance, cheers to: William Luff, Geoff Jukes, Murray Chalmers, Jack Delaney, Emma Pollock, David Brewis, Peter Brewis, Neville Judd, Matt Everitt, Paul Stokes and Tom Robinson. Shout out to my family in Scotland (Heather, Brian, Caroline, Jimmy and John) and to my pals: Anth Brown, Mike Brown, Sylvia Patterson (same old girl after all), Simon Goddard (it's a mug's game, right enough), Jon Bennett, the two Craigs (McNeil and McLean), Dave Tomlinson, Kieran Heneghan, James Hall, Lynne Roberts, Mike Soutar, Syann Gilroy, Robbie and Parm Gunn-Hamilton, Steve Wilkins, Dave Black, and Dave Scott.

Online resources: Fish People—The Official Website of Kate Bush, the incomparable Gaffaweb, Kate Bush News, Kate Bush Encyclopedia, Dreams of Orgonon, the World of Kate Bush, Kate Bush's Aquarius Moon (Twitter), Wileywindymemes (Instagram), Michael Koppelman's lolife.com blog, and the Facebook community of St Joseph's Convent Grammar School.

Print and online newspaper and magazine resources: *MOJO*, *Q*, *The Guardian*, *The Observer*, *Sunday Times*, *The Independent*, *Dazed*, *Smash Hits*, *Vanity Fair*, *Variety*, *Record Mirror*, *Stereo Review*, *Crawdaddy*, *Billboard*, *NME*, *Melody Maker*, *Daily Express*, *Daily Mail*, *Liverpool Post*, *Birmingham Evening Mail*, *Southern Daily Echo*, *Bristol Evening Post*, *Manchester Evening News*, *RCD*, *SPIN*, *Maclean's*, *Grazia*.

TV and Radio: BBC, ITV, Channel 4, RTÉ, MTV, NBC, Capital Radio, Radio Clyde, France Inter, Netflix.

Bibliography: John Carder Bush, *Cathy* (Sphere, 2014); John Carder Bush, *Inside the Rainbow* (Sphere, 2015); Kevin Cann &

Sean Mayes, *Kate Bush—A Visual Documentary* (Omnibus, 1988); Kevin Cann, *David Bowie—Any Day Now, The London Years: 1947–74* (Adelita, 2010); Rob Chapman, *Syd Barrett—A Very Irregular Head* (Faber, 2010); Krystyna Fitzgerald-Morris, Peter Fitzgerald-Morris & Dave Cross, *HomeGround: The Kate Bush Magazine Anthology One* and *Two* (Crescent Moon, 2014); Simon Goddard, *Ziggyology* (Ebury Press, 2013); Guido Harari, *The Kate Inside* (Wall of Sound Gallery, 2016); Alistair Lawrence, *Abbey Road—The Best Studio in the World* (Bloomsbury, 2016); Brian Southall, Peter Vince & Allan Rouse, *Abbey Road* (Omnibus, 2002); Graeme Thomson, *Under the Ivy—The Life and Music of Kate Bush* (Omnibus, 2010); and the programs for Tour of Life (1979); and Before the Dawn (2014).

This book is dedicated to Karen McCombie—for her toptastic bath-time subbing, her ability to do the whole "Wuthering Heights" routine when she's had enough wine (been a while!) and for reminding me to say hello to the trees and the sky and to look up—and to Eddy McCombie-Doyle, who's had quite a big bloody hill to run up these past few years, and who never fails to amaze me with their strength and resilience and ace sense of humor. Love love love.

CPSIA information can be obtained
at www.ICGtesting.com
Printed in the USA
LVHW100406210623
750159LV00001B/1